Defense Acquisition Reform, 1960–2009
An Elusive Goal

By
J. Ronald Fox

with contributions by
David G. Allen
Thomas C. Lassman
Walton S. Moody
Philip L. Shiman

CENTER OF MILITARY HISTORY
UNITED STATES ARMY
WASHINGTON, D.C., 2011

CONTENTS

    Page

Foreword vii
Principal Author ix
Preface xi

Chapter

1. **The Defense Acquisition Process** 1
   The U.S. Defense Establishment 1
   Major Weapon Systems 5
   Defense Acquisition Historical Perspective............ 7
   Defense Acquisition Versus Commercial Operation 12
   Government Acquisition Regulations 13
   Participants in Defense Acquisition 14
   Defining New Defense Systems......................... 15
   Congressional Authorization and Appropriation 19
   Stages in the Acquisition Process 20
   The Transition Between Phases 28
   Selecting a Contractor 29
   Controlling Schedules and Costs 30
   The Basis for Profits 31
   Limited Rates of Production 32
   Limitations of Government Program Managers 33

2. **Defense Acquisition Reforms in the 1960s and 1970s** ... 35
   Acquisition Reform During the 1960s—The McNamara
      Innovations 35
   The Transition from Robert McNamara to Melvin Laird .. 40
   Deputy Secretary of Defense David Packard 43
   Secretary Laird Creates the Blue Ribbon Defense
      Panel (1969) 45
   Defense Systems Acquisition Review Council 47
   Industry Advisory Council 49
   Packard Confronting Resistance 53
   Pushing Against Inertia 58
   The Blue Ribbon Defense Panel Issues Its Report (1970) .. 62
   Consolidating Gains 69
   Codifying the New Acquisition Process—DoD
      Directive 5000.1 73

Chapter	Page
Leadership in the Post-Packard Era	79
The Congressional Commission on Government Procurement	82
Office of Federal Procurement Policy	84
Procurement of Research and Development	88
Reforming Requirements	91
Legislating Reform	93
Office of Management and Budget Circular A–109	95

3. The 1980s: The Carlucci Initiatives and the Packard Commission 97
    Setting the Stage: PPBS and the Cycles of Weapons Acquisition Reform 100
    From PPBS to the Acquisition Improvement Program 106
    AIP in Action: Implementation and Execution 115
    Responding to Charges of Fraud, Waste, and Mismanagement 120
    The Packard Commission, 1985–1989 125
    Under Secretary of Defense for Acquisition 132
    The Battle for Control of Weapons Systems Acquisition 142
    The Legacy of 1980s Weapons Acquisition Reform 146
    1980s Retrospective 149

4. Acquisition Reform from 1990 to 2000 151
    A Mandate for Change 153
    Organizing the Reform Process 154
    Tools for Reform 158
    The Broad Reach of Reform 165
    Changing the Acquisition Process 175
    Results of 1990s Acquisition Reforms 180
    Views of Army Headquarters Personnel 183
    Views of the Army Program Management Community 184
    What Has Been Good About Acquisition Reform? 185
    What Has Been Bad About Acquisition Reform? 185
    Summary of Rand Findings 187

5. Conclusions 189
    The Defense Marketplace 193
    Relationships Between Government and Industry 194
    Reexamining the Program Manager Concept 198
    Differing Perceptions of Defense Acquisition 200

	Page
Government and Contractor Incentives	203
The Need for Extended Follow-up Actions	205

Appendixes

A. Four Acquisition Reform Studies Conducted from 2001 to 2009 209

B. Changes to the Acquisition Process, DoD Directive 5000.1, 1971 to 2008 221

C. Carlucci Thirty-Two Acquisition Reform Initiatives, 1983 229

D. Rand Corporation Study of Sixty-Three Acquisition Reform Initiatives, 2002 231

Abbreviations and Acronyms 235

Selected Bibliography 241

Index 255

Tables

No.
1. Defense Outlays, FY 1950–FY 2008 2
2. DoD's Budget Authority by Component 3

Figures

1. Total Federal Outlays: Non-Defense and Defense 4
2. The Defense Acquisition Management System 24
3. The Systems Acquisition Process 57

FOREWORD

Defense acquisition reform initiatives have been Department of Defense perennials over the past fifty years. Yet reforming the acquisition process remains a high priority each time a new administration comes into office. Many notable studies of defense acquisition with recommendations for changes have been published, and each has reached the same general findings with similar recommendations. However, despite the defense community's intent to reform the acquisition process, the difficulty of the problem and the associated politics, combined with organizational dynamics that are resistant to change, have led to only minor improvements. The problems of schedule slippages, cost growth, and shortfalls in technical performance on defense acquisition programs have remained much the same throughout this period.

The importance of the Department of Defense's huge acquisition projects over the years cannot be overstressed. The United States has often turned to cutting-edge technological solutions to solve strategic and operational challenges. To highlight the importance of acquisition issues, the Department of Defense began a project in 2001 to write a history of defense acquisition from the end of World War II to the start of the twenty-first century. The U.S. Army Center of Military History served as the executive agent for that project until funding was effectively withdrawn in 2009. Two volumes of that history are nearing publication, which will take the story up to 1969. To capitalize on essential information on defense acquisition reform initiatives from the three unpublished draft volumes covering the period from 1969 to 2000, the Center decided to publish extracts from those volumes, with additional analysis by J. Ronald Fox, a subject matter expert on acquisition and an adviser to the project. Much of chapter two of this acquisition reform study was written by Walton S. Moody and David G. Allen for their draft Volume III (1969–1980) of the Defense Acquisition History Project and then edited, analyzed, and augmented by Fox. Similarly, most of chapter three was taken from Thomas C. Lassman's draft chapters three and five of his Volume IV (1981–1990), and much of chapter four was written by Philip L. Shiman as chapter eight of his Volume V (1991–2000) of the Defense Acquisition History Project. Fox was able to take their chapters, provide additional analysis and insights, and consolidate and edit them with his own work to prepare this important volume focusing on defense acquisition reform. This volume is the result of all of their research and writing efforts and their collective insights into an incredibly complex system.

Professor Fox's *Defense Acquisition Reform, 1960–2009: An Elusive Goal*, provides valuable historical analysis of the numerous attempts over the past fifty years to reform the defense acquisition process for major weapons systems. It identifies important long-term trends, insights, and observations that provide perspective and context to assist current defense decision makers, acquisition officials, and the acquisition schoolhouse. It is an important work on an important subject that continues to defy solution.

Washington, D.C. RICHARD W. STEWART
31 October 2011 Chief Historian

Principal Author

J. Ronald Fox is a member of the Harvard Business School faculty where he chaired the General Management Area. His research deals with the management of large engineering and construction projects and defense acquisition. He taught courses in project management, competition and strategy, defense and aerospace marketing, and business-government relations. He holds a bachelor of science in physics, cum laude, from Le Moyne College, and a master of business administration and Ph.D. from Harvard University.

Fox served as assistant secretary of the Army in which he was responsible for Army procurement, contracting, and logistics. Prior to his appointment as assistant secretary, he served as deputy assistant secretary of the Air Force. His work in these governmental positions earned him the Exceptional Civilian Service Award from the Air Force and the Distinguished Civilian Service Award, the highest decoration for public service awarded by the Department of the Army. He chaired the Board of Visitors of the Defense Acquisition University, was trustee of the Logistics Management Institute and the Aerospace Corporation, and was director of the American Society for Macro Engineering. In 2004, he was named senior adviser on acquisitions to the Defense Acquisition History Project. In 2006, he was named to the Defense Acquisition University Hall of Fame.

He is the author of several books, including *Arming America: How the U.S. Buys Weapons* (1974); *Managing Business-Government Relations* (1982); *The Defense Management Challenge: Weapons Acquisition* (1988); *Critical Issues in the Defense Acquisition Culture* (1994); and *Challenges in Managing Large Projects* (2006).

Preface

Early in 2009, Richard W. Stewart, chief historian at the U.S. Army Center of Military History (CMH), suggested that I prepare a monograph describing the frequent recurring studies of government efforts to reform the defense acquisition process. He proposed that I present my observations on acquisition reforms, supplemented by selections of unpublished material CMH received from contract historians David G. Allen, Thomas C. Lassman, Walton S. Moody, and Philip L. Shiman. I agreed to undertake that project, resulting in this monograph.

From 1960 through 2009, more than twenty-seven major studies of defense acquisition were commissioned by presidents, Congress, secretaries of defense, government agencies, studies and analyses organizations, and universities. The U.S. Government Accountability Office (formerly U.S. General Accounting Office) has published numerous other noteworthy studies on defense acquisition. The reform studies over the nearly fifty-year period arrived at most of the same findings and made similar recommendations.

The following major studies on acquisition reform were conducted from 1960 to 2009:

1960–1962	The Weapons Acquisition Process—Harvard Business School, Merton J. Peck and Frederic M. Scherer
1970	Blue Ribbon Defense Panel (Fitzhugh Commission)
1972	Congressional Commission on Government Procurement
1974	Arming America: How the U.S. Buys Weapons—Harvard Business School, J. Ronald Fox
1979	Defense Resources Board
1979	DoD Resource Management Study
1981	Carlucci Thirty-Two Acquisition Initiatives
1982	Special Panel on Defense Procurement, House Armed Services Committee
1982	The Defense Industry—Jacques S. Gansler
1983	The Grace Commission

1985	Center for Strategic and International Studies
1986	Blue Ribbon Commission (Packard Commission)
1988	The Defense Management Challenge—Harvard Business School, J. Ronald Fox
1989	Secretary of Defense Management Review
1989	Affording Defense—Jacques S. Gansler
1989	New Weapons, Old Politics—Thomas L. McNaugher
1990	Defense Science Board Streamlining Study
1993–1994	Defense Science Board Streamlining Task Force
1993–1998	Defense Acquisition Reform Initiatives
1995	Defense Conversion—Jacques S. Gansler
2005	Reexamining Military Acquisition Reform—Rand Corporation
2006	Comparative History of DoD Management Reform, Naval Post Graduate School
2006	Office of the Secretary of Defense Acquisition Performance Assessment (DAPA)
2007	Commission on Army Acquisition and Program Management in Expeditionary Operations
2007	Defense Acquisition: Options for Congress—Congressional Research Service (CRS), Stephen Chadwick
2009	Creating a DoD Strategic Acquisition Platform—Department of Defense and the Defense Science Board
2009	CNA Independent Assessment: Air Force Acquisition

Despite the many studies and the similarity of their findings, major defense programs still require more than fifteen years to deliver less capability than planned, often at two to three times the initial cost. Most attempts to implement improvements in the management of the defense acquisition process during the past fifty years have fallen short of their objectives. It is increasingly evident that barriers to improving the acquisition process derive, not from a lack of ideas, but from the difficulties encountered by senior government managers (in Congress as well as in the Department of Defense) in identifying and changing counterproductive incentives for government and industry. There seems to be little hope of solving the chronic problems if the usual attempts at reform are tried once again. A more comprehensive approach is required—one based on a better understanding of how and why the Defense Department and its contractors work they way they do and how government and industry incentives stimulate and reinforce the seemingly intractable problems.

This monograph discusses reform initiatives from 1960 to 2009 and concludes with prescriptions for future changes to the acquisition culture of the services, Defense Department, and industry. The acquisition process has a number of built-in, even cultural, aspects that resist change. These include a workforce frequently with too little training, experience, and stable tenure to monitor and manage huge defense acquisition programs; the short tenure of senior politically appointed acquisition officials, averaging a mere eighteen months in office; an irregular and erratic flow of weapons systems appropriations; the very nature of cutting-edge, highly risky research and development; an ill-informed requirements process that virtually mandates changes to contracts as requirements are added or changed; and the many financial incentives that reward lowball contractor bids and provide negative sanctions for failing to spend all allocated funds. These cultural challenges within the current acquisition system have great value to many key participants in industry, the services, and Congress and predispose them to be generally resistant to change.

In addition to the contributions made by David Allen, Thomas Lassman, Walton Moody, and Philip Shiman, many others played an invaluable role in producing this publication. Richard Stewart, CMH chief historian, suggested this publication, reviewed the chapters, and provided helpful comments. Office of the Secretary of Defense historian Alfred Goldberg, along with historians Nancy K. Berlage and Glen R. Asner, also read my draft material and provided comments and suggestions.

Others at CMH also greatly contributed to this publication, most notably, editor Hildegard J. Bachman and visual information specialist Michael R. Gill.

I would also like to acknowledge the assistance provided by the Acker Library staff members at the Defense Acquisition University for their valuable assistance in locating names, dates, and documents useful in the study of acquisition reform: circulation manager Thelma N. Jackson and reference librarians Edward R. Fishpaw and Mary T. Klemmt.

I also benefited from my associations with Jeffrey J. Clarke, former chief of military history at CMH, who provided valuable advice and guidance throughout the early years of the Defense Acquisition History Project. Elliott Converse, senior contract historian on the Defense Acquisition History Project, and CMH contract historians Walter S. Poole, David G. Allen, Walton S. Moody, and Philip L. Shiman, all helped introduce me to the world of Defense Department historical research.

Acknowledgments would be incomplete without mentioning the immense help I received early in my career at the Harvard Business School from faculty colleagues Robert N. Anthony and J. Sterling Livingston who introduced me to the topic of defense acquisition in the 1960s. I am also indebted to the immeasurable support and assistance I received in those early years from a highly competent and dedicated public servant, Thomas D. Morris, then-assistant secretary of defense.

Finally, I am grateful for the encouragement and very helpful reviews of each draft of this manuscript by my wife and partner, Dorris. She has consistently been a morale builder as well as a careful, conscientious, and critical reader.

Any errors or inaccuracies in the text are, of course, the responsibility of the author.

Boston, Massachusetts   J. RONALD FOX
31 October 2011

DEFENSE ACQUISITION REFORM 1960–2009
AN ELUSIVE GOAL

CHAPTER **ONE**

THE DEFENSE ACQUISITION PROCESS

THE U.S. DEFENSE ESTABLISHMENT

The U.S. Department of Defense (DoD) is by far the largest and most complex business organization in the world. It operates more than 5,400 installations worldwide and executes more than 15 million contracts per year.[1] It also develops and produces the most sought-after weapons and equipment in the free world.

In 2009, the Defense Department employed more than 4.6 million Americans: 1.4 million active military personnel, 718,000 civilian DoD employees, more than 800,000 National Guard and reservists, 1.5 million military retirees, and an estimated 250,000 private-sector employees. Among full-time DoD employees are tens of thousands of military and civilian personnel who work on multibillion-dollar weapons and equipment development and production programs.[2] They include contracting officers, program managers, plant representatives, engineers, cost estimators, pricing specialists, auditors, inspectors, and their superiors up the chain of authority to the secretary of defense.

The Defense Contract Management Agency operates over 900 offices around the world, staffed by 18,697 contractors, to oversee 324,296 active contracts totaling $2.4 trillion.[3]

The defense budget is described in various ways. The term *total obligational authority* refers to the value of the congressionally approved defense programs for each fiscal year, regardless of the financing method (which could include balances available from prior years, other resources available from prior years, or resources available from the sale of items in inventory). The term *budget authority*, on the other hand, refers to the value of annual new authority to incur obligations. Outlays refer to expenditures or checks issued. Defense outlays are often presented in terms either of a percentage of the gross domestic product (GDP) or of total federal outlays (*see* Table 1).

---

[1] Office of Management and Budget, Executive Office of the President, *Management of the United States Government, Fiscal Year 2007* (Washington, D.C.: U.S. Government Printing Office, 2008).

[2] Department of Defense Statistical Information Analysis Division, Workforce Publications. See also Department of Defense, Office of the Assistant Secretary of Defense (Comptroller), "The Defense Budget and Future Years Defense Program, FY 2006–2011."

[3] Defense Contract Management Agency (DCMA) Fact Sheet (Alexandria, Va.: 31 March 2009).

Table 1—Defense Outlays, FY 1950–FY 2008

Fiscal Year	Percent of Gross Domestic Product	Percent of Total Federal Outlays
1950	4.9	27.4
1955	9.1	51.3
1960	8.2	45.0
1965	7.4	38.7
1970	8.1	39.4
1975	5.6	25.5
1980	5.0	22.5
1985	6.2	25.9
1990	5.2	23.8
1995	3.7	18.2
2000	3.0	16.5
2001	3.0	16.4
2002	3.4	17.3
2003	3.7	18.7
2004	4.0	19.9
2005	4.0	20.0
2006	4.0	19.7
2007	4.0	20.2
2008	4.1	19.3

Source: Joint Economic Committee, Office of Management and Budget, and Congressional Budget Office.

Note: See Federal Outlays table at http://www.house.gov/jec/fiscal/budget/restrain/update/tbl-4.gif and also Center for Strategic and Budgetary Assessments, Washington, D.C. The 2008 data is from the Congressional Budget Office "Total Federal Spending Outlays" and USGovernmentSpending.com.

Table 2—DoD's Budget Authority by Component (in Millions of Dollars)

	Fiscal Year 2009	Percent of Total
Army	233.0	41.4
Navy	166.1	29.5
Air Force	163.5	29.1
TOTAL	**562.6**	**100.0**

Source: Office of the Assistant Secretary of Defense (Comptroller), "National Defense Budget, Financial Summary Tables," 2009.

The defense budget is distributed among the military services and a variety of smaller defense agencies, although not equally. In the 1980s, the Army share of the budget authority was about 30 percent less than the share for either the Air Force or the Navy. In 2009, the Army share was approximately 40 percent higher than that of the Air Force or the Navy (see Table 2).[4]

In 1965, 43 percent ($50.6 billion) of the total federal outlays were devoted to national defense and 57 percent ($60.6 billion) to social programs and entitlements. In 2009, the percent devoted to national defense had fallen to 22 percent ($661.0 billion) and social programs and non-defense outlays had risen to 76 percent ($2.3 trillion) (see Figure 1).

From World War II until the 1970s, military research and development (R&D) constituted by far the largest single share of the total federal R&D effort. In 1960, for example, the Defense Department's R&D budget was $5.6 billion, of a total federal R&D budget of $8.7 billion, or 64.4 percent.[5] By 2007, the U.S. defense R&D budget had risen to $69.3 billion, accounting for 50 percent of the total federal R&D budget of $137.2 billion.[6]

---

[4] Office of the Assistant Secretary of Defense (Comptroller), "National Defense Budget Estimates," 2008 and 2009.

[5] Office of Management and Budget (OMB), *U.S. Federal Budget, 2007* (Washington, D.C.: U.S. Government Printing Office).

[6] OMB, *Special Analyses of the Budget of the U.S. Government, Fiscal Year 1972 and Fiscal Year 2007* (Washington, D.C.: U.S. Government Printing Office, 1972 and 2008).

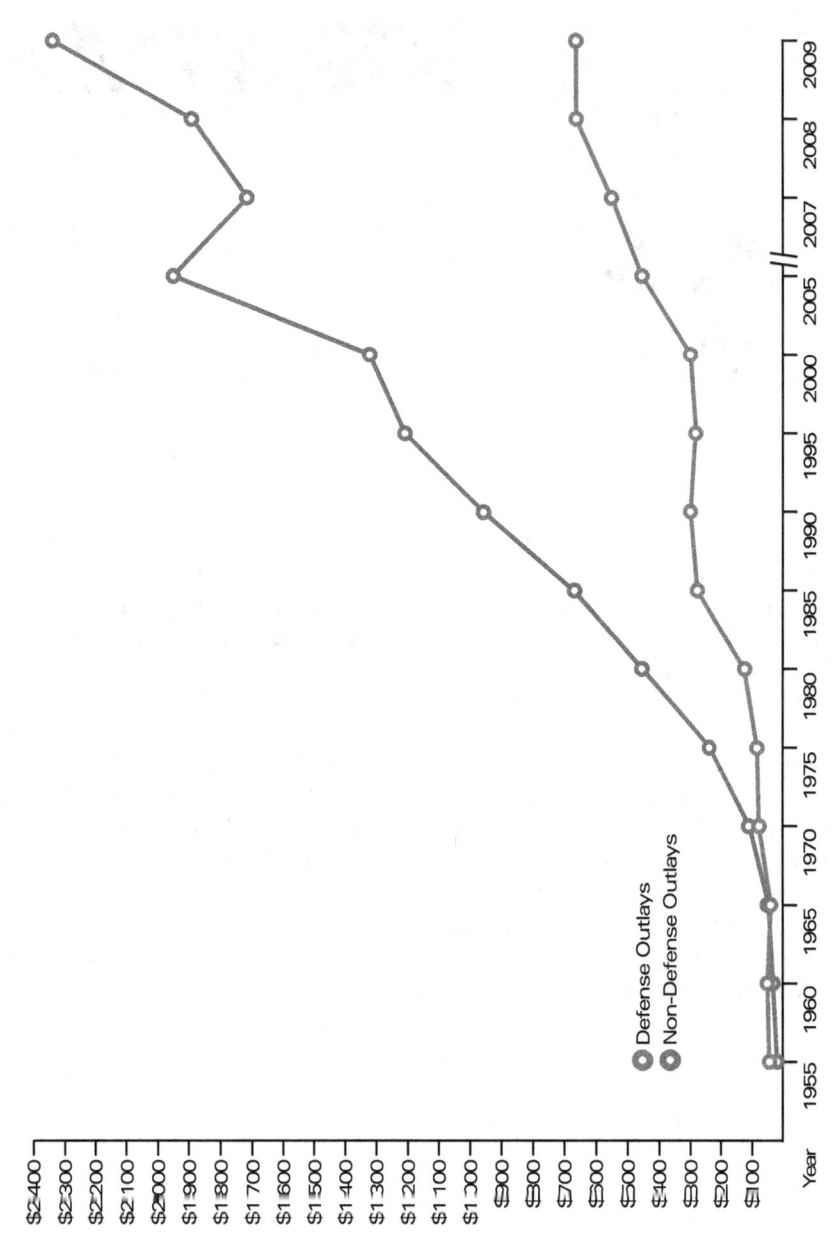

Figure 1—Total Federal Outlays: Non-Defense and Defense (in Billions of Dollars)

Source: Office of Management and Budget, Historical Tables, Outlays by Function and Subfunction

MAJOR WEAPON SYSTEMS

The Defense Department contracts for and oversees the research, development, and production of weapon systems and equipment on time and at a reasonable cost. In pursuit of this mission, DoD engages tens of thousands of prime contractors—including most of the major firms in the United States—and tens of thousands of suppliers and subcontractors.[7]

The defense acquisition structure consists of three interrelated and interdependent systems. The first is the requirements system, currently the Joint Capabilities Integration and Development System (JCIDS). The second is the Planning, Programming, Budgeting, and Execution System (PPBES, formerly PPBS), the primary resource allocation process for DoD. The third is the Defense Acquisition Process, known as the acquisition or procurement system, also referred to as "little a" acquisition. These three systems do not report to or fall under an overarching system, but they operate in a manner similar to a system of systems and are referred to as "Big A" acquisition.[8]

The PPBES was originally called the Planning, Programming, and Budgeting System (PPBS), first implemented in the early 1960s by then-Secretary of Defense Robert S. McNamara. Planning and programming activities occur in even-numbered years (called on-years) while budgeting and execution activities occur in both on-years and off-years (odd-numbered years).[9]

Since the late 1950s and early 1960s, the major products of the defense industry have been described as weapon systems. The term *weapon system*—or often major weapon systems or major programs—refers to technically complex items such as aircraft, missiles, ships, and tanks. A weapon system includes not only the major item of equipment itself but also the subsystems, logistical support, software, construction, and training needed to operate and support it. Subsystems can include power plants; armaments; equipment for guidance and navigation, ground support, test and checkout, maintenance facilities, communications, and training; spare parts; and technical data, including operating and maintenance handbooks and parts catalogs. (In 2009, major systems were those whose estimated research, development, test, and evaluation [RDT&E] costs were $365 million or more in fiscal

---

[7] DCMA Fact Sheet, 31 March 2009.

[8] Congressional Research Service (CRS) Report for Congress, "Defense Acquisition: Overview, Issues, and Options for Congress," RL34026, 20 Jun 2007, p. 3 (hereafter cited as CRS Report, 20 Jun 2007).

[9] Department of Defense (DoD) Directive 7045.14, "The Planning, Programming, and Budgeting System (PPBS)," 22 May 1984; DoD Instruction 7045.7, "Implementation of the Planning, Programming, and Budgeting System (PPBS)," 23 May 1984; CRS Report, 20 Jun 2007 pp. 7, 9.

year [FY] 2000 constant dollars, or whose production costs were estimated to be $2.19 billion or more in FY 2000 constant dollars).[10]

One result of the amorphous nature of the term *weapon system* is that there is no general agreement among DoD, Congress, Office of Management and Budget, and U.S. Government Accountability Office (GAO) (formerly the U.S. General Accounting Office) on what is and is not included in a cost estimate. (The Defense Acquisition University defines weapon systems cost simply as the sum of the procurement cost for prime mission equipment and the procurement cost for support items.) Two or more organizations (that is, Office of the Secretary of Defense, a military service, or Congress) preparing separate cost estimates for the same weapon system can make different assumptions about the development program, spare parts, logistics, training, or any of a variety of associated hardware and service costs. Hence, the same weapon system can be identified with widely differing cost estimates at different times.

During the 1980s and 1990s, increasing percentages of the defense budget were devoted to major weapon systems. In 2009, ninety-six major defense systems were at various stages of development and production. Programs included jet fighters, bombers, and transport aircraft; new combat and support vessels; and thousands of tanks and cannon-carrying troop transports, strategic and tactical missiles, and satellite programs. The GAO reported that the estimated total investment in those programs had grown from $1.2 trillion to $1.6 trillion (FY 2009 dollars) since 2003. The $1.6 trillion amount exceeds the total gross national product of all but the seven largest economies of the world (United States, China, Japan, Germany, France, United Kingdom, and Italy).[11]

Major weapon systems development and production programs are technologically advanced and complex. Indeed, they are often designed to achieve performance levels never before realized, using many components and some materials never before used in military applications. Production is characteristically low volume, with the final cost of a major system frequently running into billions of dollars. This substantial expenditure of time and money occurs in an environment of rapidly evolving technology and unexpected changes in priorities for individual programs. This predicament creates an environment of uncertainty and risk for buyer and seller alike, exacerbated by the difficulties in estimating technical performance, development time, and cost.

---

[10] DoD Instruction 5000.02, "Operation of the Defense Acquisition System," 8 Dec 2008.

[11] Major systems are those requiring more than $365 million in research and development or $1 billion in production (fiscal year [FY] 2000 dollars). DoD Directive 5000.01, "Acquisition of Major Defense Systems," 8 Dec 2008, p. 33. See also U.S. Government Accountability Office (GAO) Report, *Major Weapon Systems Continue to Experience Cost and Schedule Problems*, GAO–06–368, Mar 2006.

Military aircraft illustrate the complexity of modern weapon systems. The Air Force F–22 is an advanced fighter aircraft that replaces the F–15 as America's front-line, air superiority fighter. Prior to its full-scale development, a four-year demonstration/validation phase was conducted for the program. Thirty-nine percent of the F–22 aircraft is fabricated with titanium and 24 percent from composite materials. More than 240 firms in 37 states participate in the development and production program. The empty weight of the aircraft is 31,670 pounds and the wing area is 840 square feet. The aircraft has two engines generating 35,000 pounds of thrust, enabling the F–22 to travel at a speed of Mach 1.8 and perform tactical maneuvers at an altitude of 12 miles, twice the altitude at which other jets can perform tactical maneuvers. The F–22 was originally expected to cost $88 billion in 2009 dollars for 648 aircraft. In March 2009, the program was estimated to cost $73.7 billion for the much smaller quantity of 184 aircraft.[12]

The amount of electronics equipment in a modern fighter aircraft is astounding. An Air Force general captured the essential change: "In the past, the Air Force used to buy airplanes and add electronics. Today the Air Force buys computers and puts wings on them."[13] Forty percent or more of the funds for DoD aircraft are spent on electronics equipment.

Managing the cost, schedule, and technical performance of major acquisition programs becomes more complex as technology advances. It is virtually impossible for any one individual—or any one contractor—to comprehend every aspect of the research, engineering design, and production stages of a major acquisition program. These programs usually extend for ten years or more, during which time many thousands of components must be designed and manufactured to work together as a unit. Individuals and firms involved in defense work become increasingly specialized, as does the equipment employed. Coordination of the many operations of acquisition is itself a major Defense Department activity.

DEFENSE ACQUISITION HISTORICAL PERSPECTIVE

Since the earliest days of our nation, U.S. military forces have relied on private enterprise to supply the material, equipment, and services needed in peace and war. Although the government has always manufactured some war materials—especially ammunition—at no time have the armed forces been fully independent of

---

[12] GAO Report, *Major Weapon Systems Continue to Experience Cost and Schedule Problems*, GAO–06–368, Mar 2006. See also Artemis March, "Note on the Aerospace Industry and Industrial Modernization," Harvard Business School Note 0–687–009, under the supervision of Professor David A. Garvin.

[13] Quotation from Rick Atkinson and Fred Hiatt, "Military in a Fix," *Washington Post*, 18 August 1985.

the private sector in meeting their needs. Food, clothing, and ordinary necessities have always been supplied by contract. Ordnance and ships have also been supplied primarily by private industry, although government shipyards and arsenals have played an important role.[14]

Few would challenge the statement that U.S. defense weapons and equipment are among the best in the world. Throughout the past forty years, the defense industry has attracted outstanding scientists and engineers. The industrial firms that design and produce weapon systems are among the largest in the country. The managers of these firms are trained and experienced technical experts who understand the rewards and penalties inherent in the process, and usually produce attractive profits for defense firms.

Before and during World War II, the defense industry was usually compared with typical manufacturing industries, such as the auto industry. Since the late 1950s, however, the defense industry has been compared with custom design and development industries, in which contracting plays a major role. The *Armed Forces Journal* used the housing industry in a simple analogy.

> The housing contractor hires an architect and before the first board is cut, unless he has another development down the road, the contractor has to reduce the architect's effort to part time, or get the customer to agree to keep the architect on the payroll full time while the job requires the architect part time. The same thing follows with the carpenters, electricians, plumbers and roofers. In the aerospace business, a major effort is made by one or more firms to obtain a contract to develop and produce a defense program. Some preliminary design is accomplished, some computer modeling, and some independent research and development (R&D). Usually a large engineering team is amassed to demonstrate to the military buyers that the company has the capability in place to do the job. If the contract award is delayed, as is often the case, this high-cost team can stand virtually idle for months. In the absence of a rigorous determination to keep costs low, costs to the company and to the Government for these programs can be astronomical.[15]

In the 1950s, following a decline in the business of major defense companies after World War II, there was an expansion in the development and production of weapons and equipment. By 1959,

---

[14] Richard J. Bednar and John T. Jones Jr., "The Role of the DoD Contracting Officer," Draft Report of the American Bar Association Section of Public Contract Law, Ad Hoc Committee, John E. Cavanagh, chairman, 11 January 1987, p. 23.

[15] R. Jameson, *Armed Forces Journal,* 6 January 1969.

THE DEFENSE ACQUISITION PROCESS

the trend was away from long production runs to more research, development, testing, and evaluation.[16] Emphasis was placed on the development and production of weapon systems that incorporated the most advanced technological innovations. Toward the close of the 1950s, heavy reliance was placed on sole-source procurement. By 1960, for instance, a majority of the contract awards made by the military services were noncompetitive, and more than 40 percent were cost-plus-fixed-fee contracts.[17]

David D. Acker, a member of the Defense Systems Management College during the 1970s and 1980s, characterized the defense acquisition environment of the 1950s.

> Money was authorized to develop almost any new defense system that appeared capable of giving the United States a performance advantage over any potential adversary. Such considerations as "should cost," "design-to-cost," and "life-cycle cost" were not uppermost in the minds of defense planners until the late 1950's. Both development and production were carried out under cost-reimbursement contracts. In this environment, production costs did not pose a major constraint on engineering design. When a design was discovered to be impractical in production—or to be inoperative in field use—it was modified in accordance with government-funded engineering changes.
>
> The lack of a well-organized and integrated DoD financial management system, along with the practice of "piecemeal" procurement, led to unstable employment in the defense industry and the emergence of a transient work force. Many of the contractors being challenged to develop and produce defense systems on the outer fringes of technology found it difficult to create and maintain smoothly functioning program management teams.[18]

The Rand Corporation reports that before the 1960s there was no formal acquisition policy across DoD, largely because the secretary of defense either did not have the authority or did not choose to enforce such a policy. When the Department of Defense was established, in 1947, it was by design a loose confederation of the three military departments, and the secretary of defense was limited to providing general direction to those departments.[19]

---

[16] David D. Acker, "The Maturing of the DoD Acquisition Process," *Defense Systems Management Review* (Summer 1980): 14.

[17] Charles J. Hitch, "Evolution of the Department of Defense," in *American Defense Policy*, 3d ed., eds. Richard Head and Eavin J. Rokke (Baltimore: Johns Hopkins University Press, 1973), p. 347.

[18] Acker, "The Maturing of the DoD Acquisition Process," p. 14.

[19] Hitch, "Evolution of the Department of Defense," p. 347.

The first secretary of defense, James V. Forrestal (1947–1949), lost no time in recommending that "the statutory authority of the Secretary of Defense should be materially strengthened . . . by making it clear that the Secretary of Defense has the responsibility for exercising direction, authority and control over the departments of the National Military Establishment."[20] That power was only slowly granted, however, and throughout the 1950s, the individual services generally ran their own acquisition programs with very little interference from the Office of the Secretary of Defense (OSD), each service buying the weapon systems suitable for the kind of conflict it envisioned. The higher military budgets, resulting from the increased international role of the United States following the Korean War, presented this decentralized decision-making system with a twofold challenge: (1) efficient management of the first peacetime defense industry in U.S. history and (2) effective coordination of military R&D efforts.[21]

In the late 1950s, Brig. Gen. Bernard A. Schriever developed the weapon systems management concept and adopted the acquisition strategy of "concurrency" of development and production efforts while overseeing the development of the U.S. intercontinental ballistic missile (ICBM). At the same time, the military services began adopting program management in managing major acquisition programs. Development and production work required for each weapon or equipment program, formerly managed by functional departments within each military service, were brought together into one enterprise, known as a program (or project) management office, or, simply, program office. This change was made to smooth the transition from engineering to production and to allow for the consideration of such issues as operational support and maintenance during the early design phases. The concept of the program office meant that the development and production of a major weapon system was to be managed by a program manager, serving as the single individual in the program office responsible for all facets of the office's operations. The program manager was usually supported by a staff that could include engineers, logisticians, contracting officers and specialists, budget and financial managers, and test and evaluation personnel, who were responsible for their individual functions but would also provide guidance and advice. In addition, before a program office could engage in business with private industry, a contracting officer must become involved. Only contract-

---

[20] *First Report of the Secretary of Defense, 1948* (Washington, D.C.: U.S. Government Printing Office, 1948), p. 3.

[21] Staff Report to the Senate Committee on Armed Services, "Defense Organization: The Need for Change," 16 Oct 1985, p. 530.

THE DEFENSE ACQUISITION PROCESS

ing officers were authorized to execute contracts with industrial firms; they had a mandate to comply with government policy and to ensure fairness in government-business practices.[22] Program managers were usually military officers. Since the 1960s, each military service has organized its acquisition activities into system commands overseeing the performance of a number of research, development, and production programs and/or providing assistance to the programs.[23]

DoD program offices are responsible for ensuring that the acquisition of major defense programs is accomplished efficiently and effectively.[24] Surprisingly, however, DoD provides its contractors with few incentives to control and reduce costs. In fact, through its profit policy and source-selection process, it often inadvertently does just the opposite—rewards cost increases and penalizes cost reductions.

For each weapon system, the military services usually contract with one firm (a prime contractor) for system design and integration functions. With limited exceptions (for example, government-furnished equipment), the prime contractor directs subordinate contractors (subcontractors), who develop and produce particular subsystems and components, which the prime contractor brings together to produce a totally integrated defense weapon system.[25]

Most major defense programs encounter repeated setbacks before achieving an acceptable technical performance objective. Consequently, most of the military and civilian personnel who remain in Defense Department acquisition are, by temperament, unfailingly optimistic. In dealing with inquiries from Congress, the press, or the public, most government (and industry) managers downplay the significance of performance failures, cost overruns, and schedule changes. Their progress reports and predictions are usually positive, no matter what setbacks their programs actually experience. The gap between prediction and performance engages public attention only when there are significant increases in costs or problems in technical performance. These disparities are, however, a fact of daily life.

---

[22] GAO Report, *DoD Acquisition: Strengthening Capabilities of Key Personnel in Systems Acquisition*, GAO/NSIAD–86–45, May 1986, p. 10; Federal Acquisition Regulation (FAR), Subchapter A, Subpart 1.6, Reissue 2005.

[23] DoD Instruction 5000.02, "Operation of the Defense Acquisition System," 8 Dec 2008, p. 1; Merton J. Peck and Frederic M. Scherer, *The Weapons Acquisition Process: An Economic Analysis* (Boston: Division of Research, Harvard Business School, 1962), pp. 82–83.

[24] DoD Directive 5000.01, "The Defense Acquisition System," May 2003; DoD Instruction 5000.02, "Operation of the Defense Acquisition System," 8 Dec 2008.

[25] GAO Report, *DoD Acquisition: Strengthening Capabilities of Key Personnel in Systems Acquisition*, GAO/NSIAD–86–45, May 1986, p. 10.

Defense Acquisition Versus Commercial Operation

In the private-sector marketplace, two exchanges occur when goods are produced: income is drawn from those who buy the goods and is paid to the producers. The creation of purchasing power is matched by the sale of goods, the receipts from which absorb the purchasing power. But a government purchase—civilian or military—completes only half of the two-way transaction. Charles L. Schultze, former chairman of the president's Council of Economic Advisors, pointed out that in the defense business, although the government pays income to the producers, it does not then resell those goods in the marketplace.[26] Consequently, it does not absorb an equivalent amount of income and purchasing power. Because the extra income earned in production is not absorbed by the sale of an added supply of goods in the market, the government must borrow money or levy taxes to absorb the added purchasing power created when goods are produced for it. Although the government need not cover every dollar of its purchases by taxes, large-scale failure to absorb the added purchasing power—that is, large-scale budget deficits—can cause inflation and high interest rates. Under these conditions, purchasing power has been added to the system but not reabsorbed.

In sum, government purchases do not add to market supply in the economic sense of the term. The military nature of the goods, however, is largely irrelevant to economic consequences. If the government bought massive amounts of food, clothing, and houses and distributed them free of charge, it would add nothing to the economic supply of goods in the country. Inflation would result, no matter how "useful" the goods in question.

Schultze criticized the frequently heard proposition that the lower share of defense spending in the economy of Japan (and to a lesser extent, Germany) compared with that of the United States was an important reason for Japan's higher rate of productivity growth. That assertion is questionable. If the U.S. defense share of the gross national product (GNP) were to be at the expense of investment instead of consumption, reduction of investment might indeed lower U.S. productivity and competitiveness. But there is no economic reason, in principle, why the United States cannot alter the tax system so that it provides revenue to support defense spending by depressing consumption instead of investment. Indeed, if the United States does otherwise, the resulting fall in investment has to be recognized as a conscious choice and not a characteristic result of defense spending. In any event, Schultze pointed out that in the postwar period there was little evidence that the business investment spending share of GNP followed changes in

---

[26] Charles L. Schultze, "Economic Effects of the Defense Budget," Brookings Bulletin, Fall 1981.

the defense spending share of GNP, which ranged between 4 and 10 percent.[27] That observation has not changed from 1970 through 2009.

Hence, there is nothing inherent in defense spending that leads to inflation or lowers productivity, and that should therefore prevent the United States from maintaining the spending level it believes necessary for national security, so long as it is willing to pay for increased defense spending through higher taxes.

The rules of the game in the defense business differ markedly from those in the commercial marketplace. Many authors have sought to describe the unusual business environment of the defense industry. Defense scholar Robert J. Art points out that in the classic theory of industrial capitalism, the business firm is characteristically autonomous. Corporate management is the formal decision maker regarding what it will produce, the method of production, quantity, price, and distribution. Moreover, in the commercial marketplace, the pressures of competition compel participants to minimize costs, to a greater or lesser degree, on behalf of profits, which, in turn, are the basis for further investment by private industrial management.[28]

In analyzing the defense acquisition process, the classical concepts of the industrial firm do not apply: price is usually not an overriding factor; product and quantity are determined, not by the management of the firm, but by governmental authority; and competition normally focuses on proposed design rather than the physical product, and on promises of performance rather than the performance itself. For major acquisition programs (for example, aircraft, tanks, ships, weapon systems), the supplier often holds a monopoly and the purchaser holds a monopsony (i.e., one buyer only).[29]

Government Acquisition Regulations

DoD procurement activities are governed by three sets of federal government regulations. The first set of regulations/directives applies to the entire federal government and is contained in the Federal Acquisition Regulation (FAR). The second set of regulations applies only to DoD and is contained in the Defense Federal Acquisition Regulation Supplement (DFARS). The third set of regulations applies only to individual DoD components (Army, Navy, Air Force) and is contained in component-unique FAR supplements.[30]

---

[27] Ibid.

[28] Robert J. Art, "Bureaucratic Politics and American Foreign Policy: A Critique," *Policy Sciences* (December 1973), cited by Paul M. Bradburn, in "Strategic Postures in the Military Aircraft Industry: A Comparison of Two Companies," paper prepared at Massachusetts Institute of Technology, June 1986, p. 16.

[29] Bradburn, "Strategic Postures in the Military Aircraft Industry," p. 8.

[30] Federal Acquisition Regulation System, Jul 2009; U.S. Department of Defense, Defense Federal Acquisition Regulation Supplement, 21 Jul 2009. See also CRS Report, 20 Jun 2007, pp. 7, 9.

The regulations governing business operations of the Defense Department and private industry have increased markedly since World War II. In 1947, the Armed Services Procurement Regulation (ASPR) numbered approximately 125 pages; in 2009, Federal Acquisition Regulation and Defense supplements to the FAR, the successors to ASPR, constituted several large volumes, totaling more than 2,000 pages. Additional regulations by the military services add to the regulatory requirements.

Despite their size, these volumes do not cover all acquisition requirements. The Office of the Secretary of Defense and the military services supplement them with additional directives and instructions. A team planning to develop and produce a weapon system must conform to DoD Directive 5000.1 and DoD Instruction 5000.2, as well as hundreds of directives concerning all phases of the acquisition process, including, for example, logistics support, reliability, configuration management, parts numbering, milestone reporting, cost estimating, budgeting, measuring technical performance, training, and maintenance, as well as other matters of varying importance. Since the early 1970s, the quantity and detail of these government regulations have increased.

Participants in Defense Acquisition

The major participants in the acquisition process are Congress, the Office of Management and Budget, the Office of the Secretary of Defense, the Office of the Service Secretary, the Service Acquisition Executive, the military service materiel commands, program management offices, functional support organizations, and industry. Until these groups resolve their differences, little is accomplished. In some instances, the executive branch (through OSD and a military department) advocates a particular program, but faces serious opposition in Congress. In other instances, the administration and Congress agree to adopt one system, but industry exerts what influence it has with particular congressional members to obtain certain favorable decisions on another system.[31] In many instances, traditional areas of responsibility are blurred. For example, Congress has become more involved in specifying program technical requirements, as when it imposed a weight restriction on the Small ICBM.[32]

Each participant in the acquisition process exercises an oversight responsibility to ensure that laws and regulations are ob-

---

[31] Defense Systems Management College, "Acquisition Strategy Guide," Jul 1984, pp. 2–3.
[32] Ibid.

served and programs pursued efficiently. Consequently, there are numerous oversight and monitoring agencies. The executive branch has the Justice Department and the Office of Management and Budget; the Department of Defense and each military service have an independent inspector general and auditing office; and Congress uses the Government Accountability Office for program audits and assessment, the Congressional Budget Office for budget and program cost estimates, and the Congressional Research Service and Office of Technology Assessment for analyses. Industry has its legal resources, Washington representatives, and industry associations to protect its interests. The government manager of a major systems acquisition program must be sensitive to all participants' positions and their vested interests.[33]

(Note: The sections of this chapter beginning with "Defining New Defense Systems," below, along with four subsequent sections—"Congressional Authorization and Appropriation," "Stages in the Acquisition Process," "The Transition Between Phases," and "Selecting a Contractor"—are included for readers less familiar with the defense acquisition process. Readers familiar with the process may want to move ahead to "Controlling Schedules and Costs," near the end of the chapter.)

DEFINING NEW DEFENSE SYSTEMS

As new defense systems emerge over a period of years and improvements are made to existing systems, a large group of people in Congress, OSD, and the military services establish priorities among major acquisitions. Not only do the decision makers in this group change frequently, but so do the perceptions of the conditions on which acquisition judgments are based. An individual acquisition program, therefore, is usually subjected to frequent changes in funding, schedules, and technical performance requirements.[34]

The changes are caused by many variables, including altered perceptions of

- the current security threat;
- the future threat;
- changes in technology;
- the capability against the current threat;

---

[33] Ibid.
[34] GAO Report, *Can the United States Major Weapon Systems Acquisition Process Keep Pace with the Conventional Arms Threat Posed by the USSR?* GAO/PSAD/GP, 27 May 1980, pp. 23–24; *Defense Acquisition Performance Assessment Report* (Washington, D.C.: Office of the Secretary of Defense, January 2006), pp. 6–30.

- the best weapon mix to meet the current threat;
- the best mix of systems that can be acquired, given the available funding; and
- congressional support.[35]

Defense program managers (who must devote a significant amount of time to promoting their programs) often view this large group of decision makers as impediments to rapid completion of their programs. Overseers within the higher-level decision-making groups, reviewing a large number of complex systems on a regular basis, may easily lose sight of the uniqueness and importance of individual systems. A funding cut of a few million dollars can be disastrous to a program manager, whereas to a congressman it represents much less than .0001 percent of the defense budget and an even smaller portion of the total federal budget.[36]

The DoD budget, sent to Congress each year, is the result of a complicated consensus-building exercise. Literally hundreds of organizational units within the Defense Department contribute to decisions and their justifications. Each unit has its "staffed" positions and rebuttals representing its perspective on the myriad questions needing resolution in the course of developing plans, programs, and priorities. Each unit has written operational procedures and regulations governing the flow of information and (especially) paper work that punctuates the process. Finally, the unit position from previous years is known and offered as a starting point; most changes are therefore incremental.[37]

Congress authorizes and appropriates funds for all defense programs. As it has become much more directly involved with the technical details of the acquisition process, Congress has made numerous additions or amendments to authorization and appropriation bills, specifying constraints on and objectives for many weapon system programs.

The lack of satisfactory information appears to be one of the reasons Congress delves into the daily management of the acquisition process and changes funding levels throughout the life of a program. Three main reasons why this information may not be forthcoming from the Defense Department are as follows:

1. The complexity, advanced technology, and first-of-a-kind nature of many weapon systems preclude precise esti-

---

[35] Ibid.
[36] Ibid.
[37] Ibid.; Bradburn, "Strategic Postures in the Military Aircraft Industry," pp. 54–69.

mates of schedules, costs, or technical performance. There is frequently disagreement over how much information should be given to Congress.
2. When there is no general agreement on a well-defined mission need, program managers, their staffs, and higher headquarters cannot state confidently how effective a weapon will be. Decision makers at all levels become indecisive, and programs stretch out in time.
3. Program managers or their superiors are concerned that program funding will be curtailed and promotions may not be forthcoming if problems are candidly portrayed.

DoD Directive 5000.1, "The Defense Acquisition System," discussed in Chapter Two, provides the policies and principles that govern the defense acquisition system. DoD Instruction 5000.01, "Operation of the Defense Acquisition System," in turn establishes the management framework that implements these policies and principles. The Defense Acquisition Management System provides an event-based process whereby acquisition programs proceed through a series of milestones associated with significant program phases.

One key principle of the defense acquisition system is the use of acquisition program categories, where programs of increasing dollar value and management interest are subject to more stringent oversight. Specific dollar and other thresholds for these acquisition categories are contained in DoD Instruction 5000.02, "Operation of the Defense Acquisition System." The most expensive programs are known as Major Defense Acquisition Programs (MDAPs) or as Major Automated Information Systems (MAISs). These major programs have the most extensive statutory and regulatory reporting requirements. Major acquisition programs are defined by the following acquisition categories (ACATs).

In 2009, ACAT I programs have a dollar value estimated by the under secretary of defense for acquisition technology and logistics to require an eventual total expenditure for RDT&E of more than $365 million in FY 2000 constant dollars, or for procurement of more than $2.190 billion in FY 2000 constant dollars, or one which the under secretary for acquisition technology and logistics, as the defense acquisition executive (DAE), designates as special interest. ACAT ID programs are those ACAT I programs for which the under secretary of defense for acquisition technology and logistics retains Milestone Decision Authority (MDA); the "D" in ACAT "ID" refers to the DAE. ACAT IC programs are those ACAT I programs for which the DAE has delegated MDA to the Component Head, or if further delegated, to the Component

Acquisition Executive (CAE). The "C" reflects the delegation of MDA to the component level.[38]

ACAT IA programs pertain to the development of an automated information system (that is, a system of computer hardware and software, data, or telecommunications) that performs functions such as collecting, processing, storing, transmitting, and displaying information. Excluded are computer resources (hardware and software) that are an integral part of a weapon or weapon system or used for other highly sensitive information technology programs.[39]

ACAT IA programs either are designated by the MDA as a major automated information system or are estimated to exceed the following:

- $32 million in FY 2000 constant dollars for all expenditures, for all increments, regardless of the appropriation or fund source, directly related to the automated information system (AIS) definition, design, development, and deployment, and incurred *in any single fiscal year*; or
- $126 million in FY 2000 constant dollars for all expenditures, for all increments, regardless of appropriation or fund source, directly related to the AIS definition, design, development, and deployment, and incurred from the beginning of the Materiel Solution Analysis Phase through deployment *at all sites*; or
- $378 million in FY 2000 constant dollars for all expenditures, for all increments, regardless of appropriation or fund source, directly related to the AIS definition, design, development, and deployment, and incurred from the beginning of the Materiel Solution Analysis Phase through *sustainment for the estimated useful life of the system.*

ACAT II programs are acquisition programs that do not meet the criteria for ACAT I but have a dollar value estimated by the DoD Component Head to require an eventual total expenditure for RDT&E of more than $140 million in FY 2000 constant dollars, or for procurement of more than $660 million in FY 2000 constant dollars.

ACAT III programs are those that do not meet the above criteria for ACAT I or ACAT II.[40]

---

[38] DoD Instruction 5000.02, "Operation of the Defense Acquisition System," 8 Dec 2008, pp. 12–33.
[39] Ibid.
[40] Ibid.

Congressional Authorization and Appropriation

The contracting authority of DoD and other federal agencies is derived from congressional appropriations. Appropriations are made for a specified period of time and are usually stated in maximum dollar amounts. Those amounts are often amended one or more times a year.

There are three main types of appropriations: no-year, multiyear, and annual (single-year). No-year appropriations remain available for obligation until expended, and multiyear appropriations are available for a specific time, such as two or three years. Annual appropriations are available for obligation only during the current fiscal year, unless otherwise specified by law. Multiyear appropriations are the most prevalent form of congressional funding for the R&D and production phases of acquisition programs, and annual appropriations are used for operating expenses of federal agencies.

Subject to the availability of multiyear appropriated funds, Congress occasionally authorizes a government agency to execute a contract for more than one year's requirements for an R&D or production program in the hope of achieving schedule and cost economies. In these cases, parties to the contract are released from their mutual obligations only upon completion or termination of the contract. In contrast, a single-year contract (with options for extension beyond one year) allows the government the choice of extending the contract beyond one year, but it does not give the contractor a guarantee that it will do so. Not knowing whether the contract will be extended, the contractor usually has little inducement to make cost-reducing investments.

Congress budgets funds for an acquisition program into separate appropriations (for example, procurement, construction, or RDT&E) for each military service, and there are prohibitions against transferring funds from one account to another to accommodate unexpected short-term exigencies.

Reprogramming among appropriations is permissible within thresholds ($20 million for procurement and $10 million for RDT&E) if certain conditions are met. If thresholds are exceeded, DoD must return to Congress for reprogramming or a supplemental appropriation. The military services are allowed to reprogram funds within each appropriation without obtaining prior approval from Congress to finance cost increases for existing programs, with some exceptions.[41]

The net result of the congressional funding process is an operating budget with limited management reserves. Almost every program is underfunded, not overfunded. And the buying organizations

---
[41] Ibid.

also lack discretionary reserves. Reserves, if identified in the budget where congressional staff members can find them, are usually spotlighted, renamed slush funds, and deleted. These actions, in reality, punish prudent management.[42]

The complete absence of management reserves might be less significant if perfect short-term planning were possible. In the main, however, program budget estimates are prepared six to twelve months before their submission to Congress. Congress then spends the better part of a year deciding how much and where to increase or decrease requested program funding (usually with little awareness of the resulting imbalances across program phases). It can then be as much as two years before all the appropriated funds are actually "outlaid." Hence, the funding requirements can be three to four years out of date when the time comes to spend the money.

STAGES IN THE ACQUISITION PROCESS[43]

The acquisition of a weapon system is a two-stage process. The first stage, development, includes planning, research, testing, and evaluation; the second stage is production. Stage one is summarized below in the order in which it has generally occurred.

1. DoD identifies a security threat or defense operational mission. (A military service within DoD would normally take the lead in this and each of the following steps.)
2. DoD, often with suggestions from defense contractors, analyzes alternatives, designs an engineering development program to achieve the needed capability, and prepares an acquisition strategy and budget.
3. Congress authorizes and appropriates funds for the program.
4. The administration releases funds for the planned program.
5. DoD and interested contractors develop detailed technical approaches for the program (often simultaneously with steps 1 and 2).
6. DoD prepares a contract statement of work, with formal or informal assistance from contractors.
7. DoD issues requests for proposals (RFPs) to interested contractors and arranges pre-proposal conferences for bidders.

---

[42] Leonard Sullivan, "Characterizing the Acquisition Process," paper prepared for the Defense Acquisition Study, Center for Strategic and International Studies, Georgetown University, Jan 1986, p. E–6.

[43] DoD Instruction 5000.02, "Operation of the Defense Acquisition System," 8 Dec 2008.

8. Contractors submit proposals to DoD, where they are evaluated.
9. DoD selects one or more contractors, and the parties sign a contract for development of the weapon system.
10. The contractor begins work under the contract and each party initiates negotiated changes and modifications where required or deemed desirable (often as many as several changes a week, usually negotiated with the government monthly).
11. The contractor delivers items to DoD for testing and evaluation.

The formal acquisition process normally begins with a threat analysis, which evolves into an operational requirement. For example, if the Marine Corps defines a response to a threat for a new landing craft with access to a larger percentage of the world's beaches and with a higher speed than that of existing landing craft, a military requirement to meet such a gap would be established. If the Navy determines that a foreign power has made certain submarine advances, the Navy then defines the need to counter with an antisubmarine warfare helicopter with certain capabilities. That helicopter is then established as an operational requirement. Both requirements would reflect the estimated capabilities of potential adversaries.

There is often an earlier informal acquisition process that has its origin in defense laboratories or defense contractor firms, where engineers conceive of a new device or a new subsystem. Representatives of a firm may approach a military service, describe how they believe a device or subsystem will enhance the defense capability of the service, and then help the service prepare the justification and RFP to conduct a more formal study of the idea. This assistance nurtures the idea until it evolves into a military requirement.[44]

A defense firm wishing to obtain a contract to develop a new weapon system usually becomes involved in the program two to four years before a formal RFP is issued, or it is unlikely to qualify as a prospective contractor. This involvement generally means assisting the buying service in defining elements of the planned weapon system. The cost of conducting this initial work generally becomes part of contractors' overhead costs (for example, bid and proposal expense or independent research and development expense), which the Defense Department usually reimburses in part or in full. After several firms have completed

---

[44] Background Information, Senior Steering Group, Office of the Secretary of Defense, DoD Acquisition Study, 7–8 November 1985, pp. 8.9 to 8.10.

this work, the sponsoring service generally has sufficient information to request budget authority in the annual request of the department.

The acquisition process then proceeds from Definition of the Requirement to Materiel Solution Analysis, to Technology Development, to Engineering and Manufacturing Development, to Production and Deployment, to Operations and Support. As a system moves through the acquisition process, a program management office assumes responsibility for identifying, monitoring, and solving problems that affect schedule, cost, and technical performance. At each milestone, reviewers appraise the sources of risk and the progress achieved toward reducing it (*see* Figure 2).

The basic DoD Directive for major systems acquisition, 5000.01, version 8 December 2008, describes four key decisions and four phases of activity in the DoD acquisition process.[45] DoD Instruction 5000.02, version 8 December 2008, cites seventy-nine references containing information relevant to developing or producing acquisition systems.

The Materiel Development Decision precedes entry into any phase of the acquisition process. It is based on an analysis of user needs, technology opportunities, and resources. Competitive prototyping is required during the Technology Development Phase.

For Major Defense Acquisition Programs (MDAPs), a preliminary design review (PDR) must be conducted before Milestone B. PDRs for programs less than MDAPs may be conducted at the most appropriate time—either before or after Milestone B; however, a PDR that is conducted after Milestone B requires a post-PDR assessment by the Milestone Decision Authority (MDA).

Following the Materiel Development Decision, the MDA may authorize a program's entry into the acquisition management system at any point consistent with phase-specific entrance criteria and statutory requirements. Progress through the acquisition management system depends on obtaining sufficient knowledge to continue to the next phase of development.

User Needs and Technology Opportunities. The capability needs and acquisition management systems use joint concepts, integrated architectures and an analysis of doctrine, organization, training, materiel, leadership and education, personnel, and facilities in an integrated, collaborative process to define needed capabilities to guide the development of affordable systems. Representatives from multiple DoD communities assist in formulating broad, time-phased,

---

[45] DoD Instruction 5000.02, "Operation of the Defense Acquisition System," 8 Dec 2008, pp. 12–28.

operational goals and describing requisite capabilities in the Initial Capabilities Document. Promising technologies are identified from all sources domestic and foreign, including government laboratories and centers, academia, and the commercial sector.[46]

Evolutionary acquisition is the preferred DoD strategy for rapid acquisition of mature technology for the user.[47] An evolutionary approach delivers capability in increments, recognizing up front the need for future capability improvements. The objective is to balance needs and available capability with resources and to put capability into the hands of the user quickly. The success of the strategy depends on the phased definition of capability needs and system requirements and the maturation of technologies that lead to disciplined development and production of systems that provide increasing capability over time.

Materiel Solution Analysis Phase.[48] This phase begins with the Materiel Development Decision review as the formal entry point into the acquisition process. A Materiel Development Decision is mandatory for all programs. The purpose of this phase is to assess potential materiel solutions and to satisfy the phase-specific entrance criteria for the next program milestone designated by the MDA. Entrance into this phase depends on an approved Initial Capabilities Document resulting from an analysis of current mission performance and an analysis of potential concepts across the DoD components, international systems from allies, and cooperative opportunities.

At the Materiel Development Decision review, the Joint Staff presents the Joint Requirements Oversight Council recommendations and the DoD Component presents the Initial Capabilities Document, including the preliminary concept of operations, a description of the needed capability, the operational risk, and the basis for determining that existing capabilities and non-materiel approaches will not sufficiently mitigate the capability gap. The Director, Cost Assessment and Program Evaluation (DCAPE), or the DoD component equivalent, develops and approves the study guidance for the Analysis of Alternatives (AoA). The MDA directs initiation of the AoA, determines the acquisition phase of entry, identifies the initial review milestone, and designates the lead DoD component(s). MDA decisions are documented in an acquisition decision memorandum.

---

[46] Ibid.
[47] Ibid., p. 13.
[48] Ibid., p. 15.

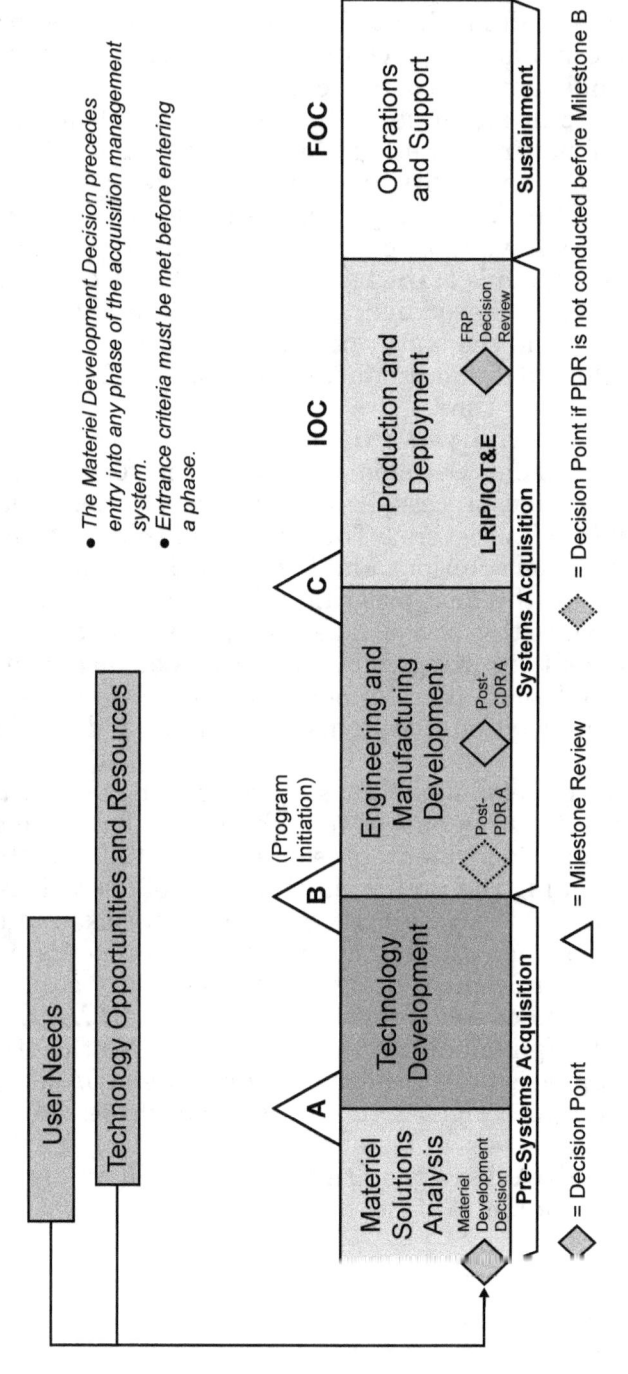

Technology Development Phase.[49] The purpose of this phase is to reduce technology risk, determine and mature the appropriate set of technologies to be integrated into a full system, and demonstrate critical technology elements (CTEs). Entrance into this phase depends on completing the AoA, identifying a proposed materiel solution, and obtaining full funding for planned Technology Development Phase activity.

Prior to Milestone A preceding the Technology Development Phase, the Technology Development Strategy (TDS) is submitted to the MDA and approved. The TDS documents the following:

a) The rationale for adopting an evolutionary strategy (the preferred approach), or using a single-step-to-full-capability strategy (e.g., for common supply items or commercial off-the-shelf items). For an evolutionary acquisition, the TDS includes a preliminary description of how the materiel solution will be divided into acquisition increments based on mature technology and an appropriate limitation on the number of prototype units or engineering development models that may be produced in support of a Technology Development Phase.
b) A preliminary acquisition strategy, including overall cost, schedule, and technical performance goals for the total research and development program.
c) Specific cost, schedule, and technical performance goals, including exit criteria, for the Technology Development Phase.
d) A description of the approach that will be used to ensure data assets will be made visible, accessible, and understandable to any potential user as early as possible.[50]
e) A list of known or probable critical program information and potential countermeasures such as antitamper in the preferred system concept and in the critical technologies and competitive prototypes to inform program protection.[51]
f) A time-phased workload assessment indentifying the manpower and functional competency requirements for successful program execution and the associated staffing plan, including the roles of government and nongovernment personnel.
g) A data management strategy.

---

[49] Ibid., p. 16.
[50] DoD Directive 8320.02, "DoD Data Sharing," 2 Dec 2004.
[51] DoD Instruction 5200.39, "Security Intelligence and Counterintelligence Support to Acquisition Program Protection," 16 Jul 2008.

h) A summary of the approved Cost and Software Data Reporting (CSDR) Plan(s) for the Technology Development Phase.[52]

Engineering and Manufacturing Development (EMD) Phase.[53] The purpose of the EMD Phase is to develop a system or an increment of capability; complete full system integration (technology risk reduction occurs during Technology Development); develop an affordable and executable manufacturing process; ensure operational supportability with particular attention to minimizing the logistics footprint; implement human systems integration; design for producibility; ensure affordability; protect critical program information by implementing appropriate techniques such as antitamper; and demonstrate system integration, interoperability, safety, and utility. The capability development document, acquisition strategy, systems engineering plan, and test and evaluation master plan guide this effort.

At Milestone B, the MDA determines the Low-Rate Initial Production (LRIP) quantity for MDAPs and major systems. LRIP quantities are minimized. The LRIP quantity for an MDAP (with rationale for quantities exceeding 10 percent of the total production quantity documented in the acquisition strategy) is included in the first selected acquisition report after its determination. Any increase in quantity after the initial determination must be approved by the MDA. The director of operational test and evaluation, following consultation with the program manager, determines the number of production or production-representative test articles required for live-fire test and evaluation and initial operational test and evaluation of programs on the OSD Test and Evaluation Oversight List.

Production and Deployment Phase.[54] The purpose of the Production and Deployment Phase is to achieve an operational capability that satisfies mission needs. Operational test and evaluation determines the effectiveness and suitability of the system. The MDA decides to commit the Department of Defense to production at Milestone C and documents the decision in an acquisition decision memorandum. Milestone C authorizes entry into LRIP (for major acquisition programs), into production or procurement (for nonmajor systems that do not require

---

[52] The Director of Cost Assessment and Program Evaluation (DCAPE) approves the CSDR Plan. DCAPE was formerly known as CAIG (Cost Analysis Improvement Group).

[53] DoD Instruction 5000.02, "Operation of the Defense Acquisition System," 8 Dec 2008, p. 20.

[54] Ibid., p. 26.

LRIP), or into limited deployment in support of operational testing for Major Automated Information System (MAIS) programs or software-intensive systems with no production components.

Operations and Support Phase.[55] The purpose of the Operations and Support Phase is to execute a support program that meets materiel readiness and operational support performance requirements and sustains the system in the most cost-effective manner over its total life cycle. Planning for this phase begins prior to program initiation and is documented in the life-cycle sustainment plan. Operations and Support has two major efforts: life-cycle sustainment and disposal.

The program manager works with the user to document performance and sustainment requirements in performance agreements specifying objective outcomes, measures, resource commitments, and stakeholder responsibilities. The program manager employs effective performance-based life-cycle product support planning, development, implementation, and management.

The company that developed the weapon system is normally awarded the first (and often subsequent) production contracts. Potential cost savings from competition may therefore not be realized because of the impracticality of introducing a second source or because of a sense of urgency; a second bidding procedure (if included) requires time and money. In addition, both the development contractor companies and the military services often argue persuasively that the expertise (acquired during the development program) required for the first production contract cannot realistically be transferred from one contractor to another because so many modifications to the design are made during initial production engineering. The policy of awarding production contracts before prototypes are completely tested makes it even more difficult to award the initial production contract to any firm other than the developer. For obvious reasons, the development contractor encourages this overlap (i.e., concurrency) between development and production.

There is good reason for the impatience of the military to proceed to production. The beginning of the acquisition process—DoD's planning and congressional budget hearings—can last from 12 to 24 months, or longer. Further, more than half the DoD procurement account (for items other than ammunition) is not spent until three or more years after Congress appropriates the funds. From initial planning to expenditure of funds for production, there can be a time lag of eight years.

---

[55] Ibid., p. 28.

The Transition Between Phases

An acquisition program can enter the above framework at any one of the three milestones (A, B, or C), depending on factors such as technological maturity, when the capability is required and when resources are available for the acquisition. Each phase has different purposes and entrance criteria, which can be regulatory or statutory. During Materiel Solution Analysis, an initial concept developed during the Joint Capabilities Integration and Development System (JCIDS) effort is refined, an AoA is conducted, and a TDS is developed based in part on results from the AoA. If a program receives Milestone A approval at the end of Materiel Solution Analysis, technology risk reduction efforts outlined in the TDS are conducted to determine what technologies are appropriate to be introduced into the intended system.[56]

If a program receives a Milestone B approval, then the program proceeds to begin development of the capability and reduction of integration and manufacturing risk.[57]

Milestone C represents the beginning of low-rate initial production, which is intended both to prepare manufacturing and quality control processes for a higher rate of production and to provide production-representative articles for operational test and evaluation (OT&E). Upon completion of OT&E and demonstration of adequate control over manufacturing processes, a full-rate production decision may be granted, allowing the program to produce the remaining assets planned for the program. When enough systems are delivered and other predefined criteria are met, and initial operating capability can be attained, some degree of operations can be achieved. Eventually, full operational capability would be achieved when the system is ready to operate as much as required.[58]

In practice, the lines between phases of the acquisition process are frequently blurred because of the iterative nature of development and initial production. Indeed, it has been management of the transition from one phase to the next that has posed significant problems for senior defense managers over the years.

Program appraisal has many possible approaches. Usually, one or more technical experts identify particular components of a system being developed and then describe or rate the risk associated with each component. Their ratings reflect the level of risk and

---

[56] Ibid., pp. 2–28.

[57] CRS Report, 20 Jun 2007, p. 12n23. DoD's approach to proceeding with detailed design and integration of mature technologies while continuing risk reduction of other less mature technologies that will be integrated later is called evolutionary acquisition.

[58] CRS Report, 20 Jun 2007, p. 12.

THE DEFENSE ACQUISITION PROCESS

sometimes the consequences of potential technical problems for the cost, schedule, or technical performance of the overall system.[59]

Prolonging the acquisition process is a common occurrence. The lengthy acquisition process (ten years or longer) for major weapon systems is a central problem and causes substantial cost increases as well.

SELECTING A CONTRACTOR

The government source selection process includes preparation and issuance of an RFP and the selection of one or more contractors. The RFP requests whatever information is needed to select contractors who can accomplish the development or production program at a reasonable cost. Included in the RFP, and available to contractors when preparing their proposals, are the technical, managerial, and cost criteria against which the proposals are to be evaluated.[60]

The secretary of a military service designates the service acquisition executive (or sometimes the secretary himself) to be the source selection authority (SSA), and three or more people are assigned to serve as members of a Source Selection Advisory Council (SSAC). After a military service has issued an RFP to prospective contractors and the contractors have responded with their (multivolume) proposals, the SSAC convenes a temporary committee called the Source Selection Evaluation Board (SSEB).[61] The time and effort spent on these evaluations vary widely, but six months or more is typical for major acquisition programs.

Most contractor proposals for the development of complex weapon systems are subdivided into the areas of technical, management, and cost information corresponding with the evaluation criteria. In evaluating the technical information, for example, the SSEB normally identifies a number of key technical items that are further divided into factors, with chairmen assigned. Factor chairmen evaluate each contractor proposal according to their specialty. On large proposals there can be more than eighty factors and the total number of source selection personnel may exceed two hundred. Factor scores are tallied to arrive at an item score; item scores are tallied to arrive at an area score.

The SSEB then prepares and submits an evaluation report to the SSAC. If the SSAC decides to assign weights (their use is not mandatory) to areas of contractor proposals, the weights must be assigned before receiving contractor proposals. After analyzing the SSEB's findings and applying any weights, the SSAC prepares a report for

---

[59] GAO Report, *Technical Risk Assessment*, GAO/EMD 86–5, Apr 1986.
[60] Bradburn, "Strategic Postures in the Military Aircraft Industry," pp. 54–69.
[61] Ibid.

the SSA. The report may or may not recommend a specific contractor, depending on the SSA's preferences. The SSA then selects the winning contractor or contractors based on (1) comparative evaluations of proposals, (2) costs, (3) risk assessment, (4) past performance, (5) contractual considerations, and (6) surveys of contractor capabilities.

During the source selection process, government personnel at times, often through suggestions to improve the quality of all proposals, disclose the technical and design approaches of a company as described in its proposal, to other prospective contractors to allow them to consider incorporating the proposal's better or less costly features (or both) into their own proposals. Industry generally considers this practice, known as technical leveling, unethical, particularly because it has no counterpart in the commercial marketplace. The possibility for technical leveling to unduly influence the ultimate selection of a contractor is substantial.

Controlling Schedules and Costs

Notwithstanding substantial budget increases during the past thirty years, major defense programs have repeatedly experienced significant schedule delays and cost increases. About nine in ten programs exceed initial cost estimates, excluding the effects of quantity changes and inflation.[62]

A review of the history of major weapons procurement reveals that the discrepancies between estimated and actual costs have been significant for many years. Some believe the discrepancy is due to deficient cost estimating; others believe it is due to deficient cost control, or due to both. A 1962 Harvard University study (discussed in Chapter Two), based on twelve major weapon programs of the 1950s, concluded that development costs were generally significantly higher than originally estimated.[63] Production costs also tended to exceed original estimates by significant margins. These systems also experienced schedule delays, which averaged 36 percent beyond the projected time for completion. In the 1960s, cost increases continued to occur on major systems. No systems were found that had been completed at the cost projected, and none was found to have cost less than predicted.[64]

---

[62] U.S. Congress, Senate, testimony of Norman Augustine, president of Martin Marietta and former under secretary of the Army, Hearing before the Committee on Governmental Affairs, *Acquisition Process in the Department of Defense*, 21–27 October and 5 November 1981; Jacques S. Gansler, "Program Instability: Causes, Costs, and Cures," paper prepared for the Defense Acquisition Study, Center for Strategic and International Studies, Georgetown University, 1 Mar 1986.

[63] Peck and Scherer, *Weapons Acquisition Process*, 1962, pp. 429–30; U.S. Congress, House, Committee on Government Operations, *Inaccuracy of Department of Defense Acquisition Cost Estimates*, 16 November 1979, p. 4.

[64] Report of the Acquisition Cycle Task Force, Defense Science Board, 1977 Summer Study, 15 Mar 1978, p. 68; House, Committee on Government Operations, *Inaccuracy of Department of Defense Acquisition Cost Estimates*, 16 November 1979, p. 4.

Whereas the 1960s and 1970s saw numerous cases of significant cost increases in defense acquisition programs, the 1980s and 1990s witnessed even greater cost increases, evidenced by OSD records and GAO analyses of cost growth on major acquisition programs.[65]

In an insightful report issued in 1979 titled *Impediments to Reducing the Costs of Weapon Systems,* the GAO outlined several aspects of the acquisition process that contribute to the cost of large defense programs.[66]

On government programs, annual congressional review of the DoD budget and changing priorities, whether political or military, often mean a change in funding levels on a major program one or more times a year. Pentagon and congressional reductions in quantities and delays in approving funds frequently disrupt the development or production process, thereby increasing the unit cost of a weapon system. In particular, funding uncertainty makes long-term production planning extremely difficult and decreases the probability that contractors will benefit from any attempt to reduce production costs, increase productivity, or both. Because increasing and decreasing labor resources is easier than acquiring and disposing of capital investments to cope with fluctuating business volume, defense contractors may elect not to invest in labor-saving equipment. As a result, production costs remain high.

The Basis for Profits

The bulk of major defense systems acquisition money is expended through contracts. Once the contracting parties agree on the estimated costs, profit is negotiated largely as a percentage of these costs.

Unfortunately, this method of contracting also provides little incentive for contractors to reduce costs; in fact, it often encourages higher costs. For the past four decades, studies by DoD, the Logistics Management Institute, the GAO, and other organizations have concluded that changes in the method by which profits are earned are necessary to motivate contractors to reduce costs. In the late 1970s and 1980s, OSD directed DoD negotiators to place more weight on invested capital and less on cost in the negotiation of profit. In fact, however, this directive produced no

---

[65] GAO Report, *Major Weapon Systems Continue to Experience Cost and Schedule Problems,* GAO–06–368, Mar 2006; GAO Report, *Assessments of Selected Weapon Programs,* GAO–09–326SP, Mar 2009.

[66] GAO Report, *Impediments to Reducing the Costs of Weapon Systems,* PSAD–80–6, 8 Nov 1979.

more than a minimal shift away from cost-based profit determination. It is not yet clear whether this is because of limited potential benefits to the contractors or the lack of implementation skills by government personnel. Although the Defense Department has devised various theoretical incentives for cost reduction, the costs actually incurred on a prior contract usually serve as the baseline for negotiating costs of follow-on contracts. Thus, a cost-based profit structure discourages the acquisition of plants and equipment or any other actions by management that could lower the overall acquisition costs to the government.[67]

One of the most common complaints from defense contractors has been that doing business with the government is difficult, time consuming, and costly, particularly when compared to commercial practices. Indeed, there is no doubt that government procurement practices are complex, time consuming, and costly. Two factors contributing to these results are the perceived need by government to protect its interests and to provide safeguards for the proper expenditure of public funds.

In addition, the government may seek to use the procurement process to help accomplish its socioeconomic objectives. Eligibility for government contracts thus depends on compliance with regulations promoting a variety of social objectives.[68] These objectives include maintaining employee health and safety, protecting the environment, supporting small business, supporting minority businesses and employment programs, maintaining wage-level supports, aiding the economy and protecting domestic business, encouraging NATO (North Atlantic Treaty Organization) standardization, and providing employment for the handicapped.

Limited Rates of Production

In the commercial sector of the U.S. economy, production volume is largely determined by company management based on production efficiency and market analyses. In the case of defense systems, however, production rates are often dictated by constraints set by Congress, Office of Management and Budget, OSD, and the military services and in part by product efficiencies. Major weapon systems, subject to annual review, are often revised numerous times. Again, either Congress, OSD, or the military services can (and often do) dictate that production of items be conducted at less-efficient low rates to ensure that an active industrial base, that is, an in-place production capability, is maintained.[69]

---

[67] Ibid. The comments in this report were as relevant in 2009 as they were in 1979.
[68] Ibid.
[69] Ibid.

Uneconomical production rates of new DoD hardware can also result from concurrent development and production, dictating that a limited production rate be maintained until the hardware has been tested and proved effective. Both new and standard hardware may also be produced at a limited rate because sufficient funds are not available in the DoD budget to produce a greater number in a given year. Whatever the reasons for limiting production to less than the optimal rate, the result is often a loss of productivity and an increase in the cost of major weapon systems.[70]

Limitations of Government Program Managers

The acquisition of large defense development and production programs poses one of the most challenging industrial management problems in the world. Controlling and reducing costs is difficult in any industry, but even more so in larger and more complex engineering development and production programs. Costs tend to rise in all organizations unless managers and their staffs are skilled in industrial management and determined to control or reduce costs. Yet the Army, the Navy, and, to a lesser extent, the Air Force provide limited industrial management training for military officers whom they assign to key managerial positions in major acquisition programs. Military officers assigned to acquisition programs often have extensive combat arms experience (for example, as pilots, ship captains, armor commanders). Government civilians as well as military officers assigned to acquisition programs frequently have little or no advanced training and experience in contractor operations and the planning and control of large industrial development and production programs.

A procurement system with few cost-reduction incentives, directed by government managers with limited industrial knowledge, skills, and minimal industrial management experience, understandably will have significant cost problems. Given the variety of factors described in the preceding paragraphs, it would be surprising if defense programs did not experience significant cost increases.

---

[70] Ibid.

CHAPTER **Two**

DEFENSE ACQUISITION REFORMS IN THE 1960s AND 1970s

In 1962 and 1964, two innovative books resulted from a three-year research project at the Harvard Business School on the development of advanced weapons: *The Weapons Acquisition Process: An Economic Analysis,* by Merton J. Peck and Frederic M. Scherer, and *The Weapons Acquisition Process: Economic Incentives,* by Frederic M. Scherer.[1] The first volume described the basic structure of the acquisition process and presented a comprehensive economic analysis. The second volume built on the first but focused on economic incentives inherent in defense acquisition.

Peck and Scherer examined six specific problems in the management of research, development, and production programs conducted by industry and Department of Defense (DoD): (1) schedule slippage, (2) cost growth, (3) lack of qualified government personnel, (4) high frequency of personnel turnover, (5) inadequate methods of cost estimation, and (6) insufficient training in the measurement and control of contractor performance. Fifty years later, acquisition reforms continue to seek remedies to the same problems.

Acquisition Reform During the 1960s—The McNamara Innovations

The Department of Defense Reorganization Act of 1958 authorized the defense secretary to assign the development, production, and operational use of weapon systems to any military department or service. Although this legislation provided the groundwork for the expanding role of the Office of the Secretary of Defense (OSD) in the management of defense acquisition programs, the authority to direct and control DoD was not fully exercised until 1961 when Robert S. McNamara, a former Ford Motor Company executive, became secretary of defense. McNamara believed in active management from the top, choosing to play a role in all aspects of programs rather than wait for problems to be brought to his attention.[2]

---

[1] Merton J. Peck and Frederic M. Scherer, *The Weapons Acquisition Process: An Economic Analysis* (Boston: Division of Research, Harvard Business School, 1962); Frederic M. Scherer, *The Weapons Acquisition Process: Economic Incentives* (Boston: Division of Research, Harvard Business School, 1964).

[2] Alain C. Enthoven and K. Wayne Smith, *How Much Is Enough? Shaping the Defense Program, 1961–1969* (New York: Harper & Row, 1971), p. 32.

During Secretary McNamara's first year in office, he decided to centralize authority and planning for the defense establishment at the OSD level and to decentralize operations to the military services. He achieved the centralization of the planning and operational decisions during his term of office, but only partially achieved decentralization of operations.[3]

The OSD and the military services produced innovations in three acquisition areas during the 1960s: program planning and selection, source selection and contracting, and management of ongoing acquisition programs.

During the administrations of John F. Kennedy and Lyndon B. Johnson (1960–1968), in response to numerous cost overruns of the 1950s and early 1960s, OSD discouraged the use of cost-plus-fixed-fee contracts in favor of fixed-price and incentive contracts, attempting to stimulate more rigorous control of costs. In the early 1960s, Secretary McNamara (1961–1968) and his Pentagon management team developed and sought to implement a number of additional improvements. McNamara centralized the functions of planning, programming, and budgeting (subsequently called the Planning, Programming, and Budgeting System, or PPBS) in the Pentagon and assigned more decision-making authority to a new staff of younger military and civilian systems analysts working in OSD. PPBS provided the secretary and the president with an organized approach to major program decisions and to the allocation of resources within DoD, though it was not designed to have a major impact on the acquisition process. These organizational changes were intended to improve efficiency and cost effectiveness, reduce waste, and also mitigate strong interservice rivalries, which had generated overlapping—and in some cases, such as long-range missiles—duplicate weapons programs.

Another improvement was the creation of the Office of Systems Analysis to perform cost-effectiveness studies aided by improved cost estimating, with the help of research at Rand Corporation.[4] Subsequently, the military services each adopted or strengthened their own systems analysis organizations. Some in the military services saw this development as a matter of self-preservation, the only means by which to survive the more rigorous program evaluations being conducted by the Office of the Secretary of Defense.

To enhance contractor source selection and contracting, several improvements were adopted: parametric cost estimating,[5] formal

---

[3] David D. Acker, "The Maturing of the DoD Acquisition Process," *Defense Systems Management Review* (Summer 1980): 14–17.

[4] Background Information, Senior Steering Group, Office of the Secretary of Defense, DoD Acquisition Study, 7–8 November 1985.

[5] Parametric cost estimating derives cost estimates from employing historical costs related to physical or performance characteristics.

source selection procedures, contractor performance evaluations, total package procurement, contract definition, and incentive contracting. In the management of ongoing programs, innovations in the 1960s included the adoption of the program manager concept; the consolidation of contract administration across the military services; the Program Evaluation and Review Technique (PERT) for scheduling; the Cost and Schedule Control System Criteria (C/SCSC), which subsequently became the Earned Value Management System (EVMS); Systems Engineering; Cost Information Reports; Contractor Funds Status Reporting; Configuration Management; and Technical Performance Measurement (TPM). The large number of management innovations taxed the capabilities of the services to implement the new techniques.

While these reforms produced a number of positive results, especially in terms of matching available resources to mission requirements, the services continued to resist OSD's control of the weapons acquisition process. Moreover, several well-publicized procurement fiascos, most notably the Air Force's ill-fated F–111 fighter-bomber and C–5A cargo transport programs, revealed the limits of McNamara's centralized management policies vis-à-vis the services.

The McNamara team also developed and implemented, to greater or lesser degrees, a variety of acquisition organizations and techniques, including the Defense Supply Agency, Defense Contract Administration Service (DCAS), Defense Contract Audit Agency (DCAA), Total Package Procurement (TPP), and the Development Concept Paper (DCP), as well as increased competition among prospective contractors.[6]

Among McNamara's acquisition improvements, TPP appears to have encountered the most serious difficulties in its implementation. It required firms to contract, on a fixed-price basis, for both the acquisition program development and production stages at the same time, as a means of preventing a winning contractor (for the development program) from facing little or no competition in bidding on the subsequent production stage. TPP was applied on acquisition programs such as the Lockheed C–5A cargo plane, the General Dynamics F–111 fighter aircraft, and the Grumman F–14A Tomcat fighter aircraft. Each of these acquisition programs experienced large cost overruns. TPP was judged to be ineffective for two reasons: (1) the military services introduced or allowed numerous contract changes in the programs, thereby obscuring any incentives for cost control and accountability for cost growth; and

---

[6] U.S. Congress, Senate, testimony of Laurence E. Lynn, Professor Public Policy, Harvard University, hearing before the Committee on Governmental Affairs, 21–27 October and 5 November 1981, pp. 133–35.

(2) the services, reluctant to incur delays by shifting to new contractors, decided not to enforce most of the fixed-price TPP contracts. In 1966, Secretary McNamara abandoned the TPP concept.[7]

One of the most important elements in the McNamara approach to management during the 1960s was the commitment to centralized decision making in OSD. The new Planning, Programming, Budgeting System correlated resource inputs with categories of performance (e.g., strategic retaliatory forces, tactical air forces, general-purpose forces, and research and development). The newly created office of assistant secretary of defense for systems analysis employed more than one hundred professional personnel preparing and using parametric cost estimates in cost-benefit analyses for use by the secretary of defense and other decision makers in the Pentagon. In addition to these centralization initiatives, Secretary McNamara's office issued a number of new acquisition policies and directives, including:

- Planning procedures for integrated logistics support for systems and equipment (the integration of supply and maintenance considerations and planning into the systems engineering and design process);
- Procedures for contractor proposal evaluation and source selection;
- Procedures for improved quality assurance (the enforcement of technical criteria governing the quality of materials, data, supplies, and services);
- Information systems for planning and control of acquisition schedules and costs;
- Value engineering (a program to eliminate or modify unessential equipment features and thus minimize costs);
- Configuration management (technical and administrative procedures to [1] identify and document functional and physical characteristics of a configuration item, [2] control changes to those characteristics, and [3] record and report change processing and implementation status); and
- Work breakdown structure (WBS) frameworks (product-oriented family trees used to subdivide large programs into their parts consisting of hardware, software, services, and work tasks that result from engineering efforts during development and production of defense systems or equipment).[8]

---

[7] Gordon Adams, Paul Murphy, and William Grey Rosenau, *Controlling Weapons Costs: Can the Pentagon Reforms Work?* (New York: Council on Economic Priorities, 1983), pp. 19–20.

[8] Acker, "The Maturing of the DoD Acquisition Process," pp. 35–37.

New planning and control techniques for streamlining the acquisition process were introduced at a school for Army, Navy, and Air Force prospective program managers established by OSD at Wright-Patterson Air Force Base in Dayton, Ohio. Several private consulting firms also developed and offered acquisition courses for training DoD and contractor personnel in these new techniques.

McNamara promoted the program management concept as a means of centralizing responsibility for major acquisition programs. One person was to direct and be held accountable for the development and/or production of a weapon system. In testimony before the House Appropriations Committee in 1964, McNamara stated:

> I want to look to a point of central control and information in the form of a program manager for each major weapon system. . . . He shall be rewarded in his career for prompt and analytical disclosure of his problems as well as for his successes. This is a key position in our military departments, demanding the best managerial talents on which I want to place full reliance for our future weapons inventories.[9]

Unfortunately, limited managerial training available to DoD acquisition managers during the 1960s fell far short of the level of knowledge and skill required to implement the new policies, directives, and techniques.[10] After several years of sustained effort, serious cost, schedule, and technical performance problems continued to disrupt the acquisition process. Defense critics made frequent allusions to the costly discrepancies between projected and actual performance by defense contractors. Although the reform concepts appeared sound, their implementation had fallen far short of expectations.

Seven years later, in 1971, Deputy Secretary of Defense David Packard told the same committee:

> With the long tradition of putting a general in charge of the battle, or putting an admiral in charge of a fleet, one would think it would be easy to get the services to accept the proposition that you should have one man with authority in charge of a weapon development and acquisition program. We have been able to get this done in a few isolated cases, but it simply has not been fully accepted as a management must by any of the services.[11]

---

[9] U.S. Congress, House, testimony of Robert S. McNamara, Secretary of Defense, before the Appropriations Committee, 1964.

[10] J. Ronald Fox, *Arming America: How the U.S. Buys Weapons* (Boston: Division of Research, Harvard Business School, 1974), pp. 198–213.

[11] U.S. Congress, House, testimony of David Packard, Deputy Secretary of Defense, before the Appropriations Committee, 1971.

Military officers assigned to program management positions usually failed to have the requisite training and experience in procurement and general business management to oversee and negotiate effectively with industrial contractors. Their management assignments were frequently brief due to the established military policy of assignment rotations.

Problems of cost, schedule, and technical performance continued to plague defense acquisition throughout the 1960s. In 1968 Robert Charles, the assistant secretary of the Air Force, told an audience at George Washington University: "A review of six recent contracts indicates that actual technical performance of the operational equipment came to less than 86% of the contractor's proposed technical performance on which the decision to proceed was based."[12] In 1969 Robert Benson, who had just completed two years as an analyst in the Office of the Secretary of Defense, testified during government hearings that "about 90% of the major weapon systems that the Defense Department procures end up costing at least twice as much as was originally estimated." Also in 1969, Richard Stubbing, an analyst in the U.S. Bureau of the Budget, told the same congressional committee: "Of eleven major weapon systems begun during the 1960's, only two of them had electronic components that performed up to standard. One performed at a 75% level of the technical performance requirement and two at a 50% level. But six—a majority—of the eleven performed at a level 25% or less of the technical performance standards and specifications set for them."[13] In the same year, the U.S. General Accounting Office (later called the U.S. Government Accountability Office) performed a survey of thirty-eight ongoing major weapon systems programs and found cost estimates already 50 percent higher than the original contract figures.[14]

THE TRANSITION FROM ROBERT MCNAMARA TO MELVIN LAIRD

After serving more than seven years as secretary of defense, Robert McNamara left the Pentagon in March 1968 to become president of the World Bank. Cost growth, schedule slippages, and technical performance shortfalls in major acquisition programs, combined with the failure of the Total Package Procurement method, prompted President Richard M. Nixon in 1970 to appoint the

---

[12] Address by the Honorable Robert Charles, Assistant Secretary of the Air Force (Installations and Logistics) to the George Washington University R&D [Research and Development] Contracts Conference, Washington, D.C., 7 November 1968.

[13] U.S. Congress, Joint Economic Committee, testimony of Richard Stubbing, U.S. Bureau of the Budget, Hearings on Defense Procurement, Washington, D.C., 10 March 1969.

[14] Comptroller General of the United States, Report to the Congress on Major Weapons Programs, 1969.

Blue Ribbon Defense Panel (Fitzhugh Commission). In 1972, Congress appointed the Congressional Commission on Government Procurement to identify the causes of weapons cost overruns and to propose new methods of cost control.[15]

As the 1970s began, critics of the Defense Department within Congress and the media became more vocal and more persistent. In March 1970, the Washington-based Logistics Management Institute prepared a preliminary report on government-contractor relationships in defense acquisition. The report summarized the most common shortcomings of the Defense Department management of the acquisition process:

> *First* is the observation that the defense acquisition process apparently is out of control. Initial time and cost estimates—and even updated estimates—cannot be depended upon. Mandatory engineering changes arise continually throughout the process. Management information and control systems do not identify impending problems in time for preventive action to be taken.
>
> *Second* is the claim that bargaining positions (between government and contractors) are unbalanced; first one side, then the other has the advantage. The theory of countervailing pressures acting to produce fair and realistic contract terms does not hold. With emphasis on economies of scale and series production, there are only a small number of weapon systems competitions each year and prospective contractors believe that their very existence may be jeopardized by failure to win. Hence, the Department of Defense (DoD) is in the dominant position and can compel an unreasonable bargain. Following award of the contract, the DoD, committed to the timely success of the program, is in the weaker position as the sole source contractor negotiates for contract changes, product acceptance, and follow-on business.
>
> *Third* is the assertion that incentives both for efficient operation and for candor about expectations are lacking. Heavy reliance on historical costs in pricing, lack of adequate consideration of capital required in negotiating profit rates, and the high risk of low future utilization of contractor-owned facilities impede investment and modernization of contractor plants. The hazard to program survival, of high-costs, schedule delays, or looming technical difficulties, as each program competes with others in and out of the DoD, motivates optimistic and less than candid forecasts of program performance by DoD and contractor personnel alike.
>
> *Fourth* are allegations of confusion, connivance, and deception by the DoD-contractor combination. Close cooperation and

---

[15] Adams, Murphy, and Rosenau, *Controlling Weapons Costs*, 1983, pp. 19–20.

common interest are held in contrast to the arm's length relationship preferred by much of regulation and policy. Policy notwithstanding, the military departments receive advice and assistance from prospective contractors in preparation of requests for proposals. Contractors receive aid from Government personnel in performance of contracts, reducing the effectiveness of contracts as instruments of control.[16]

In 1969, at the beginning of Richard Nixon's first presidential term, Melvin R. Laird was appointed secretary of defense. Laird was determined to end the Vietnam War he inherited from the prior administration and to improve his department's standing with the American people and Congress. An eight-term representative from Wisconsin, Laird had served on the House Appropriations Subcommittee on Defense.

Laird's mandate for change grew out of an increasing perception that the military establishment, in Vietnam as well as in the area of weapons acquisition, had somehow gone astray. The massive defense expenditures of the sixties had seemingly failed to provide the United States with any discernable military advantage over the Communist bloc. Television images in American homes every night demonstrated that in Vietnam, expensive high-tech weapons did little to affect the bloody stalemate that continued to sap the nation's political will. In both nuclear and conventional arms, the Soviet Union appeared to be capable of outproducing the United States, threatening to swamp the nation's forces with relatively unsophisticated but nevertheless effective weapons if an all-out war ever came.

In his quest to reform the Defense Department, Laird wanted to move quickly. He needed to end the war in Vietnam and to restructure the department's defense posture in the postwar period. In addition, Laird had a self-imposed time limit. The new secretary had publicly vowed not to serve beyond the end of Nixon's first term.[17]

In many ways, the new secretary's background had prepared him for tackling procurement reform. Laird's connections with House and Senate leaders would help smooth over relations between DoD and Congress, while his knowledge of the political aspects of defense acquisition would help him navigate the interrelationship between the military and commercial elites.

---

[16] Report, Logistics Management Institute, *The DoD-Contractor Relationship—Preliminary Review*, Task 69–21 (McLean, Va.: Logistics Management Institute, March 1970), pp. 8–10.

[17] Interv, Defense Acquisition History Project (DAHP) with Melvin R. Laird, 18 Nov 2004, Office of the Secretary of Defense (OSD) Historical Office, Washington, D.C., p. 6.

Although Vietnam absorbed most of Laird's energies, he refused to let the war sidetrack his determination to study and implement changes to the Pentagon procurement practices. High-profile failures and cost overruns had eroded congressional confidence in Defense Department acquisition management, and Laird hoped reforms would improve both results and his department's standing on Capitol Hill.

DEPUTY SECRETARY OF DEFENSE DAVID PACKARD

In seeking a strong acquisition reform program, Secretary Laird brought aboard one of the nation's most successful industrial managers as deputy secretary of defense. David Packard had honed his management skills as the head of Hewlett-Packard (HP), where he helped grow the company from a garage workshop into a leading electronic instrument manufacturer with over 13,000 employees and hundreds of millions of dollars in revenue. Packard was widely recognized as a management expert and was well regarded in his dealings with the Defense Department relating to the management of defense acquisition programs.[18]

Packard's position as a major shareholder of his company initially created a potential problem: how could he, as the secretary of defense's point man on the acquisition of weapons and equipment, make decisions that might affect the value of his massive holdings in a major defense contractor? On the other hand, Packard explained at his confirmation hearing that he would have to sell over three million shares of company stock in order to comply with federal conflict-of-interest laws; such an enormous volume of stock sales would depress the HP share price and hurt ordinary shareholders.[19]

Packard solved this problem by arranging to put his holdings in trust during his tenure at defense, foregoing all company dividends and even any appreciation in the value of his stock.[20] Laird also barred Packard from taking any official actions relating to Hewlett-Packard.[21] This arrangement satisfied conflict-of-interest rules but cost Packard millions. In his autobiography, he noted that after three years in office his "HP stock had increased in value and I estimated that I'd given

---

[18] Interv, OSD Historical Office with David Packard, 9 Nov 1987, p. 4.

[19] "Nominations of Laird, Packard, and Darden," Hearings before the Senate Armed Services Committee, 91st Cong., 1st sess., 14 January 1969, pp. 61–62.

[20] Interv, OSD Historical Office with Packard, 9 Nov 1987, p. 3.

[21] Memo, Melvin R. Laird, Secretary of Defense, for Listed Parties, 24 Jan 1969, sub: Matters Involving the Hewlett-Packard Company, Comptroller Subject Decimal File, 1969 (75–0089), box 11, 020 OSD, 69, Record Group (RG) 330, Washington National Records Center (WNRC), Suitland, Md.

away about $20 million."²² Eventually his commitment to his company played a major part in his decision to leave DoD.

Laird gave Packard a free hand to run research, development, and procurement functions within DoD and appointed a new team to work with Packard in these fields. A key participant was Barry Shillito, a former business executive and assistant secretary of the Navy for installations and logistics, to serve as assistant secretary of defense for installations and logistics. In that position, Shillito would oversee weapons system procurement under Packard's direction.²³

Other important members of the Defense Department acquisition team included Assistant Secretary of Defense (Comptroller) Robert C. Moot, who had entered office the previous summer and had already earned accolades. John S. Foster continued to serve as director of defense research and engineering (DDR&E), a post he had held since 1965. DDR&E had responsibility for formulating a department-wide plan for research, development, test, and engineering, based on the latest threat assessments, technological possibilities, and the requirements of the services.²⁴ As the secretary's point man on research and development, Foster also reviewed the development status of weapons systems that the services presented to Laird for production approval decisions.

The Office of Systems Analysis presented a special case. This controversial DoD component played a major role in defense acquisition but had fallen into disfavor with Congress.²⁵ The office under its initial director, Alain C. Enthoven, took the blame for many of the errors that occurred during McNamara's tenure and became the target of service complaints when the office proposed procurement targets that differed from the services' own stated requirements.²⁶ Congressman L. Mendel Rivers, who chaired the House Armed Services Committee and often sided with the military services, had especially intense feelings against the Systems Analysis office. During an appearance by Laird and Packard before this committee, Rivers lashed out against the office:

> [A]s sure as the sun rises in the heavens and you are sitting in that seat, if you retain this organization you are headed for trouble with this committee. . . . We have had trouble with that Systems Analysis, and we have sworn by the eternal gods that it will not run this country any longer, like it did in the other ad-

---

[22] David Packard, *The HP Way: How Bill Hewlett and I Built our Company*, eds. David Kirby and Karen Lewis (New York: HarperBusiness, 1995), p. 185.
[23] Interv, DAHP with Barry Shillito, 6, 8 Jun 2005, p. 17.
[24] Interv, DAHP with John S. Foster, 19 Feb 2003, p. 3.
[25] Interv, OSD Historical Office with Packard, 9 Nov 1987, p. 6.
[26] Interv, DAHP with Foster, 19 Feb 2003, p. 17.

ministration. It just about ruined NATO, and it sure ruined the Department of Defense.[27]

Mendel Rivers and other members of Congress resented and were unaccustomed to the strong analytical arguments supporting McNamara's weapons acquisition decisions—arguments that sometimes undermined the non-quantitative judgments of influential members of Congress and of a number of senior military officers. Laird named outgoing Assistant Secretary Alain Enthoven's deputy, Ivan Selin, as acting assistant secretary for systems analysis. But a number of members of Congress expected him to clean house so far as Systems Analysis was concerned; simply replacing Enthoven with his deputy would not do. Congressman Rivers warned Laird about congressional opposition to the Systems Analysis office personnel who, in Rivers' view, allegedly "had injected their own views in strategic and tactical decisions to such an extent that they negated the statutory functions imposed on the Joint Chiefs of Staff."[28] Not surprisingly, Selin was tarred with the same brush as his former boss and could never get Senate confirmation. Senator Barry M. Goldwater wired Secretary Laird in August that he was "shocked" to learn that Laird's nominee "was author of [the] report [Senator William] Proxmire used indicating Air Force does not want a second buy [of the] C–5A. [He] thought this man [i.e., Selin] had departed long ago, for the best interests of defense, urge separation immediately."[29] After nearly a year of tension and frustration, Selin gave up and submitted his resignation in late 1969.[30] The secretary reluctantly accepted it and replaced Selin with Gardiner Tucker, who served as assistant secretary of defense for systems analysis for the remainder of Laird's term.

SECRETARY LAIRD CREATES THE BLUE RIBBON DEFENSE PANEL (1969)

With his acquisition team in place, Secretary Laird began a two-track effort to change the way the Pentagon did business. While Packard provided the internal push for adoption of his progressive management techniques, an independent outside panel reviewed DoD's practices and organization with the goal of recommending improvements to both. The panel resulted in part from

---

[27] U.S. Congress, House, Hearings before the Committee on Armed Services, 91st Cong., 1st sess., *Military Posture*, pt. 1, 1970, p. 1710.
[28] Ltr, Congressman L. Mendel Rivers to Packard, 7 May 1969, Deputy Sec Subject File, 1969 (74–132), box 2, RG 330, WNRC.
[29] Ltr, Barry Goldwater to Laird, 21 Aug 1969, Comptroller Subject Decimal File (75–0089), box 57, 452 (Jun–Aug), RG 330, WNRC.
[30] Memo, [Ivan] Selin [Acting Assistant Secretary of Defense for Systems Analysis] to Laird, n.d. [11 Dec 1969?]; Memo, Laird to Selin, 17 Dec 1969, both in Comptroller Subject Decimal File, 1969 (75–0089), 020 Systems Analysis (Jul 69), RG 330, WNRC.

one of Nixon's campaign promises to conduct an in-depth study of DoD, a proposal that Laird had supported as a congressman. In early April 1969, the secretary publicly announced that he would appoint a panel to carry out Nixon's promised study and began the process of selecting its members.

Laird drew the members of the Blue Ribbon Defense Panel, as it was known, from a broad spectrum of professions and areas of expertise. DoD vetted prospects from non-defense businesses such as insurance and cruise lines, from organized labor, and from the legal field. The prospects also included bankers, economists, educators, and journalists, though spots were also created for engineers and others with a more direct interest in military affairs.[31] Laird eventually chose Gilbert W. Fitzhugh, the chairman of Metropolitan Life Insurance Company, to chair the panel. Fifteen other successful candidates joined Fitzhugh on the panel, including other corporate executives, attorneys, educators, and even a representative from the NFL Commissioner's office.[32]

In July 1969, the Blue Ribbon Defense Panel was ready to begin work, with a goal of completing its analysis and submitting its recommendations to the president by 1 July 1970. Laird gave the panel a four-point charter. He expected them to conduct a one-year study on: (1) department organization and management, including the Joint Chiefs, defense agencies, and services, as they affected the department's mission performance and decision-making process; (2) defense research and development efforts and their impact on mission fulfillment, costs, organization, time, and relations with the scientific and industrial community; (3) department procurement policies and practices as they related to costs, time, and quality; and (4) other matters submitted at the secretary's request.[33] Such a broad charter could potentially produce an overly inclusive and therefore useless survey, so Laird urged the panel members to focus on how to help DoD run smoothly, rather than try to determine the direction it was headed.[34] (The panel recommendations are discussed later in this chapter.)

As Fitzhugh and his colleagues organized their staff and began work, the internal activities of Laird's reorganization effort, led by Packard, picked up speed. The secretary had always expected that

---

[31] Prospect List, Blue Ribbon Defense Panel, n.d., Comptroller Subject Decimal File, 1969 (75–0089), box 10, Blue Ribbon Defense Panel, RG 330, WNRC.

[32] *Report to the President and the Secretary of Defense on the Department of Defense,* Blue Ribbon Defense Panel (Washington, D.C.: U.S. Government Printing Office, 1 July 1970), p. iii (hereinafter cited as Blue Ribbon Panel Report).

[33] Blue Ribbon Panel Report, p. v.

[34] Outline of Remarks of Secretary of Defense Melvin R. Laird to Blue Ribbon Defense Panel (24 July 1969), Comptroller Subject Decimal File, 1969 (75–0089), box 10, Blue Ribbon Defense Panel, RG 330, WNRC.

his deputy would manage the day-to-day operations of the department while he provided strategic direction and handled external affairs, such as relations with Congress. Laird viewed the arrangement like a corporation; he would fill the role of a chief executive officer, while Packard would serve as chief operating officer.[35]

DEFENSE SYSTEMS ACQUISITION REVIEW COUNCIL

Given primary authority for determining how the Pentagon did business, Packard wasted little time in trying to integrate his HP management philosophy into DoD operations. The management by objective method had been a "fundamental part of HP's operating philosophy since the very early days of the company," Packard later wrote. Management by objectives moved away from a tightly controlled military management style to "a system in which overall objectives are clearly stated and agreed upon, and which gives people the flexibility to work toward those goals in ways they determine best for their own areas of responsibility. It is the philosophy of decentralization in management and the very essence of free enterprise." The philosophy had worked well with HP, a highly trained, highly motivated workforce in the private sector. Packard's management by objective and decentralization would be seen repeatedly in the changes he would bring to DoD acquisition.[36]

Packard's vision of acquisition reform extended beyond his management style. Given his background, it was not surprising that he relied on improved technology and believed that the United States could field more capable forces with fewer troops and lower financial costs.[37] Beginning in early 1969, he set about trying to change the way the military procured such technology in its weapon systems. Shortly after taking office, he circulated a letter to all DoD personnel reminding them that they needed to continue to improve practices and urging them to come forward with specific suggestions on improving operations.[38] Whatever practical effect it may have had, the message served notice that the new deputy secretary intended to shake things up.

In May 1969, Packard took a major step to modify DoD's acquisition practices at the highest level, creating a new body to advise him of the "status and readiness of each major system to proceed to the next phase of effort in its life cycle."[39] He named this

---

[35] Interv, OSD Historical Office with Melvin R. Laird, 2 Sep 1986, p. 15.

[36] Packard, *HP Way*, 1995, pp. 152–54.

[37] Interv, OSD Historical Office with Packard, 9 Nov 1987, p. 18.

[38] Msg, Packard to all DoD Personnel, 14 Feb 1969, IV B, box 558, OSD/DOD Organization, 1969–1972, OSD Historical Office Subject Files; Packard, *HP Way*, 1995, pp. 176–78.

[39] Memo, Packard for Service Secretaries, Assistant Secretary of Defense (ASD) Comptroller, ASD (Installation and Logistics [I&L]), Director of Defense Research and

new organization the Defense Systems Acquisition Review Council (DSARC) and placed it within the Office of the Secretary of Defense. In essence, the new group was to act as a high-level source of advice to Packard and Laird on how major weapons programs were progressing as they reached critical decision points.

In creating this body, the deputy secretary had not acted alone. The idea for DSARC, or something like it, had been circulating within OSD prior to Packard's announcement; Assistant Secretary of Defense (Comptroller) Robert Moot and Assistant Secretary of Defense for Installations and Logistics Barry Shillito had exchanged proposals on the subject earlier that month. Moot's belief that "the major systems acquisition process needs to be improved, coordinating OSD attention from just after the force level decision through at least the first production buy." Moot's proposed Weapons System Acquisition Review Committee closely resembled the body that Packard created.[40] According to one source, the concept of a review council may have actually originated with Packard's assistant secretaries. Whatever the source, Packard embraced and expanded the idea.[41]

An advocate of pragmatic, flexible management, Packard conceived of the DSARC as a temporary ad-hoc advisory group to help him improve the quality of acquisition decisions within DoD.[42] Like many of the programs that DSARC evaluated, this simple concept eventually evolved into a more complex entity, adding new features, growing in size, and extending in time far more than its creator had imagined. Packard had hoped that DSARC would become a forum in which representatives of the services and members of his staff could implement his goal of management by objectives. Ideally, the various parties would use DSARC reviews to agree on objectives for each weapon system, which the service managing the program would then be free to pursue with minimal OSD interference.[43]

Packard distributed a charter for DSARC, in which he detailed the council's functions. The council would consist of Packard's prin-

---

Engineering (DDR&E), and ASD (Systems Analysis), sub: Establishment of a Defense System Acquisition Review Council, 30 May 1969, with attachment, Charter, Defense System Acquisition Review Council, VIIIA, box 992: Management, 1969–1970, OSD Historical Office Subject Files.

[40] Memo, Assistant Secretary of Defense (Comptroller) for Assistant Secretary of Defense (Installations and Logistics), 19 May 69, sub: Major Weapon System Acquisition, Comptroller Subject Decimal File, 1969 (75–0089), box 54, 400.13 (May 1969), RG 330, WNRC.

[41] Interv, DAHP with Shillito, 6, 8 Jun 2005, pp. 19, 26–27.

[42] Interv, OSD Historical Office with Packard, 9 Nov 1987, pp. 20–21.

[43] Ibid., pp. 21–22.

cipal deputies, the director of defense research and engineering, the assistant secretary of defense for installations and logistics, the assistant secretary of defense (comptroller), and the assistant secretary of defense for systems analysis. The charter directed DSARC to evaluate each major weapons system at three major decision points, or milestones, in the life of a program as it moved from definition to production and deployment. At each stage, DSARC members would draw guidance from the Development Concept Paper (DCP), which laid out each program's characteristics, objectives, plans, and performance targets as the basis for approval of program initiation. Thereafter, the DCP served as the basis for monitoring the program against the standards that had been set and for approving or disapproving changes beyond the threshold limits set therein.[44] Packard envisioned DSARC as a complement to the DCP, which would continue as the formal Pentagon management and decision-making system for major weapons programs.

Packard's creation of DSARC marked his first major step to use organizational changes to impose his management philosophy on DoD acquisition practices. Ideally, DSARC reviews would act as a filter, preventing seriously flawed weapons programs from moving downstream through the procurement process from initiation to production. The knowledge that major weapons systems would have to pass a formal OSD review at three separate stages would presumably motivate the sponsoring service to correct major deficiencies before bringing the program before a DSARC review.

Packard viewed DSARC as only a partial and interim step in reforming the acquisition process. In the months following the establishment of this body, Packard's deputies worked on implementing broader changes that would encompass the entire life span of a weapons system, not just three decision points. Efforts to achieve more far-reaching reforms raised the question of the extent to which OSD could or should become involved in the actual management of acquisition programs. Defining the scope of DoD responsibilities for program management would presumably help clarify where Packard and his team might most profitably direct their ideas for management reforms.

Industry Advisory Council

Shortly after establishing DSARC, Packard began preparations for more fully integrating his management philosophy into the Pentagon acquisition process. He started with the Industry Advisory Council (IAC) to the Department of Defense, an influential ad-

---

[44] Memo, John S. Foster for Packard, 7 Jul 1969, sub: Management of Weapons Systems Acquisition, Comptroller Subject Decimal File, 1969 (75–0089), box 54, 400.13 (June 1969), RG 330, WNRC.

visory group of about twenty-five business executives (largely from defense contractor firms) who met three times a year at the Pentagon from 1962 to 1972. Packard, who had been chairman of the IAC, was highly critical of and had strong opinions about military procurement, especially the catastrophic results brought about by Total Package Procurement.[45]

As defense deputy secretary, Packard established several IAC panels to study the acquisition process and recommend changes. In early 1969, Packard created "Panel A," chaired by Foster, to "study and review ways and means of increasing the effectiveness of the major systems acquisition process."[46] Panel A presented its preliminary findings in mid-June. It reported that during the 1950s and 1960s, acquisition programs suffered from chronic cost overruns and development delays, despite attempts by earlier defense secretaries to fix the process. Given the complexity of the systems involved, Panel A warned that "although we can expect improvement, we can never expect perfection."[47] In addition to cost growth and schedule slippage, the panel identified other current problems such as changes inserted in operational performance objectives and a lack of clearcut delegation of authority to and within the services.

The panel criticized both the concept formulation and program execution stages of current acquisition programs. The concept formulation problems included inadequately defined operational performance objectives, insufficient hardware demonstration, unreliable cost estimates, insufficient initial funding, and premature commitment to system development that left major technological problems unsolved. Once acquisition programs were under way, management weaknesses contributed to poor control over results. Panel A found program management deficient due in part to excessive high-level meddling in details of development and production. The proliferation of management systems among different government offices added to these difficulties, as did a lack of highly qualified program managers in the services. All of these management weaknesses exacerbated the problems created when the services

---

[45] On Packard's independently arrived at views on Total Package Procurement and competitive prototyping, see Michael S. Malone, *Bill & Dave: How Hewlett and Packard Built the World's Greatest Company* (New York: Portfolio, 2007), pp. 257–60.

[46] Memo, Office of the Assistant Secretary of Defense (Installations and Logistics) for Laird and Packard, 9 Oct 1969, subj Industry Advisory Council, 10–11 October 1969, Comptroller Subject Decimal File, 1969 (75–0089), box 43, 334 Industry Advisory Council (July 1969), RG 330, WNRC.

[47] *Report by Panel A of the Industry Advisory Council on the Major Systems Acquisition Process,* 14 Jun 1969, Comptroller Subject Decimal File, 1969 (75–0089), box 54, 400.13 (July 1969), RG 330, WNRC.

rushed systems into production before solving the major development problems and without securing adequate funding.

Panel A recommended addressing concept formulation weaknesses by slowing down the process, requiring formal risk analyses, and increasing the emphasis on studying possible trade-offs among cost, schedule, and technical/operational aspects of a system. The report proposed setting cost, schedule, and technical performance targets and challenging suppliers to design the best system within those limits. This approach would encourage study of possible trade-offs at the earliest point in a system's life cycle. The panel also suggested reducing risk by relying more on prototypes and less on paper studies, especially in critical technical areas. Bringing costs under control would require improved cost-estimating capabilities within the military services, while OSD would need the capability to review service cost proposals. Panel A also suggested that OSD establish policies to discourage the unrealistic optimism in cost estimating that had become the norm in Pentagon procurement. There was no mention of increasing contractor incentives to meet program technical objectives with more effective cost control.

The industry panel concluded that improved program management required more clarity on the roles and responsibilities assigned to OSD and to the services. OSD should approve a program's objectives and thresholds on key characteristics, then stand back and monitor the program so long as it remained within those thresholds. By contrast, the sponsoring service should manage the program within the thresholds and periodically report to OSD for review at specified milestones. Program budgets should include reserves for inevitable design changes during development, and the lead military service for a program should control such changes within program thresholds. The panel also wanted the services to improve their program management training and capabilities while reducing the number of management systems, cutting excessive documentation, and limiting the number of Defense Department program reviews and reviewers.[48]

Packard showed his interest in the industry panel by attending the meeting where the panel presented its preliminary report. The deputy secretary discussed Panel A's findings with IAC members, asking the attendees to offer suggestions on prioritizing the virtual wish list of recommendations it had developed. Those present at the meeting included Eugene G. Fubini, author of the existing department acquisition directive, who formerly served in DoD as assistant secretary of defense for research and engineering under Defense Secretary Harold Brown in the early 1960s. Fubini declared that he

---
[48] Ibid.

had erred in drafting the existing directive by placing too much emphasis on contract definition instead of stressing the importance of concept formulation, and he suggested that DoD revise its existing contract definition directive—3200.9—accordingly.

In early July 1969, DDR&E reported to Packard that while Panel A's findings were still in draft form, OSD had begun to implement some of the less controversial proposals. These included a thorough review of the Defense Weapons Systems Management Center, at Wright-Patterson Air Force Base, Ohio, where DoD had trained future program managers since 1964. DoD had also undertaken a study analyzing management systems and data requirements, with a view toward reducing documentation requirements that increased contractor overhead. The study also considered plans to augment the department's internal cost-estimating capabilities.[49] Foster concluded that the Defense Department should apply specific agreed-upon management improvements to existing programs rather than issue a series of broad policy directives. Using that approach, Packard and his deputies could learn which reforms actually worked in practice. He reiterated the view that OSD should manage major programs only by "thresholds," allowing the sponsoring service to perform the detailed management within the agreed-upon parameters contained in the DCP. After approving these thresholds at program initiation, OSD could review them at key predetermined "achievement milestones."[50] Between those milestones and within the thresholds, the sponsoring service would manage the program, submitting periodic progress reports to OSD with information about costs, schedules, technological problems, and proposed solutions. Barry Shillito, the assistant secretary of defense for installations and logistics, agreed that OSD had to emphasize its nonparticipation in the conduct of weapon system procurement functions. After reading Foster's memo to Packard, Shillito cautioned DDR&E against using the phrase "OSD management" in reference to acquisition programs so as to avoid any inference that OSD actually played a managerial role.[51]

When the IAC's Panel A issued its report in mid-July 1969, its recommendations essentially mirrored those presented to Packard and others a month earlier. As analyzed later that year, the recommendations dealt with initial program activities and included thorough concept formulation, greater reliance on critical experiments, increased cost-estimating capabilities at the services and OSD levels, and contractor competitions that stressed design at-

---

[49] Memo, Foster for Packard, 7 Jul 1969.
[50] Ibid.
[51] Memo, Barry Shillito for John S. Foster, 22 Jul 1969, Comptroller Subject Decimal File 1969 (75–0089), box 54, 400.13 (July 1969), RG 330, WNRC.

tributes rather than simply costs. To better execute and manage a program, the panel recommended clarifying OSD and service roles, relying on milestone achievement to measure progress, providing funding reserves, employing a flexible contracting policy, reducing documentation and reviewing overhead costs, improving program management, and controlling engineering changes.[52]

Foster reminded Packard that DDR&E had already begun implementing some of the suggestions, while other suggestions required more study. Foster believed that Packard could take immediate action by clarifying OSD-service responsibilities, applying improvements to individual programs, and streamlining management by reducing documentation. Other improvements, such as designing to cost, requiring realistic cost estimates from contractors, and employing more prototypes, would require more study and possibly the drafting of new management directives.[53]

Because the services would have responsibility for program management between DSARC reviews, OSD would have to rely on them to implement most of Panel A's recommendations for improving acquisition management. Commenting on Foster's report to Packard, Shillito wrote: "I suggest that there not be any inference that OSD manages any programs. We monitor, we approve, we set parameters, we establish policy, but we attempt to continuously ensure that management responsibilities are retained in the services." This demarcation of responsibility presented a potential problem for Packard. While he could fine-tune OSD's acquisition-related activities, reforming the management practices of three very different and nominally independent services would prove more difficult. At the same time, he would need the services' help in convincing defense contractors to accept the possible burdens his new management practices might impose.[54]

Packard Confronting Resistance

In mid-1969, Packard explained his management reform objectives directly to the service secretaries. In a three-page memorandum, he first noted that the need for improvements in weapons system acquisition had been obvious from the day he took office, but that he had wanted to study the situation before taking ac-

---

[52] Memo, Office of the Secretary for Defense for Industry Advisory Council and Defense Participants, 4 Nov 1969, sub: Summary Minutes of the 10–11 October 1969 Meeting, Table B, Chart 1, VIII G, Installations and Logistics (1969–2000), Industry, 1969–1971, box 1022, OSD Historical Office Subject Files.

[53] Memo, Foster for Packard, 18 Jul 1969, sub: Report by Panel A of the Industry Advisory Council, Comptroller Subject Decimal File, 1969 (75–0089), box 54, 400.13 (July 1969), RG 330, WNRC.

[54] Memo, Shillito for Foster, 22 Jul 1969.

tion.[55] With the panel reports in hand, the deputy secretary believed the time had come to try out some of the recommendations with an eye to making the successful reforms part of DoD policy. Packard wanted each service to focus on three areas to reduce cost overruns: improved cost estimates (both from contractors and the services), better system definition to reduce the need for mid-program changes, and earlier identification and analysis of risk factors during the concept formulation stage. Packard also urged the services to rely more on prototypes and less on paper studies and to carry out adequate tests before making a production commitment. Finally, Packard asked each secretary to report on how his service was implementing the changes.

Packard saw his July 1969 memo on acquisition management practices as merely the beginning of his effort to reform the way the services handled their major weapon systems programs. In October, he told a meeting of IAC that the services could achieve success in managing major programs only if they selected the right people for the program management jobs and established ground rules that would enable good managers to carry out their responsibilities successfully. He believed that the OSD could most effectively improve management practices by issuing broad policy edicts and delegating other responsibilities.[56] At this meeting, Foster emphasized that the services would exercise greater control over acquisition and management; consequently, they would have to develop their own capabilities to evaluate contractor estimates of cost and scheduling and would need to select appropriate program managers.

In addition to exhorting the services to improve weapon system management, Packard also acted that summer to improve the training of potential program managers. In June 1969, he ordered a study of the Defense Weapons Systems Management Center at Wright-Patterson Air Force Base, the services' joint school for weapons system planning and acquisition. This study, headed by the deputy DDR&E, recommended moving the school to the Washington, D.C., area to provide access to senior DoD officials and suggested the development of a new curriculum to enhance the depth and quality of training the students received. The Army volunteered to provide facilities for the school at Fort Belvoir, Virginia, and to operate the school at that location where it began developing and offering courses on program manage-

---

[55] Memo, Packard for Service Secretaries, 31 Jul 1969, sub: Improvement in Weapon System Acquisition, 31 July 1969, Comptroller Subject Decimal File 1969 (75–0089), 400.13 (July 1969), RG 330, WNRC.

[56] Memo, Office of the Secretary of Defense for Industry Advisory Council and Defense Participants, 4 Nov 1969.

ment. The school was renamed the Defense System Management School; later it changed from school to college[57] and in 1992 served as the core organization in the creation of the Defense Acquisition University.

In response to Packard's demand for reports on acquisition reform in the services, the three service secretaries duly replied that their organizations had already instituted procedures and initiated changes guaranteed to improve major weapons system procurement results. Army Secretary Stanley R. Resor reported that he fully agreed with Packard's reform objectives, but noted that the Army would require "far-reaching revisions to our acquisition processes" to fully implement the deputy secretary's program. The Army had taken immediate measures to reduce overoptimism in cost estimates, control changes, improve risk assessment, and to meet Packard's other goals. It also had "an integrated approach to address the problems of the acquisition of a weapon system, beginning with concept formulation and extending through production." In light of these initiatives, Resor concluded that the Army required no further directives or policy guidance from Packard's office.[58] In a similar vein, Navy Under Secretary John W. Warner assured the deputy secretary that, consistent with Packard's desire to test the proposed reforms, the Navy had "initiated a series of remedial action experiments vectored to meet the objectives you have discussed."[59]

Facing more scrutiny than the other services, due to the highly publicized problems with the C–5A and F–111, the Air Force produced a more detailed response to Packard's query. The secretary of the Air Force passed on a letter from his service's chief of staff detailing the improvements that the Air Force had made to its acquisition practices and addressing the deputy secretary's major areas of concern. The Air Force claimed to have improved its cost estimating capabilities, including those relating to design changes. It also had embraced Packard's views on controlling design changes, emphasizing contract flexibility, and using more analytical studies early in the acquisition process. Finally, the Air

---

[57] David D. Acker, *A History of the Defense Systems Management College* (Washington, D.C.: U.S. Government Printing Office, 1986), p. 15. For a more extensive treatment of the Defense Systems Management School/College, see Chapter 9.

[58] Memo, Stanley R. Resor, Secretary of the Army, for Packard, sub: Improvement in Weapon System Acquisition, 2 Oct 1969, attached to memo, Packard for Resor, 10 Oct 1969, Comptroller Subject Decimal File (75–0089), box 54, 400.13 (October 1969), RG 330, WNRC.

[59] Memo, John W. Warner, Navy Under Secretary, for Packard, sub: Improvement in Weapon System Acquisition, 20 Oct 1969, Comptroller Subject Decimal File 1969 (75–0089), 400.13 (October 1969), RG 330, WNRC.

Force had increased its reliance on competitive prototypes and hardware testing, especially in the F–15 development program.[60]

These assurances by the secretaries that they had adopted or were studying his earlier directives failed to satisfy Packard. He was concerned that without a major push from above, each service would continue with business as usual. Shortly after receiving the service responses to his requests, Packard circulated a series of detailed charts that explained in some detail the powers and responsibilities of the major players during each phase (discussed in Chapter One) of the DSARC review of acquisition programs. These charts divided the acquisition process and each major acquisition program into phases and decision points, from conception through deployment.[61] Each program began with a conceptual phase, where DDR&E took primary responsibility for overseeing the service sponsor and initiating a DCP. This phase ended when DDR&E presented the completed DCP at the program decision meeting, where it also chaired the DSARC. Upon approval the validation phase followed, where the service had primary responsibility—with DDR&E oversight—for developing the system's major characteristics and reporting any breaches of DCP thresholds to OSD. The phase led to the ratification decision, where the DDR&E-chaired DSARC decided whether to continue on to full-scale development. During the full-scale development phase, the service and its contractor(s) would design, build, and test the system, including supporting elements, while protecting against breaches of the DCP thresholds. At the production decision meeting, the assistant secretary of defense for installations and logistics assumed the chair of DSARC, though DDR&E, having monitored the previous phase, would still have responsibility for preparing the DCP. If successful, the system would move on to the production and deployment phases. This Packard-era acquisition process is shown in Figure 3 and is contrasted with the procedure followed in the 1960s.

Packard's charts clearly stated that between decision points, the sponsoring service would have primary responsibility for reporting to OSD any breaches of agreed-on thresholds for its programs. In May 1970, Packard expanded on this requirement, explaining in a memorandum to the services and his staff that the responsible service secretary had to report immediately to DDR&E any threshold breaches or failures to meet milestones in the de-

---

[60] Memo, Robert C. Seamans Jr. [Secretary of the Air Force] for Packard, 5 Dec 1969 with attached letter, Gen. J. C. Meyer to Seamans, sub: Improvement in Weapon Systems Acquisition, 20 Oct 1969, Comptroller Subject Decimal File 69 (75–0089), 400.13 (September 1969), RG 330, WNRC.

[61] Memo, Packard for Service Secretaries, 15 Dec 1969, sub: Responsibilities in the Process of Acquiring Major Weapon Systems, app. to "Policy Changes in Weapon System Procurement," House Committee on Government Operations, 91st Cong., 2d sess., 22 September 1970.

Figure 3—The Systems Acquisition Process

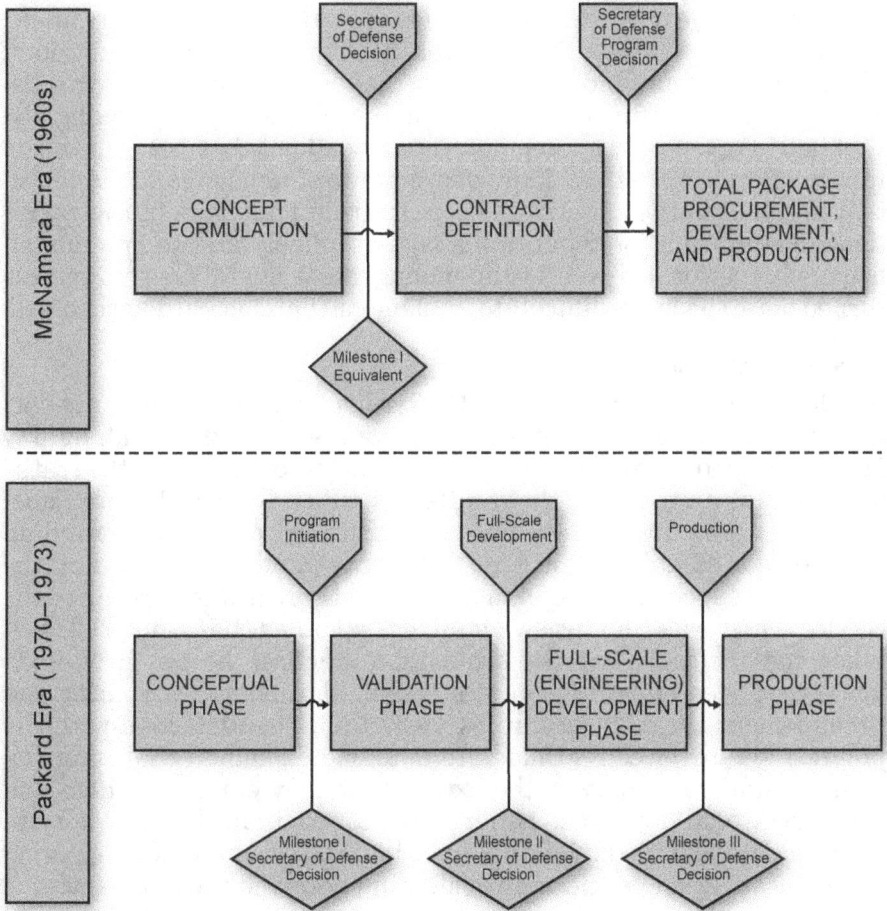

velopment schedule. Otherwise, in keeping with Packard's aim of reducing reporting requirements, the service program manager could limit communications regarding a program to quarterly reports and informal communications with OSD staff.[62]

Although most of these changes affected only internal DoD operations, the deputy secretary's new policies had to pass muster

---

[62] Memo, Packard for Listed Parties, 14 May 1970, sub: Reports to the Secretary of Defense by the Military Departments and Defense Agencies on Approved Major Weapon Systems during Development, app. to "Policy Changes in Weapon System Procurement," House Committee on Government Operations, 91st Cong., 2d sess., 22 September 1970.

outside the Pentagon as well. In March 1970, Packard testified before the Senate Armed Services Committee regarding military appropriations for fiscal year 1971. Amid a series of questions about the troubled C–5A program, he took the opportunity to give a brief description of his reform program and noted that he had established procedures designed to prevent future technical problems like those plaguing the Lockheed transport. The deputy secretary added that his acquisition reform effort emphasized improved program management. He promised to convince the services to keep program managers in their positions long enough for them to manage effectively and to promote officers who performed well in the management field.[63] These promises turned out to be more difficult to implement than Packard anticipated.

Pushing Against Inertia

During his first year in office, Packard approached his reform effort in a piecemeal fashion and the services had responded in kind. In May 1970, he issued a broad policy edict in an attempt to change the status quo. Perhaps anticipating the results of the Blue Ribbon Defense Panel study that was due that summer, the Packard policy memorandum included additional guidance for the services and OSD regarding the changes he expected to see in major weapons programs. Writing to the service secretaries and his own staff, he explained that while DoD had taken some steps to improve acquisition practices, he was now ready for "a concerted effort to firmly establish additional new policies and to implement them."[64] Packard expressed his dissatisfaction with the progress the services had made to date. He explained that improvements would come only to the extent that they embraced them and that they would have to do better in the future than they had done in the past. He reminded them that OSD had responsibility for approving service acquisition policies and evaluating how well they implemented approved policies, as well as deciding whether major programs should move forward at each major milestone.

The policy guidance focused on four areas: management, development, production, and contracting. Because actual management of acquisition programs and assignment of management personnel remained a service responsibility, Packard could only indirectly affect the makeup and day-to-day operations of the management team. He sought to accomplish this by directing the services to ensure that program managers had the required management skills,

---

[63] U.S. Congress, Senate, Armed Services Committee, 91st Cong., 2d sess., *Military Procurement for Fiscal Year 1971*, 10 March 1970, pp. 857–60.

[64] Memo, Packard for Listed Parties, 28 May 1970, sub: Policy Guidance on Major Weapon Systems Acquisition, IV B, OSD/DOD Organization, 1969–1972, box 558 (1970–1971), OSD Historical Office Subject Files.

give them adequate authority to make major decisions at each stage of the program, and minimize the layers of authority between the program manager and the service secretary. In addition, program managers could use their increased authority effectively only if they stayed with a program long enough to thoroughly understand it and implement the new procedures. In that regard, the services would have to offer successful program managers career advancements and other rewards comparable to military operations officer advancements and rewards in order to convince talented managers to accept program manager assignments. Packard's statement of requirements had a mixed reception within the services that understandably preferred to have military operations officers as program managers responsible for acquisition programs and for deciding when to report acquisition problems through the traditional chain of command.

Packard expressed his views on the issue of overdocumentation and unneeded layers of authority in a letter later that year to George P. Shultz, director of the Office of Management and Budget. Packard quoted with approval a long statement by Admiral Hyman G. Rickover regarding the reporting burdens of weapon program managers.

> So long as the bureaucracy consists of large numbers of people at many levels who believe they perform their function of evaluation and approval properly, by requiring vast and detailed information to be submitted through the many levels of the bureaucracy, program managers will never be found who can effectively manage their jobs. A program manager today would require at least 48 hours a day of his own time just to satisfy the requests for detailed information from the Navy and DoD bureaucracies, the Congress, the General Accounting Office [GAO], and various other parties who have the legal right—and use it—to place demands on his time. As long as we operate a system where the checkers (those charged with the responsibility of evaluating and approving) outnumber the doers (those responsible for carrying out the work), the doers are condemned to spend their time doing paper work for the checkers.[65]

Packard stressed the need to improve the process of system development, both at the conceptual and full-scale engineering stages. He argued that the control over system costs ultimately depended on a management team's ability to make intelligent trade-offs between operating capabilities and engineering designs at each stage of a program and to provide contractors with sufficient

---

[65] Ltr, Packard to George P. Shultz, director of the Office of Management and Budget, 27 Oct 1970.

incentives to exercise effective cost control. The program schedule should allow sufficient time to resolve the inevitable design and performance problems in a logical fashion, avoiding unnecessary overlapping of different development stages.

Packard's proposed management plan focused on reducing technical risk at the conceptual stage. First, managers should assess the risk involved in the design, decide how much effort would be needed to solve the engineering problems, and accurately assess the consequences of failure of each program element. The manager should continually consider and update the cost-benefit trade-offs between operating requirements and engineering design possibilities. Finally, actual testing of components would provide the only sure way to determine whether the technical risks had been resolved. Proposals for OSD approval at the conceptual stage would have to include a description of how the program manager intended to handle risk assessment, trade-offs, and testing. These tasks appeared to exceed the skills of many program managers.

In order to move beyond the conceptual stage to full-scale development, the program manager would have to convince OSD (through the DSARC) that management had adequately addressed the risks during the conceptual stage. This would require proof of successful hardware tests for key subsystems and components. During the full-scale development stage, managers would need to shape contracts and procedures to eliminate unnecessary reports and documentation, focusing instead on perfecting and validating the system design.

Before seeking approval for actual production, the responsible service would have to certify that all milestones demonstrating the achievement of a practical engineering design had been met and that all engineering problems encountered during development had been resolved with trade-offs that optimized production, maintenance, and operating costs. Plans for production startup would need to minimize financial commitments until the service could demonstrate that it had resolved all development problems, including production engineering and production tooling.

In the area of contracting, Packard expected the services to tailor system contracts to the risks involved. He favored cost-reimbursement contracts for the development stages of major systems, with subcontracts that maximized competition for vital system components. Finally, Packard noted that his new management rules might conflict with existing DoD directives and instructions. In all such cases, he ordered that his new rules take precedence and revealed that he had given DDR&E the task of rewriting the existing regulations to reflect his policy reforms.[66]

---

[66] Memo, Packard for Listed Recipients, 28 May 1970.

The generic tone and broad scope of Packard's policy directive illustrated the nature of his dilemma in attempting to reform Pentagon procurement. He had committed to the principle that OSD would refrain from interfering in the management of major system acquisition programs, a philosophy that fit with his belief in the efficacy of management by objectives. His office would confine itself to establishing general policy guidelines that would govern how the services managed their programs. It would measure compliance with these guidelines through periodic reports and during the scheduled reviews of programs by DSARC, both of which were designed to determine whether a system had met its agreed-upon targets for cost, technical performance, and scheduling. As a practical matter, this arrangement allowed Packard's staff to enforce program management practices only through the threat of cancellation or delay if DSARC members disapproved of the progress the system had made since the last milestone.

Packard's policy of management by objectives assumed that the acquisition managers in the military services would be skilled to oversee and manage large engineering and production programs on budget and on schedule. But this assumption turned out to be only partially correct. The absence of detailed oversight practically invited the services to continue their established management methods, trusting that they could use political or economic arguments to get their programs through the DSARC review process when necessary. In a task as vital and complicated as managing the acquisition of major weapons and equipment for a military service, senior officials in the service could often do what they believed was best for the acquisition process and best for their individual service, irrespective of the wishes of OSD officials whose tenure was likely to be less than three years. The military services could wait them out.

The deputy secretary obviously believed that his May 1970 memorandum represented a significant step in the process of reforming Pentagon procurement. Shortly after circulating his new rules for acquisition, Packard held a press conference announcing the changes. He explained that his goals included improving the services' performance, noting that he had "come down to the proposition that we have just got to get the services to do a better job; that we can't sit up here topside, and make decisions, and run the programs, and have it make any sense." He also stressed his continuing emphasis on empowering program managers with greater authority and incentives but also insisted on trade-offs within programs as a continuing part of the management process "at every stage in the program." He concluded by explaining that his approach contained nothing really new but represented a significant improvement over how the Pentagon had handled major procurement programs in the past.[67]

Packard must have realized that his reforms could only take effect once the services had individually adopted his management practices. The first step toward institutionalizing his guidance involved rewriting the standing DoD regulations on acquisition policy to reflect the deputy secretary's views. OSD undertook this task almost immediately following the distribution of the policy guidance memorandum. In early June 1970, Packard informed an IAC meeting that he had established a task force to review and revise all policies and regulations affected by his proposed reforms.[68]

The process of reviewing and rewriting key procurement directives would take some time. Meanwhile, Packard wanted his new methods implemented immediately. In late July, DDR&E's John Foster wrote the Joint Chiefs and service secretaries notifying them that "Mr. Packard does not want the application of these policies to await changes in DoD Directives and Instructions and corresponding regulations in the military departments and defense agencies." Therefore, the recipients were instructed to review all their ongoing programs to (1) identify for each program where the program failed to comply with the deputy secretary's new policies from the May 28 memorandum; (2) recommend changes to bring them into compliance (or explain why a change would be impractical); and (3) identify decision layers between the program managers and the service secretaries.[69]

The Blue Ribbon Defense Panel Issues Its Report (1970)

Shortly before Packard issued his order for the military services to begin implementing his new policies, the Blue Ribbon Defense Panel published its report on the issues. After a year of study, the panel issued a book-length report (1970)[70] that covered a broad

---

[67] Statement of Deputy Secretary of Defense to the Press, 9 Jun 1970, app. to "Policy Changes in Weapon System Procurement," House Committee on Government Operations, 91st Cong., 2d sess., 22 September 1970.

[68] Statement of Secretary of Defense to Industry Advisory Council, 13 Jul 1970, sub: Summary Minutes of the Industry Advisory Council Meeting on 12 and 13 June 1970, VIII G, Installations and Logistics (1969–2000), Industry, 1969–1971, box 1022, OSD Historical Office Subject Files.

[69] Memo, Foster for Listed Recipients, 29 Jul 1970, sub: Application of New Policy Guidance to Major Weapon Systems, app. to "Policy Changes in Weapon System Procurement," House Committee on Government Operations, 91st Cong., 2d sess., 22 September 1970.

[70] Blue Ribbon Panel Report. The Blue Ribbon Defense Panel, chaired by Gilbert W. Fitzhugh, was appointed by the president and the secretary of defense in July 1969 to examine the following areas: (a) organization and management of DoD, including the Joint Chiefs of Staff, the defense agencies, and the military services; (b) defense research and development efforts from the standpoint of mission fulfillments, costs, organization, time, and interrelation with the scientific and industrial community; (c) defense procurement policies and practices, particularly as they

range of management issues affecting the Department of Defense. The panel had divided itself into four committees to study the four topics requested by Secretary Laird. The committees on Organization and Personnel Management and on Management of Material Resources directly addressed the areas affecting Packard and the acquisition process.

Fitzhugh certainly had sufficient access to top DoD officials to develop a clear picture of Packard's plans to reform the procurement process for major weapons. He took an office close to Secretary Laird's, and the two met twice weekly so that Fitzhugh could update Laird on the Blue Ribbon Defense Panel's progress.[71] Barry Shillito, the assistant secretary of defense for installations and logistics, and one of Packard's most active assistants in the reform effort, sat just down the hall and worked closely with Fitzhugh on the panel's study.[72] Packard also worked with the panel, though Fitzhugh and his colleagues independently investigated some areas that the deputy secretary and his staff had not considered in any detail.[73]

Not surprisingly, the panel's final report adopted some of Packard and Laird's views on changing the acquisition system. The panel concluded that DoD's established policies had "contributed to serious cost overruns, schedule slippages and [technical] performance deficiencies," and that reform would "require many interrelated changes in organization and procedures."[74]

To address this and other problems, the panel recommended a sweeping high-level reorganization of the department. It suggested creating three major internal groups, each headed by a deputy secretary of defense. One would deal with operations. The second, under a deputy secretary of defense for resource management, would manage resources, including acquisition. The office would include assistant secretaries for research and advanced technology and for engineering development. The third body, under a deputy secretary of defense for evaluation, would evaluate functions ranging from accounting to weapon system performance. This office would include an assistant secretary of defense for test and evaluation responsible for DoD test and evaluation policy, and for the Defense

---

relate to costs, time, and quality; and (d) such other matters as the secretary of defense may submit to it from time to time. (Melvin Laird was the Secretary of Defense.) The 237-page report contained six chapters: (1) Organization, (2) Management of Materiel Resources, (3) Management and Procedures, (4) Management of Personnel Resources, (5) Other Management Considerations, and (6) Conflicts of Interest.

[71] Interv, OSD Historical Office with Laird, 2 Sep 1986, p. 9.
[72] Interv, DAHP with Shillito, 6, 8 Jun 2005, p. 29.
[73] Interv, OSD Historical Office with Packard, 28 Nov 1988, p. 2.
[74] Blue Ribbon Panel Report, p. 2 (quotation).

Test Agency, which the panel believed should design and conduct tests on systems and equipment.

Based on these recommendations, the Blue Ribbon Panel would have—administratively, at least—separated the testing function from the procurement process, dividing Packard's authority between two bodies just as he was working to integrate prototype and component testing into the developmental stage of each weapon system program. Just a few months earlier, Packard had issued a DoD directive explicitly charging DDR&E with responsibility for "research, development, test and evaluation of weapons, weapons systems, and Defense materiel."[75] This same directive assigned Foster to recommend research and engineering responsibilities for new weapon systems development. Clearly, Packard intended to keep control over testing and evaluation of major weapon systems. DDR&E believed that separating testing and development made no sense, as the development team would have the best ideas on how to model and interpret the tests.[76]

The report failed to set out a clear rationale for separating weapon systems testing from research, engineering, and development. In calling for the creation of an assistant secretary of defense for testing, the panel's report seemed to focus its concerns on problems with operational testing and evaluation. It noted that each service had a different system for operational testing, that neither OSD nor the Joint Chiefs had much control over these testing organizations, and that the services had no effective mechanism to conduct operational testing across service lines. The creation of an assistant secretary for testing and evaluation would presumably help coordinate service testing policies and ensure that the services devoted adequate resources to this area.[77]

The panel's report appeared to analyze the existing major weapon system acquisition process from industry's point of view. It noted that problems at each stage of the process cumulatively created the conditions for delays, cost overruns, and technical deficiencies, and then blamed a good part of this on the existing acquisition directive 3200.9. The panel reported that, pursuant to DoD Directive 3200.9, the initial, or concept formulation phase of a program involved comprehensive studies and experimentation intended to bring the program to a point where: (1) experiments were complete and the needed technology available; (2) performance requirements were defined; (3) the best technical approaches had been selected; (4) tradeoffs thoroughly analyzed; (5) cost effectiveness had been determined

---

[75] DoD Directive 5129.1, "Director of Defense Research and Engineering," 13 Mar 70.
[76] Interv, DAHP with Foster, 19 Feb 2003, p. 37.
[77] Blue Ribbon Panel Report, pp. 88–90.

on a competitive basis; and (6) credible cost and schedule estimates were available. However, the report concluded that the prescribed prerequisites for obtaining a decision to proceed to engineering development "prove to be largely idealistic for application to the totality of a large weapon system and have not been strictly adhered to in practice."[78]

The panel saved its strongest criticism for the contract definition phase of the process mandated by DoD Directive 3200.9, which occurred once OSD decided to proceed with engineering development. During this phase, the government issued a request for proposals, chose a number of would-be contractors to prepare and submit competing "detailed and voluminous" proposals for the engineering development stage of a program, and selected a winner. The Blue Ribbon Panel concluded that the scope of the proposals at this stage of the program required too much speculation and estimating by industry:

> The central purpose of the contract is concerned with engineering development, a matter of considerable technical uncertainty. To expect and require through contract definition that a contractor have the capability even to identify all end items of the system, let alone develop detailed specifications for each, in an advanced technological product, and concurrently to prepare reliable predictions in detail on the maintainability, reliability, and the requirement for operational training to use the product, is impractical.[79]

An additional problem arose because industry relied on paper studies prepared in "concept formulation." As a result, their proposals tended to rest on the often erroneous assumption that technical risks had been reduced; the resulting cost estimates almost always proved unreliable. Due to "the unwarranted reliance on paper analysis" during concept formulation, potential contractors often found to their surprise that "the necessary technology to proceed with Engineering Development had not been accomplished."[80]

Like Packard, the Blue Ribbon Panel recommended formulation of a new weapons development policy aimed at reducing technical risks by relying more on hardware testing of competitive prototypes and less on concurrent development and paper studies prior to approving full-scale development. The panel's report mirrored Packard's desire to increase flexibility in selecting contract types consistent with anticipated technical risks during system develop-

---

[78] Ibid., p. 70.
[79] Ibid.
[80] Ibid., p. 73.

ment and to reduce unnecessary paperwork (in this case, contract definition documents).[81]

The panel also seemed to support the deputy secretary's view that improving management of programs required better selection, training, retention and empowerment of program managers. It found that military officers assigned to manage programs frequently had inadequate training and lacked scientific and industrial management knowledge and experience. They were usually rotated at short intervals (often at critical points in acquisition programs), giving the departing officers little or no opportunity to train their successors.[82] They saw little potential for career advancement in program management and often viewed their assignment as a stepping stone to private-sector employment with industry.[83]

To compound the problems created by personnel policies, program managers remained bogged down by heavy reporting and documentation requirements that added to overall management costs. These requirements stemmed, in part, from the numerous command levels between managers and top service decision makers, which produced a demand for innumerable briefings while diluting the manager's authority to make management decisions. While program managers were saddled with increasingly complex tasks and ever-widening responsibilities, the services had yet to establish a clear division of authority among the program manager, contracting officer, and contract auditor.

The Blue Ribbon Panel laid some of the blame for acquisition problems on weaknesses in the DCP and its use as a tool for program initiation and management. The panel noted that DCPs varied in quality and that their very brevity—a twenty-page maximum—tended to obscure differences among the various contributors as to how a program should develop. While praising the flexibility the DCP provided to high-level decision makers, the panel warned against using it to justify an unstructured, ad hoc approach to program management. The report suggested better training of the personnel who prepared these documents as the best way to minimize this risk.[84]

The panel concluded that the Defense Department could not fix the problems in existing management practices on an ad hoc basis and recommended that the Pentagon revise basic directives and

---

[81] Ibid., p. 74.
[82] Ibid., p. 79.
[83] Ibid.
[84] Ibid., pp. 120–21.

create new ground rules to resolve these fundamental weaknesses. The report advocated the use of more civilian managers and the creation of a program manager career path within the military, including industrial management training and experience, while giving program managers greater and more clearly defined authority. Once again, the panel's proposals were consistent with Packard's guidelines distributed two months earlier to the services. Either the panel had been swayed by Packard's arguments or he had anticipated the panel's findings.

The Blue Ribbon Panel believed that all parties, including Congress and the public, placed too much faith in the accuracy of cost estimates, despite the inherent technical uncertainties in developing new advanced weapons systems. While the irreducible level of technological risk created unavoidable inaccuracies, other factors contributed to the problem of inappropriately low estimates, especially the incentive to gain strong and continuing support for a program from the end user and Congress. Fitzhugh and his colleagues believed that DoD could reduce—though never eliminate—the inherent unreliability of cost estimates by relying more on historical cost data for similar programs. Therefore, the panel concluded that the military services and contractors should be prepared to continually revise cost estimates as programs progressed from inception through production.[85] In the absence of creating stronger incentives for the services and contractors to exercise vigorous cost control, and by playing down the importance or value of early cost estimates, the panel was essentially admitting that what most observers would consider "cost overruns" had become an inescapable part of producing major weapons systems.

Although the panel's report blamed DoD management shortfalls for most of the problems with weapons systems acquisition, industry did not escape censure entirely. The business-dominated panel argued that industry's problems actually stemmed from companies' eagerness to accommodate the Pentagon. This, in turn, led to "over responsiveness to every expressed or implied desire" of DoD and the military services. The supposedly obsequious attitude of contractors resulted in the acceptance of contract changes, adding program features, inefficient management rules, and increasing costs. It also resulted in industry reluctance to point out technical risks and uncertainties of certain complex systems, and reliance on overly ambitious design solutions to meet user requirements—all frequently imposing higher costs on the military services. The panel could suggest little to remedy this situation other

---
[85] Ibid., p. 84.

than urging contractors to use greater objectivity in their evaluations of proposed developments.[86]

Apart from the proposal for a radical restructuring of the Defense Department at the highest level, Fitzhugh and his colleagues generally recommended following the same reform course that Packard had already undertaken on his own. Packard and Laird agreed that DoD did not need a triumvirate of deputy secretaries, which left them free to implement those recommendations that fit in with their management reform goals.[87] Speaking at the dinner of the Armed Forces Management Association a month later, Packard explained that while he supported many of the Blue Ribbon Panel's suggestions, he opposed creating three deputy secretaries. He noted that he favored greater decentralization of responsibility within the Pentagon and that the proposal to create additional high-level posts would undercut that goal. "We do not want to create a structure that adds more top-level involvement in the workingman's business," he said. "Three deputies would tend to pull even more decision making up to the top, and we do not want to move in that direction."[88]

In the same address to several hundred defense industry representatives, Packard referred to the current state of defense procurement as "a mess":

> I suppose that some of our critics will call this a meeting of the military-industrial complex. So be it. I am not embarrassed by the fact that we need industry to help the Department of Defense. I am only embarrassed that we haven't done a better job. Many of you, and certainly those *not* in the industry, may expect me to talk about what a grand job we have all done and how necessary we are for one another. I am not going to do that. I am going to talk about the things we do wrong and the things we have to do better.
>
> Let's face it—the fact is that there has been bad management of many defense programs in the past. We spent billions of the taxpayers' dollars; sometimes we spent it badly. Part of this is due to basic uncertainties in the defense business. Some uncertainties will always exist. However, most of it has been due to bad management, both in the Department of Defense and in the defense industry. We can and are doing something about that. I am not talking just about cost overruns as so many of our critics do. Overruns are the end product of our mistakes rather than the key

---

[86] Ibid., p. 85.
[87] Interv, OSD Historical Office with Packard, 28 Nov 1988, p. 1.
[88] Address by David Packard to the Armed Forces Management Association, 22 August 1970, app. to "Policy Changes in Weapon System Procurement," House Committee on Government Operations, 91st Cong., 2d sess., 22 September 1970.

issue to be addressed. I am surprised that our critics took so long to discover cost overruns. They have been around a long time, and many of the cost overruns that receive the most publicity were organized by defense and industry years ago. We are now paying the price for mistakes in contracting, in development, and in management.

Frankly, gentlemen, in defense procurement, we have a real mess on our hands, and the question you and I have to face up to is what are we going to do to clean it up.[89]

Packard also admitted that the services had not yet fully embraced his reforms. Referring specifically to his proposals for selecting, retaining, and empowering program managers, he complained that "all four services have accepted my recommendations—and their letters say that they agree. But on at least two occasions they have taken actions exactly contrary to those suggested." At the same time, he clearly distanced himself from the Blue Ribbon Panel's pro-industry views on who was to blame for problems in procurement. He told his audience of industry representatives that "the Defense Department has been led down the garden path for years on sophisticated systems that you promised would do all kinds of things for some optimistic [i.e., low] cost. Too frequently we have been wrong in listening to you, and more frequently you have been unable to deliver on either of these promises—what it would do or what it would cost."[90]

Consolidating Gains

A month after his speech to the Armed Forces Management Association, Packard returned to Congress to promote and explain his proposed changes in weapons procurement policy. In his testimony before the House Committee on Government Operations in September 1970, he once again stressed the importance of employing the best trained, skilled, and motivated program managers and giving them sufficient leeway to make necessary decisions, especially regarding trade-offs among capability, schedule, and cost that arose in all major programs.[91]

The deputy secretary testified that most problems pertaining to major programs stemmed from unrealistic assumptions made at the program's inception. Military planners tended to overstate the threat and demand unnecessary capabilities, while industry engineers promised more than they could deliver, leading to "a form

---

[89] Ibid.
[90] Ibid.
[91] "Policy Changes in Weapon System Procurement," House Committee on Government Operations, 91st Cong., 2d sess., 22 September 1970, p. 25.

of management euphoria" that created unreasonably low cost estimates. In turn, those low estimates account for part of the cost overruns that draw so much public criticism.

Packard argued that a well-managed, flexibly organized program could avoid many of the mistakes that had dogged DoD acquisitions over the previous decade. Rigid requirements for capabilities and scheduling should give way to an approach that allowed trade-offs at any point throughout the life of a program. Such trade-offs could be considered by the program manager on a continuing basis, while DSARC would examine at selected intervals whether the program had adequately used this method to address technical challenges that arose during development. He claimed that by empowering program managers, the services could assume near-total responsibility for managing each program. This approach could work only if the services improved their personnel policies so that skilled managers remained on a program long enough to attain a high level of knowledge about the system they were managing and to have an effect on a program. The services would have to change their organizational structures in a way that removed the ability of various command levels to interfere with the trade-offs that would have to occur on nearly every program—command levels that also had a strong influence on whether a program manager would or would not be promoted. One congressman summed up this portion of Packard's vision with a single word, "Utopia."[92]

The following day, Packard's subordinates filled in the details of the reform program for interested committee members, but they also faced probing questions over whether the changes represented anything more than window dressing. V. Adm. Vincent De Poix of DDR&E testified that he chaired an OSD committee that had the task of harmonizing directives and regulations with the deputy secretary's acquisition policies. De Poix and his group had completed the first phase of their work, which included reviewing existing acquisition directives and recommending changes or cancellation of those in conflict with the new regime. The second phase, already under way, involved drafting new, more comprehensive directives on weapons systems acquisition that would incorporate much of the substance of Packard's May 1970 policy memorandum.[93]

Some members of Congress remained skeptical about the actual impact this process would have on contractors and military services determined to push through their desired programs and performance characteristics. Asked whether the services would ac-

---
[92] Ibid., p. 18 (quotation).
[93] Ibid., pp. 57–64.

tually seek out trade-offs that compromised technical performance, De Poix could reply only that they would have no choice because the secretary had told them to look for trade-offs rather than coming back asking for more money. He explained that in future programs "if you find that it is going to take more money to hold to the original specifications of performance characteristics, you look at that aspect. You examine it to save yourself money, and because you have been told to do it by guidance from the Deputy Secretary of Defense."[94] Such assurances did little to assuage the members' concerns, especially when De Poix admitted that the procedure reflected "very little change from the previous method."[95] One member suggested that the mood of the country, rather than the details of procedure, would prove decisive: "The directives, of course, come from the Secretary and from the Deputy Secretary, but basically it is the attitude of the country and what the country will accept. The military has got to accept it because they are being cut back in these areas so they cannot have Cadillacs all the time. They have got to have Chevrolets sometimes."[96]

Early in 1971, Laird wrote Senator John C. Stennis, the chairman of the Senate Armed Services Committee, summarizing DoD's progress in improving the acquisition of major weapons systems and describing the impact of the recommendations of the Blue Ribbon Panel. The secretary highlighted seven major areas of improvement, most of which echoed Packard's earlier directives. Laird noted that his deputy had directed the service secretaries to improve the quality and increase the authority and longevity of program managers, while cutting away the layers of bureaucracy that inhibited the decision-making process.[97]

Laird's letter to Senator Stennis also emphasized the creation of DSARC and the revitalization of the DCP as tools for guiding, recording, and implementing decisions on major weapons systems programs. He noted that DSARC had already conducted twenty-seven decision reviews on nineteen major programs, approving service recommendations twelve times and ordering the services to rework or redirect their programs fifteen times. He also explained how the Pentagon now used the DCP as a contract between the sponsoring service (or its program manager) and the secretary of defense, setting agreed-upon program objectives

---

[94] Ibid., p. 93 (quotation).
[95] Ibid., pp. 69–70 (quotation).
[96] Ibid., p. 93 (quotation).
[97] Ltr, Laird to Senator John C. Stennis, 18 Mar 1971, with attachment, DoD Steps Taken to Improve the Acquisition of Major Weapon Systems, Comptroller Subject Decimal File, 1971 (76–0197), 400.13 (February 1971), RG 330, WNRC.

against which DSARC could measure a weapon system's progress at crucial decision points.

Laird pointed out the progress his office had made in eliminating excess departmental instructions and updating directives in order to consolidate management authority and increase efficiency, especially by purging unnecessary paperwork. He explained that these changes facilitated the decentralization of Defense Department acquisition operations, giving the services more management responsibility while retaining for OSD the tasks of setting policy and performing oversight through DSARC reviews. Finally, DoD had recognized the need to tailor contract types to the perceived risk of a specific acquisition program, relying on cost-plus-incentive contracts for the development of major systems. At the same time, it had mandated increased controls over and limitations on mid-program changes. It was still studying what it would require in the way of updated information on cost, schedule, and technical performance from contractors.

Laird also informed the senator that he had established a DoD Blue Ribbon Action Committee under the assistant secretary of defense for administration to implement his decisions regarding the Blue Ribbon Panel's recommendations. He claimed that the Defense Department had already enacted some of the panel's most important recommendations in slightly different form, pointing out that Packard's May 1970 memorandum on major weapons acquisition had effectively created a new policy that would reduce technical risks and increase acquisition flexibility, as the panel had suggested. Laird promised to issue a new policy directive for major systems to codify the changes. He added that Packard had already taken steps intended to improve the training, motivation, and authority of program managers in line with the panel's proposals and was engaged in trying to reduce the reporting requirements and decentralize program management. In addition, OSD had cancelled the old acquisition Directive 3200.9, which had drawn the ire of defense contractors on the panel.

On the issue of reorganizing his department at the highest levels, Laird told Stennis that the current organization required no such major changes. He reported that he had rejected the Blue Ribbon Panel's recommendation to create an assistant secretary of defense for testing and evaluation reporting to a deputy secretary for evaluation. He claimed that splitting responsibility for testing between DDR&E and the chief of military operations would be sufficient to satisfy the panel's desire to improve the stature and quality of operational testing and lead to the wider use of scientific testing techniques. These areas, therefore, required no major reorganization. Nor was Laird willing to require that the Advanced Research Projects Agency (ARPA) provide a formal risk assessment for each new weapon system prior to the approval of the DCP for that program. He would leave this in the hands of the services and defense agencies directly involved, under the oversight of DDR&E.[98]

With agreement that their reform project had covered the most significant flaws in the procurement process, Packard and Laird felt free to praise Fitzhugh and his colleagues without accepting their conclusions regarding major changes at the Department of Defense. As a result, the Blue Ribbon Panel's report had only a marginal impact on acquisition. In November 1970, the deputy secretary issued a memo announcing that the department would adopt eight of the Blue Ribbon Panel's less sweeping recommendations.[99]

Overall, the panel's study and report had reinforced Packard's reform effort by highlighting the need for systemic changes to the Defense Department acquisition process. Given the panel's limited time and resources, its study of an organization as large and complex as DoD naturally lacked depth. The report's lack of detail allowed Laird and Packard to pick and choose the recommendations they supported. Not surprisingly, these recommendations tended to reflect their predetermined views on the subject—views they had undoubtedly made clear to Fitzhugh and his colleagues. In areas where the secretary and deputy secretary disagreed with the panel's proposals, they could fall back on their superior knowledge of existing organizations and procedures, as opposed to the report's often sketchy rationale for particular changes to the status quo. Laird and Packard agreed not to oppose the creation of a second deputy secretary that Congress created in 1972, but Laird left office with that position still unfilled.[100]

CODIFYING THE NEW ACQUISITION PROCESS—DOD DIRECTIVE 5000.1

With the Blue Ribbon Panel's study completed and its findings integrated into the reform effort, Packard could focus on translating his management by objective improvements into standard departmental acquisition procedures. During early 1971, De Poix led a joint OSD/service/agency task force that worked for several

---

[98] Ibid.

[99] Memo, Packard for Listed Parties, 3 Nov 1970, sub: Blue Ribbon Decision Memorandum No. 1, IV B, Blue Ribbon Defense Panel, 1969–1970 (1), box 549, OSD Historical Office Subject Files.

[100] On the implementation of the Blue Ribbon Defense Panel's recommendations, see Mark M. Lowenthal, "Defense Department Reorganization: The Fitzhugh Report, 1969–1970," Congressional Research Service, CRS–76–153F, 19 August 1976, pp. 19–27; on an assessment of problems with blue ribbon commissions, including the Blue Ribbon Defense Panel, see William E. Kovacic, "Blue Ribbon Defense Commissions: The Acquisition of Major Weapon Systems," in *Arms, Politics, and the Economy: Historical and Contemporary Perspectives,* ed. Robert Higgs (New York: Holmes & Meier, 1990), pp. 61–104.

months on a new acquisition directive to replace the now-discarded 3200.9 and codify the changes announced in Packard's 28 May 1970 memorandum. The proposed directive went through a number of drafts during the spring of 1971, as different offices aired their views.[101] Exactly one year after issuing his program for acquisition reform, Packard circulated the new "Directive on the Acquisition of Major Defense Systems" for review.[102] Packard signed this directive, Number 5000.1, on 13 July 1971. It encapsulated in six pages the major elements of his management reform philosophy.

DoD Directive 5000.1 applied to major acquisition programs only—those exceeding a development cost of more than $50 million, a production cost of over $200 million, or a program meeting some urgent national need.[103] The directive began by stressing Packard's determination to decentralize responsibility for these programs and to place them under the authority of a single program manager with enough clout, skills, and independence to accomplish the program goals. To that end, it spelled out the division of responsibility between OSD and the services. (See Appendix B for a description of the changes made to DoD Directive 5000.1 during the period 1971 through 2008.)

The services had responsibility for identifying requirements and developing and producing the systems to meet those requirements, including the selection of contractors. DoD Directive 5000.1 specified that reporting demands on program managers would be kept to a minimum and that OSD's oversight function centered on approving the DCP and performing the threshold reviews assigned to DSARC. Thus, Packard and Laird would limit themselves to monitoring a program's progress against agreed objectives, with the secretary making decisions for further program commitments based on the advice of DSARC.

DoD Directive 5000.1 stated that the DCP, as the key program planning and evaluation document, would include the rationale for each program, along with a plan for meeting the stated requirement and an assessment of major issues, including technological risks. The sponsoring service would prepare the DCP based on the service's conceptual formulation of the best answer to a particular operational requirement, coordinating with the appropriate OSD entity—usually DDR&E, but also the assistant secretary of

---

[101] Covering Brief, Foster to Packard, ca. May 1971, Comptroller Subject Decimal File, 1071 (76-0197), 400.13 (April-May 1971), RG 330, WNRC.

[102] Memo, Packard for Listed Parties, 28 May 1971, sub: DoD Directive on the Acquisition of Major Defense Systems, Comptroller Subject Decimal File, 1971 (76–0197), 400.13 (April-May 1971), RG 330, WNRC.

[103] DoD Directive 5000.1, "Acquisition of Major Defense Systems," 13 Jul 1971. See also Appendix B.

defense for telecommunications for communications programs—to reach mutually agreeable thresholds on performance, schedules, cost, and other issues. The service would submit the program to DSARC review for approval of full-scale development and again at production initiation.

The new directive admonished the services to structure program schedules around actual achievement of key objectives. Program managers should consider schedules as subject to trade-off, to the same extent as cost and technical performance parameters, and should allow for unforeseen problems and delays to avoid unnecessary overlapping of different phases. To manage risk, the sponsoring service would need to assess continually the progress achieved in meeting technical challenges, committing more resources only when confident that problems could be solved. This confidence could come only from early and frequent use of realistic tests, with results of operational testing presented to the DSARC at the time of the production decision. Whether the services would find it within their interest to adopt these changes remained to be seen.

DoD Directive 5000.1 left to the services the responsibility for choosing contractors and contract terms but warned against total package procurement of complex new systems. The services were advised that cost-type contracts made sense on high-risk development programs, while the services could use fixed-price agreements once development had solved major problems. The directive enjoined the services to require would-be contractors to identify risks and uncertainties in their proposals, but at the same time to minimize the contractor's expenses in the solicitation process. The services were free to penalize contractor proposals that included unreasonably low-cost estimates. Each program would require an effective management control system that would allow the service to plan assignments and monitor progress. Program managers should utilize contractor management and information systems for this task to the extent possible and hold paperwork to a minimum.

The drafters of DoD Directive 5000.1 had clearly borrowed heavily from Packard's memorandum of May 1970, to the extent of using the same language to admonish the readers regarding key items. For instance, in reference to the conceptual development stage of a program, the May 1970 memorandum held that "it is crucial that the right decisions be made during the conceptual stage. If wrong decisions are made during this period the problems that are generated cannot easily be overcome later in the program." The 1971 directive matched this warning nearly word for word: "It is crucial that the right decisions be made during this conceptual effort; wrong decisions create problems not easily overcome later in the program."

In addition to borrowing the language of Packard's May 1970 memorandum in places, the authors of DoD Directive 5000.1 followed his reasoning. In both documents, the services were directed to rely on program managers with long-term assignments to run their programs, including plans for risk reduction in the DCP, and to tailor contract terms to the perceived level of technological risk. In addition, both DoD Directive 5000.1 and the May 1970 memorandum mandated that programs could progress only on demonstrated achievement of agreed development objectives such as completion of final engineering designs or successful component tests.

However, DoD Directive 5000.1 went beyond a mere repetition of Packard's earlier memorandum and reflected a more comprehensive approach to the acquisition process. The July 1971 directive concentrated largely on ensuring that programs identified technological risks and documented the solution to engineering problems. Thus, the directive made these steps prerequisites for moving a weapon system from one stage to the next through the Defense Department screening process. By the following year, OSD seemed willing to pass judgment on the operational requirement for and comparative value of weapon systems, in addition to their technological progress. This broadening of OSD authority, perhaps only making explicit what the services had already accepted in practice, was spelled out in the requirements for weapon system DCPs. Although DoD Directive 5000.1 gave the services responsibility for "identifying needs and defining, developing and producing systems to satisfy those needs," OSD's responsibilities included "assuring that major defense systems are pursued in response to valid needs." The sponsoring service therefore had to include a justification for the proposed system as part of the DCP submitted for OSD approval. At each stage, DSARC review would cover "the need for the selected defense system in consideration of threat, systems alternatives, special logistics needs, estimates of development costs, preliminary estimates of life cycle costs and potential benefits in context with overall DoD strategy and fiscal guidance." The new directive also stated that the rationale for each system "shall be challenged throughout the acquisition process." Although obviously the secretary could cancel any program he believed had become superfluous, DoD Directive 5000.1 made assessing the justification for a weapon system an ongoing part of the OSD oversight function.

DoD Directive 5000.1 also covered topics that the Blue Ribbon Panel had raised in its report issued after the Packard memorandum. The new directive addressed the contractor selection process, mandating that the services choose contractors based on capability to perform rather than just price. Its requirement that the services plan the solicitation and evaluation of proposals with the aim of minimizing contractor expense obviously reflected the concerns raised by the Blue Ribbon Panel over the extent and cost of such proposals. In addition, DoD Directive 5000.1 explained that system development would depend on an advanced technology base maintained by basic research and prototype testing divorced from any particular weapon system program. This part of the directive mirrored the panel's recommendation for continued exploratory development of subsystems and advanced technologies, independent of a specific weapon system.[104]

Packard saw the publication of DoD Directive 5000.1 as the culmination of his attempt to reform acquisition practices at the OSD level, noting in September 1971 that it "completed a major DoD-wide effort which included a review of OSD-level Directives and Instructions relating to systems acquisition."[105] He further explained that a review of DoD acquisition publications resulted in replacing 125 old directives and instructions with only 59 new ones and urged the service secretaries to make similar reviews of their own organization's publications and effect similar efficiencies. Packard expressed his appreciation that the services had already implemented some of the changes he had ordered in his May 1970 memorandum, including greater emphasis on testing and evaluation. He concluded that new service acquisition regulatory documents would speed the reform process by removing unnecessary procedures.

In some respects, the introduction of DoD Directive 5000.1 produced few encouraging changes within the military services. Reassignments for additional tours of duty to program management positions were rare, except in the case of nonrated (nonflying status) officers in the Air Force. Promotion to the several hundred flag officer positions in the Army, Navy, and Air Force continued to be based largely on combat arms assignments and performance. There appeared to be little or no accountability for cost growth on acquisition programs.

In December 1971, Packard left the Department of Defense to return to private life. Financial considerations apparently played a large part in his decision. Hewlett-Packard had flourished in his

---

[104] Blue Ribbon Panel Report, p. 74.
[105] Memo Packard for Listed Parties, 23 Sep 1971, sub: Defense Systems Acquisition Policy, Comptroller Subject Decimal File, 1971 (76–0197), 400.13 (August-September 1971), box 47, RG 330, WNRC.

absence, and under the terms of the trust established when he took office he would have had to sacrifice an additional $20 million worth of company stock if he remained.[106] After leaving office, Packard stayed on for a couple of months informally to help the department in the transition to a new deputy, and then returned to California to become chairman of Hewlett-Packard Company.

In 1972, the Cost Analysis Improvement Group (CAIG) (earlier recommended by Packard) was formed as part of OSD to provide staff with independent program cost estimates to present to DSARC and to determine uniform DoD cost-estimating standards.[107] Equally important, Packard sought ways to limit the expensive practice of putting a weapon system into production before completing its development. This reform, called fly-before-buy, entailed the development of prototypes and competitive fly-offs before choosing a contractor and entering production.[108] Nonetheless, defense acquisition programs continued to experience significant cost increases throughout the 1970s, due in part to the fact that the incentives for program managers and contractors intended to implement the initiatives remained largely unchanged.

In early 1972 in preparation for budget hearings, Packard wrote Secretary Laird a lengthy memo summarizing his views of the Laird-Packard team's accomplishments over the preceding three years in the area of weapons development and procurement. The services had followed his vision, Packard believed, in part because he had struck a workable balance between OSD oversight responsibilities and service prerogatives. By restraining OSD offices from becoming involved in program management except at certain milestones through DSARC procedures, Packard encouraged the services to accept responsibility for improving the management of their programs. He believed that freeing the services from the threat of OSD interference (so long as the program was going well) had improved service attitudes toward OSD and their performance in program management.

Addressing the issue of cost growth, Packard laid the blame for politically embarrassing overruns on unrealistic industry bidding practices and the military's willingness to suspend disbelief when selecting contractors. The result, he noted, was "we implicitly agreed to either see companies go into bankruptcy or else that we would cover the increased cost through one device or another in the future."[109] Better contracting procedures could help, but the

---

[106] Interv, OSD Historical Office with Packard, 9 Nov 1987, p. 3.

[107] Staff Report to the Senate Committee on Armed Services, "Defense Organization: The Need for Change," 16 October 1985, p. 532.

[108] Adams, Murphy, and Rosenau, *Controlling Weapons Costs*, pp. 19, 20.

[109] Ibid.

twin problems of cost overruns and underbidding remained. These factors contributed to and were a symptom of the general malaise in the nation's defense industry. Packard hoped that the use of different contract types for different phases of a weapons system program and the move away from total package procurement would improve the Defense Department's relationship with industry. DoD also had several initiatives in place to support industry's profits and encourage capital investment.

Laird evidently agreed with his former deputy's analysis. A month later, he incorporated Packard's memo into his testimony before the House Appropriations Committee on the DoD fiscal 1973 appropriations bill. The secretary praised Packard's plain talk and warned the committee that a rough road lay ahead in procurement reform, but concluded that "thanks to Dave Packard, the road ahead is going to be easier."[110]

The years in which Melvin Laird and David Packard worked to reform the acquisition process were marked by continuing debates in Congress over the role of the military-industrial complex. At the same time, the defense budget experienced downward pressures following the end of the Vietnam War. These pressures were intensified by increased government spending on programs aimed at social improvement and the strains of an inflationary economy. Although OSD had made great strides in improving the atmosphere between OSD and the services, Congress was troubled by the slowness of reform. The result was the creation of the study project known as the Congressional Commission on Government Procurement (1972), or the McGuire-Holifield Commission discussed later in this chapter.

LEADERSHIP IN THE POST-PACKARD ERA

After David Packard left the Pentagon in December 1971, President Nixon chose Kenneth Rush as deputy secretary of defense.[111] Thirteen months later, he left the Pentagon to accept an appointment as deputy secretary of state in January 1973 at the beginning of Nixon's second term. (Rush had previously been ambassador to West Germany.) During that same month, Melvin Laird stepped down as secretary of defense, in accordance with his commitment to serve no more than four years.

To lead the Defense Department after Laird's departure, President Nixon turned to Elliot L. Richardson, then secretary of Health,

---

[110] U.S. Congress, House, *Department of Defense Appropriations for 1973, Hearings before a Subcommittee of the Committee on Appropriations*, 92d Cong., 2d sess., 22 February 1972, pp. 210–18.

[111] Obituary of Attorney D. Kenneth Rush, former president of Union Carbide and Carbon Corporation and former ambassador to Germany, *New York Times*, 13 December 1994.

Education, and Welfare. Moving from an agency with one of the largest budgets in the federal government to another, Richardson, who had no previous experience in defense acquisition or with the Defense Department other than his World War II service in the Army combat medical corps, had to present the Defense program and budget for fiscal 1974 to Congress and assess uncompleted acquisition reforms from the Laird-Packard era.[112] Nixon simultaneously nominated William P. Clements Jr. of Texas to succeed Rush as deputy secretary. Clements was the founder of Southeast Drilling Company, a pioneering multimillion-dollar firm in the offshore oil-drilling business. He had served on the Blue Ribbon Panel in 1970–1971 and in 1972 had co-chaired the Nixon re-election campaign organization in Texas. Richardson and Clements took the helm at DoD at the end of January 1973.[113]

Throughout 1973, attention to acquisition reform was eclipsed by changes in secretaries of defense and other presidential appointees throughout the government. The turmoil of the Watergate scandal began to affect OSD in the early months of 1973. On 30 April, President Nixon reorganized the administration in response to further Watergate revelations. Attorney General Richard G. Kleindienst was among those resigning, and Richardson, after spending less than four months as secretary of defense was called on to replace him. The president then called for the recently named head of the Central Intelligence Agency (CIA), James R. Schlesinger, to become secretary of defense.

Schlesinger, an economist by training, worked at the Rand Corporation and was familiar with defense issues. He served in the Nixon administration as chairman of the Atomic Energy Commission before moving to his brief tenure at the CIA.[114] Schlesinger was not confirmed by the Senate for a month. Senator Proxmire put a hold on the nomination until he could question Schlesinger on his views on strategy in Southeast Asia. Schlesinger served meanwhile in an acting capacity until the hearings late in June 1973, after which the confirmation went through and he took office on 2 July.[115]

---

[112] U.S. Congress, House, testimony of Secretary of Defense Elliot L. Richardson before the Committee on Armed Forces, FY 1974 Defense Budget and FY 1974–1978 Program (10 April 1973): 1–20.

[113] "The Pentagon's New No. 2 Man," *Business Week* (27 January 1973). 10.

[114] Roger R. Trask and Alfred Goldberg, *The Department of Defense, 1947–1997: Organization and Leaders* (Washington, D.C.: Office of the Secretary of Defense Historical Office, 2000), pp. 92–93.

[115] Interv, Goldberg and Matloff with James R. Schlesinger, 12 Jul 1990, p. 1, OSD Historical Office; Trask and Goldberg, *Department of Defense, 1947–1997*, pp. 90–93.

By this time, the Nixon administration's appointments tangle was taking its toll on OSD. The positions of assistant secretary of defense for installations and logistics and comptroller had been vacant since January, and Secretary of the Air Force Robert C. Seamans Jr. had left the Air Force without a replacement. John Foster was still DDR&E, but Clements' lack of confidence in him was public knowledge.[116] But by July 1973, the DoD team was finally filling in. The new DDR&E was Malcolm R. Currie, a business executive in the technology field with a doctorate from the University of California at Berkeley and naval service in the Second World War. The comptroller was Terence E. McClary, a business executive specializing in financial issues. The assistant secretary of defense for installations and logistics was Arthur I. Mendolia. Richardson had downgraded the position of assistant secretary of defense for systems analysis when Gardiner Tucker left the position. The new director of program analysis and evaluation reporting to the DoD comptroller was Leonard Sullivan. His position was reestablished at the assistant secretary level in 1974. Schlesinger persuaded John L. McLucas (Air Force under secretary since March 1969) to accept an appointment as secretary of the Air Force.[117]

In the fall of 1975, Schlesinger publicly voiced his objections to the budget cuts then under consideration in Congress, amounting to possibly $5 billion. His continual disagreements with Henry A. Kissinger over SALT (Strategic Arms Limitation Treaty); his quarrels with Clements, his deputy secretary; and a personal style many considered abrasive had weakened him with the genial President Gerald P. Ford. Accordingly, the president called for his resignation and Schlesinger left office on 19 November, completing seventeen months as secretary of defense.[118]

To succeed Schlesinger, President Ford turned to Donald H. Rumsfeld, a member of the White House staff. The 43-year-old Chicago native had served in Congress during the 1960s but joined the Nixon administration to hold a number of positions, including that of representative to NATO. Taking office as the 1976 election campaign was beginning, he was able to regain some of the funding that had been cut from Schlesinger's budget.[119] But funding for the Safeguard installation disappeared, and real spending decreased.

---

[116] "The Pentagon's New No. 2 Man," *Business Week* (27 January 1973): 40.

[117] Trask and Goldberg, *Department of Defense, 1947–1997*, p. 93.

[118] Interv, Goldberg and Matloff with James R. Schlesinger, 7 Feb 1991, pp. 30–36, OSD Historical Office; Trask and Goldberg, *Department of Defense, 1947–1997*, p. 93; Interv, Goldberg and Trask with Donald H. Rumsfeld, 12 Jul 1994, OSD Historical Office, pp. 16–20; Gerald R. Ford, *A Time to Heal: The Autobiography of Gerald R. Ford* (New York: Harper & Row, 1979), pp. 320–30.

[119] Trask and Goldberg, *Department of Defense, 1947–1997*, pp. 94–95.

Rumsfeld gave a high priority to developing a political consensus for increases in defense. He instituted a series of conferences with legislators and opinion leaders designed to present evidence about the Soviet buildup and the strategic balance.[120]

THE CONGRESSIONAL COMMISSION ON GOVERNMENT PROCUREMENT

In 1970, Congress had been paying increased attention to all aspects of defense management. Weapons acquisition was only one aspect of the problems that concerned Congress. Procurement throughout the federal government seemed in need of study. Despite the work of the Blue Ribbon Defense Panel, several congressional members continued to favor a major study of procurement throughout the government.[121] Beginning in 1966, congressional hearings and proposals had examined the need for such a study, and by 1970, when the panel turned in its report, a congressional commission on government procurement was already being formed.

The Congressional Commission on Government Procurement (also called the Commission on Procurement and the McGuire-Holifield Commission) was to address the entire scope of procurement across the government. With the rise of spending in the civilian agencies, problems were not confined to defense. Still, the experience of the Defense Department as the government's dominant buyer was a major focus for the commission. The acquisition of entire systems was a related issue, and notwithstanding the Blue Ribbon Panel's report, the commission devoted an entire study to major systems in defense and elsewhere. Likewise, such issues as the procurement of research and development were connected to systems acquisition. Congress hoped that the commission would look at problems of cost and competition. Also, because a large body of law governed procurement, and Congress was often blamed for having created the problem through its legislation, the commission was to investigate the need for changes in the statutes. The commission addressed several controversial issues, including centralization, the independence of the Defense Contract Audit Agency, the role of the private sector in research and development, the role of industry in advancing technology, and the nature of the acquisition process itself.[122]

---

[120] Interv, Goldberg and Trask with Donald H. Rumsfeld, 12 Jul 94, pp. 20–21.

[121] *Report to the President and the Secretary of Defense on the Department of Defense*, Blue Ribbon Defense Panel, 1 July 1970.

[122] *Report of the Commission on Government Procurement* (Washington, D.C.: U.S. Government Printing Office, 31 December 1972), vol. 1, pp. vii–viii. The report referred to an "agency head," which in the case of DoD meant the secretary of defense. The military services were defined as "agency components."

On 26 November 1969, soon after the Blue Ribbon Panel had started work, Congress passed the law creating the Commission on Government Procurement. It was to have twelve members: three appointed by the presiding officer of each house of Congress, five appointed by President Nixon, and the Comptroller General of the United States. Two members of each house and two officials of the executive branch were to be included. The two senators chosen were Henry M. Jackson (D-Wash.) and Edward J. Gurney (R-Fla.). Gurney's colleague, Lawton M. Chiles Jr. (D-Fla.), replaced Jackson early in 1972. Congressmen Frank Horton (R-N.Y.) and Chet E. Holifield (D-Calif.) came from the House of Representatives. Holifield became one of the two cochairmen, the other being Perkins McGuire, who was working as a consultant in Washington, D.C., but who had served as assistant secretary of defense for supply and logistics in the Eisenhower administration. The two executive branch officials were Frank P. Sanders, under secretary of the Navy, and Robert L. Kunzig, administrator of the General Services Administration, who was replaced by his acting successor, Arthur F. Sampson, in mid-1972. Elmer B. Staats, the comptroller general and head of the General Accounting Office, served ex officio. Besides McGuire, the private-sector members included business executives and, as a replacement, James E. Webb, former head of the National Aeronautics and Space Administration (NASA).

The commission appointed thirteen study groups and submitted its final report on 31 December 1972, over a year after the Blue Ribbon Report. The heads of the study groups represented a variety of backgrounds extending from business and consulting firms to government agencies. A civilian official from the Air Force headed the research and development group, while John Russell Clark of LTV Aerospace Corporation chaired the group covering major systems acquisition. Other members of the group were from the public and private sectors.[123]

The experience of the Defense Department was central to the findings of the congressional commission. Although the commission addressed the full range of government procurement issues, the first one they mentioned was public concern over cost growth in weapons programs. Procurement was then taking up one-fourth of the federal budget, and defense acquisition was two-thirds of federal government procurement. The next agency in scale was the Atomic Energy Commission, which spent most of its procurement money in connection with nuclear weapons programs, in support of the Defense Department.

---

[123] Ibid., pp. iii–iv, 139–51.

The congressional commission attempted the task of addressing procurement throughout the government while dealing with the primary importance of defense programs.[124] The issues addressed included research and development, acquisition of major systems, commercial products, construction, grant assistance programs, and such legal thickets as administrative remedies, liability, and intellectual property. Formal recommendations numbered 149 in all, covering everything from proposals for legislation to editorial revisions in current regulations.[125]

The commission concluded that procurement in the federal government was in need of modernization and simplification, as well as better management. Reform would require legislation, since much of what was wrong lay embedded in practices Congress had sanctioned over the years. At the same time, reform within the executive branch seemed to require congressional attention, beginning with the creation of an office to oversee procurement throughout the government. In the acquisition of major systems, the report called for a more open and competitive process in the early phases of programs, or "competition at the front end."[126]

Office of Federal Procurement Policy

The congressional commission's leading recommendation was that a law be passed creating a single office of federal procurement policy, preferably within the Office of Management and Budget. In analyzing the process of planning, solicitation, source selection, negotiation, awards, and contract administration, the report furnished an agenda for the proposed office. The report gave especially high priority to two issues: (1) the relationship between the government and the private sector and (2) the need for timely payment of contractors.[127] But it also addressed an array of complaints about government procurement based on years of experience. They included the disjunction between the Armed Services Procurement Act, which applied to defense acquisition, and the Federal Property and Administrative Services Act, which affected the civilian agencies of the government. A series of recommendations sought to bring coherence to procurement regulations and make procedures more in tune with current reality. For instance, the process that made negotiated contracts the exception to the rule of formal advertising and sealed bids justified by one of seventeen possible exceptions as stated in "determinations and findings" needed

---

[124] Ibid., pt. A, "General Procurement Considerations," pp. 2–5.
[125] Ibid., pp. 185–99.
[126] Ibid., pp. 2–5.
[127] Ibid., pp. v, 12–14.

change.[128] As the commission noted: "The point is not that there should be more negotiation and less advertising but that competitive negotiation should be recognized in law for what it is; namely, a normal, sound buying method which the government should prefer where market conditions are not appropriate for the use of formal advertising."[129]

Existing laws seemed to encourage practices such as technical leveling and "auctioning" in which the government brought on exchanges of information among bidders, until all bids were the same, and the most innovative bidder gained no benefit but instead had to keep its bid low to win.[130]

One contribution the proposed office of federal procurement policy could make was to simplify regulations, adopting a uniform structure and process, with the chance of reducing the "five-foot shelf" of regulations every office had to keep. The commission was also concerned with the quality, motivation, and state of training of the contracting officers and the procurement workforce throughout the government.[131]

Frequent statements of policy had supported the principle that favored reliance on the private sector for the acquisition of major weapon systems. Since 1966, Bureau of the Budget Circular A–76 had proclaimed that the government should rely on private sources for goods and services except in specific cases, one of which was, in essence, military necessity. Most politicians treated this principle as indisputable. The McGuire-Holifield Commission recommended writing A–76 into law, and the only dissenting views were those business members who favored procedures for stronger enforcement of the privatization standard. The view put forward by such critics as the economist John Kenneth Galbraith that the defense firms were really public assets and should be nationalized got short shrift.[132]

Concerning government-owned, contractor-operated facilities, the historic government defense plants, the commission simply noted that they seemed to give their operators an unfair competitive advantage and urged the proposed office of federal procurement policy to review the guidelines.[133]

---

[128] Ibid., pp. 18–25.
[129] Ibid., p. 21.
[130] Ibid., pp. 20–25.
[131] Ibid., pp. 31–38, 43–55; Interv, DAHP with James D. Schlesinger, 7 Feb 1991, p. 28.
[132] *Report of the Commission on Government Procurement*, vol. 1, pt. A, pp. 57–65; John Kenneth Galbraith, "The Big Defense Firms Are Really Public Firms and Should Be Nationalized," *New York Times Magazine*, 16 November 1969.
[133] *Report of the Commission on Government Procurement*, vol. 1, pt. A, p. 66.

The commission devoted much attention to the issue of timely payment. For small businesses, the problem of delays in government payments could be a matter of survival. Likewise, subcontractors might suffer if the prime contractor chose to pass along funding delays to them. Undoubtedly, Congress had been concerned over constituents who had suffered from delayed government payments. But the commission devoted a good deal of attention to Congress' own role in the problem, which was the failure to pass appropriations promptly. Continuing resolutions often failed to cover expenses of ongoing contract work and forced delays in beginning new work.[134] The commission accordingly pointed the way toward reforms that were to emerge in the Budget Reform Act of 1974.

On such matters as cost accounting, the commission simply urged that the proposed office of federal procurement policy set uniform standards, so that contractors could follow the same procedures for all government work, regardless of the agency. Contractors needed a uniform standard on prices and allowable costs, including overhead, as well as profit and risk. The commission also feared that many contractors were overburdened by management and reporting requirements from a variety of government agencies.[135]

The government maintained field organizations for management and support of its contracts. The commission noted the wide range of agencies with such field organizations and the inefficiency and incoherence of the system of "plant cognizance," even within the Defense Department. The Defense Contract Administration Service (DCAS), created to provide a unified approach to plant management, had not fulfilled its potential. As of 1972, the Army still had cognizance of five plants, the Navy fifteen, and the Air Force nineteen. Although willing to allow government-owned plants and all shipyards to remain under service cognizance, the commission urged centralizing the oversight of remaining plants under DCAS. To strengthen the service further, the report proposed separating it from the Defense Supply Agency and consolidating the Defense Contract Audit Agency (DCAA) with DCAS.[136]

The commission was far from united on the consolidation proposal. The majority report contended that the DCAA existed solely to audit contractors doing government work. It was accordingly a part of the management team for defense oversight of contractors and supported the contract management function. Although the commission mentioned the frequent suggestions from business that DCAS and DCAA be consolidated, opposition by the Defense

---

[134] Ibid., pp. 67–73.
[135] Ibid., pp. 75–79.
[136] Ibid., pp. 103–10.

Department, confirmed by David Packard during his tenure, was also noted. Congressional committees had been opposed to the consolidation, as had the General Accounting Office. On the commission itself, Senator Chiles, Congressman Holifield, and Comptroller General Staats all lodged objections.[137] Former NASA Director Webb not only objected but also asserted that an independent auditing function was an essential element of leadership in an agency. The quality and motivation of the procurement workforce depended on the knowledge that an independent auditing activity was receiving the full support of the top management of the agency.

The commission also addressed two politically sensitive issues: the use of procurement to implement national policies and the role of small business. Congress and the White House had given a number of groups leverage to influence procurement policy. Organized labor, civil rights advocates, environmentalists, and business groups seeking to limit foreign competition had all seen their concerns legislated. Much duplication had resulted as, for example, the Buy American Act and DFARS, Subpart 225.7004, restricting the acquisition of foreign buses, were general and specific applications of the same concern. Moreover, objectives often conflicted. Procurement officials had become compliance officers for such concerns as limiting the use of nonunion labor, prohibiting racial discrimination, and ensuring compliance with the Clean Air Act, let alone efforts to ensure fair and honest procurement practices. Their need to report on these topics added to the cost and time needed to complete procurement actions. This burden was not often acknowledged as a factor in the costs and delays of weapons acquisition. The report of the commission called for a review of these policies, increasing the visibility of costs and establishing standard procedures for enforcement.[138]

Legislators who were closely involved with procurement seemed to be especially aware of the number of their constituents who were the owners of small businesses. Problems included defining what a small business was, what was a fair share of government procurement for small firms, the effectiveness of set-aside requirements, and the status of subcontractors. The commission called for a review of small business policy by the Small Business Administration and the new Office of Federal Procurement Policy. But it was clear that Congress would define competition in the procurement process in part in terms of the opportunities for small businesses to bid.[139]

---
[137] Ibid.
[138] Ibid., pp. 112–18.
[139] Ibid., pp. 125–32.

Procurement of Research and Development

The role of the defense industry in research and development paralleled that of private-sector nonprofit organizations. Universities and, to a lesser extent, nonprofit foundations, performed essential research. But the post-1945 era had produced a group of independent nonprofit research organizations specifically organized to do work under contract with the government. These were the federally funded research and development centers (FFRDCs), long known in the Defense Department as federal contract research centers (FCRCs). Some of these were connected to educational institutions, while others had spun off from defense contractors. Most had a connection with a specific component of the Department of Defense.[140]

The FCRCs varied in size and specialization. The largest in 1969 was the Aerospace Corporation, which worked with the Air Force, and specifically with the Air Force Space and Missile Systems Organization (SAMSO), with over 3,000 employees and programs valued at $74 million a year. Next in monetary value was the Lincoln Laboratory, connected with the Massachusetts Institute of Technology, at $68 million a year. Lincoln Laboratory performed work for the Air Force, largely connected with the Electronic Systems Division. Other groups included the Johns Hopkins University's Applied Physics Laboratory; the Center for Naval Analyses; the Logistics Management Institute, which performed work for OSD and the military services; and the Army-connected Human Resources Research Organization (HumRRO). The Institute for Defense Analyses (IDA) worked for OSD. The Rand Corporation, which spun off from the Douglas Aircraft Corporation in 1948 to do work for the Air Force, had more than 1,200 employees and annual funding of over $20 million.[141]

At the same time, the military services continued to operate their own laboratories throughout the United States. As the emphasis on competition and the role of the private sector continued, questions about the role of the federal laboratories were inevitable. The Procurement Commission alleged that few of the service laboratories had a strong reputation. The Army's Harry Diamond Laboratory, then still in Washington, D.C., and the Navy's Naval Weapons Center at China Lake, California, were singled out as deserving of their high reputations.[142]

---

[140] Ibid.
[141] Ibid., pp. 16–18.
[142] Ibid., pp. 13–16.

The Procurement Commission favored utilizing the government laboratories in support of contract research and development. It also believed that FCRCs needed strong oversight. The strongest suggestion of the commission was that federal agencies needed to be open to competition from unsolicited proposals. Encouraging innovative ideas was the essence of competition in research and development. For this reason, the commissioners saw no difficulty in sustaining a variety of research and development organizations.[143]

The commission preferred cost-reimbursement contracts over fixed-price contracts for research and development projects. These projects were likely to be too high risk for fixed-price instruments, while the need for the government to manage research closely fit well with managing costs. The commission also supported DoD's use of standing agreements with research and development contractors that simplified negotiation for specific projects.[144]

The commission's support for research in the private sector led to its main policy recommendation, which was to provide for covering the cost of research by contractors. The manufacturers of major defense systems hoped to finance their research and development from the proceeds of their work on government contracts. Known as contractor independent technical effort (CITE), this work was normally funded from contractor overhead. The commission noted that in sealed-bid procurement, as in production for the commercial market, competition ensured that the manufacturer would control costs for research as well as production. When DoD or other agencies negotiated cost-reimbursement contracts, the contractor hoped to recover a fair share of overhead as an allowable cost, which normally included the cost of CITE.[145]

It had long been the practice in defense contractor accounting to subdivide these costs into independent research and development (IR&D) and bid and proposal (B&P), as well as development testing and evaluation (DT&E), a fairly recent addition. For bid and proposal work, it was the task of government to make sure that a winning bidder was qualified to do the work. The commensurate right of the bidder was to demonstrate qualifications for performing the required work. Development test and evaluation broke out the specific costs of testing, which in the wake of Packard's reforms was a serious concern.[146] The Procurement Commission, in keeping with its support for the private sector, recommend-

---

[143] Ibid., pp. 23–28.
[144] Ibid., pp. 45–46.
[145] *Report of the Commission on Government Procurement*, vol. 2, pt. B, "Acquisition of Research and Development," pp. 31–34.
[146] Ibid.

ed "a policy recognizing IR&D and B&P efforts as necessary costs of doing business."[147]

Since the introduction of the Armed Services Procurement Regulation (ASPR) in 1949, the normal government practice had been to allow contractor reimbursement for independent technical effort. But the process of determining a fair reimbursement had undergone change. Though often interpreted as allowing simply the expenses of product development, the ASPR had been cited as authority for allowing research costs as well. A 1959 revision of the ASPR attempted to set distinct procedures for research and for development. In the early 1960s, DDR&E led a task group to work out a better solution. The proposed answer was to include all reasonable CITE in overhead. But the rising tide of criticism of the military-industrial complex led Congress in 1969 and 1970 to impose a ceiling on the amounts a contractor could recover. Following a study by GAO and congressional hearings early in 1970, legislation removed the ceiling but imposed a "relevancy test" to determine appropriate expenses. Accordingly, OSD issued a revision to the ASPR on 1 September 1971.[148]

The revisions established definitions for recoverable costs as overhead for IR&D and B&P. The main feature was a requirement that major contractors negotiate annually with the government to establish a ceiling of allowable costs for research. This requirement in effect established that the big defense contractors would be operating government-subsidized research and development programs aimed at supporting their work in producing weapon systems for national defense. The Procurement Commission essentially supported this approach, as it engaged the private sector in furnishing technology to the government.[149]

The Procurement Commission's recommendation asserted the principle that IR&D and B&P expenses should be treated in a uniform manner throughout the government. Businesses that relied primarily on fixed-price contracts or commercial sales should be allowed to treat research expenses as normal overhead. Those that relied on cost-reimbursement contracts would have to demonstrate the relevancy of the research to the mission of the agency (i.e., the Defense Department). But the commission was far from unanimous in its recommendation.[150]

The controversy was deep-seated. The commission agreed that ideally a contractor could take research costs out of profit. But it

---
[147] Ibid., p. 31.
[148] Ibid., pp. 32–38.
[149] Ibid.
[150] Ibid., pp. 31–32.

noted: "It is axiomatic that a business must generate income in excess of all of its costs if it is to survive." In view of the controversy over the appropriate level of profit in the defense industry, it was prudent to treat CITE expenses as allowable costs (overhead) rather than as contractor deductions from profit. Critics of the defense industry tended to define bid and proposal as advertising. The entire issue of CITE was intensely controversial. It was easy for critics to believe that overhead costs, including IR&D and B&P, were rationalizations for waste.[151]

Dissenting commissioners included three of the legislators (Chiles, Holifield, and Horton), as well as Staats of the GAO and Webb. The dissenters favored the existing procedures as outlined in the ASPR, with an explicit requirement for visibility, allowing the government access to contractors' records to make sure the costs were reasonable. Sanders, the under secretary of the Navy, supported in part by Sampson, the acting GSA (General Services Administration) administrator, suggested inventive ways to get around the "IR&D/B&P dilemma." These included such ideas as allowing contractors to establish nonprofit subsidiaries to do their research, awards, grants, and tax breaks. Changes in overhead rules or profit policy could incentivize desired behavior.[152]

REFORMING REQUIREMENTS

The report of the Congressional Commission on Government Procurement included a penetrating assessment of the issues of systems acquisition based on the experience of the Defense Department over the years. From this, civilian agencies might profit in their own expanded concerns with systems acquisition. John Russell Clark, who headed the study group on acquisition, was general manager of the Vought Division of LTV as well as an aeronautical engineer with a degree from the Massachusetts Institute of Technology. The group included representatives from industry and government, one member being an employee of the Aerospace Corporation, an FCRC.[153]

The report on acquisition described a process that included contractors who overpromised technical performance in order to obtain work, military services that overmanaged the design process, defense secretaries who lacked the means to control the process, and a Congress bogged down in detail. In place of "patchwork" solutions, the commission urged an attack on the underlying prob-

---

[151] William Proxmire, *Report from Wasteland* (New York: Praeger Publishers, 1970), pp. 114–15.
[152] *Report of the Commission on Government Procurement*, vol. 2, pt. B, pp. 39–42.
[153] Ibid., vol. 1, app. B, p. 149.

lems, instituting a systematic process by which all participants could have the needed information.[154]

The report's most penetrating argument concerned the requirements process for weapon systems, in which the focus on predetermined technical solutions actually increased risk. The proposed solution, "competition at the front end"—an increased emphasis on competitive alternate solutions—involved increasing the role of industry in the development of weapons. Packard's known interest in competitive prototypes suggested an even more all-embracing reliance on competition in the earliest phases of a weapons program. In place of the commonly understood requirements process, firms might be invited to submit a solution to a problem, a mission need rather than a design to meet predetermined specifications.[155]

In December 1972, the Congressional Commission on Government Procurement presented its report. The following five items were its principal findings and recommendations:

- Congress was ill-equipped to evaluate performance, costs, and schedules for new defense systems programs in the context of national security objectives and priorities. Congress should establish an office of federal procurement policy, to be headed by a presidential appointee, to oversee procurement policies and systems throughout the government.
- Congress should consolidate all statutory procurement regulations into a single statute.
- DoD should upgrade the acquisition workforce by establishing an institution to provide necessary education and services.
- DoD should reduce the management and administrative layers between policy makers and program offices.
- Congress should have greater visibility in the acquisition process to exercise its responsibilities, i.e., provide the information needed to make key program decisions and commitments.

Pentagon officials adopted the position that DoD was already moving in the direction recommended in the commission's report.[156] Implementing the report of the McGuire Holifield Commission was under way for several years but was never fully carried out.

---

[154] Ibid., vol. 2, pt. C, pp. 69–73.
[155] Ibid., pp. 77–82.
[156] Acker, "The Maturing of the DoD Acquisition Process," pp. 41–43.

A scorecard of recommendations adopted would probably be impressive, but the soundness of the changes might never be fully assessed. Perhaps the greatest strength of the report can be attributed to the fact that Congress had commissioned it. Accordingly, the commission had been free to suggest ways in which the legislative branch had contributed to the problem and how legislation might bring change. At the same time, the executive departments were also forced to pay attention and to make careful arguments if they preferred to reject any of the commission's proposals. The Defense Department could argue for its part that the report reflected its own experience. Indeed, many of the recommendations paralleled DoD's own thinking.[157]

The response in the Defense Department proved to be slow. A study of the acquisition process by a group with extensive experience in the Pentagon asserted that the reform of requirements was not really needed. DoD devoted its attention to the internal reforms that Clements and others saw as necessary.

Legislating Reform

During 1974, Congress adopted two major reforms. One was only tangentially connected with the commission's report but was a critical issue in executive-legislative relations. This was passage of the Budget Act. The other was the creation of an Office of Federal Procurement Policy.

Although Congress often voiced its criticisms of the acquisition process in DoD and the federal government in general, many members were aware of the deficiencies of Congress. The most urgent issue was the continuing delays in adopting appropriations, especially for the Defense Department, a practice known to impose serious hardships. Among the victims were smaller contractors who could not afford delays in payment. One recommendation of the McGuire-Holifield Commission had been to expedite payments to contractors.[158]

The Budget Act of 1974 was the most far-reaching reform of the congressional budget process since 1921. Broadly speaking, it was designed as an attack on the weakened President Nixon to end his practice of impounding funds that Congress had appropriated. It added reforms in the way Congress handled the budget, creating the Congressional Budget Office, revising the committee process, and changing the fiscal calendar of the federal government. Fiscal Year 1976 would be the last to end on 30 June. A transitional quarter running from July to September would be followed by fiscal

---

[157] *Report on the Commission on Government Procurement*, vol. 1, pp. vi–viii.
[158] Ibid.

1977, ending on 30 September of that year. The act also mandated that by 1978 agencies were to provide Congress with budget data on research in a format designed to highlight mission needs. In the process, the reform of the fiscal calendar was designed to resolve the problem of late payments.[159]

A month later, Congress passed the legislation creating the Office of Federal Procurement Policy. In the Defense Department there was considerable doubt that such an office was necessary. Given the unique nature of defense acquisition and the scale of DoD's procurement budget, senior defense officials believed that reform within the Defense Department was best managed in the Pentagon rather than in an organization outside DoD. Nonetheless, Congress concluded that an outside voice for reform was needed, and the law was passed in August 1974, the month of President Nixon's resignation.[160] The Office of Federal Procurement Policy was to be an element of the Office of Management and Budget. President Ford nominated Hugh E. Witt, then working in OSD under the assistant secretary for installations and logistics, to be the first administrator of the Office of Federal Procurement Policy. The Senate confirmed Witt in December 1974. In the meantime, other legislation was introduced to overhaul procurement legislation, help small business, reform bid contract protest procedures, and extend the Renegotiation Board.[161]

A number of changes came about within a year or two after the McGuire-Holifield Commission submitted its report. The Office of Management and Budget (OMB) assigned the recommendations of the commission to task groups headed by different federal agencies. It also updated OMB Circular A–76, which set policy on the role of private business in procurement.[162] The Defense Department adopted a number of changes but took a stand against others. It formally rejected the proposals to reform the structure of DCAS and DCAA. Separating DCAS from the Defense Supply Agency would create too much duplication of staff, and the independence of the DCAA remained a fundamental principle of defense management. The question of independent research and development remained open as the Office of Federal Procurement Policy explored agency and industry views. Nonetheless, the effect of the commission's at-

---

[159] Ibid., pp. 37, 69–73.

[160] Remarks by Senator Sam Nunn, *Congressional Record*, 93d Cong. 2d sess., S. 7575–7577, 1974.

[161] GAO Report, *Legislative Recommendations of the Commission on Government Procurement: 5 Years Later*, PSAD–78–100, 31 Jul 1978, pp. 7–11.

[162] Ibid., pp. 11–15.

tention to this topic was to encourage a more supportive view of the efforts of private enterprise in research.[163]

OFFICE OF MANAGEMENT AND BUDGET CIRCULAR A-109

In 1976, the Office of Federal Procurement Policy published Circular A-109, which required more competition throughout the acquisition process and mission area analysis in the early stages of the process. Nonetheless, its implementation by successive defense secretaries often encountered resistance from the military services and contractors.[164]

Under A-109 requirements, the acquisition cycle began with a military service determination of a need for a particular weapon system to perform a mission. The service then prepared a mission-need statement, which expressed the need in terms of operational requirements rather than performance specifications or system characteristics. To acquire control over this portion of the acquisition cycle, OSD added a new Milestone Zero to the acquisition process, signifying OSD approval of a mission need proposed by a military service. This approval was required before the acquisition program could proceed.[165]

During the administration of Jimmy Carter (1977–1981), Defense Secretary Harold Brown (a former director of defense research and engineering) sought to regain some of the authority in weapons acquisition that Packard had relinquished to the services. Secretary Brown also issued a formal requirement to comply with OMB Circular A-109 for mission area analysis and mission-need statements.[166]

Throughout the 1970s, the Defense Department expended much effort to improve the Planning, Programming, and Budgeting System. The efforts involved identifying long-term mission needs and matching them to resource requirements, reviewing the outcomes against a variety of alternatives, and finally translating the results into firm budget proposals. By the end of the 1970s, however, several major initiatives undertaken during the Nixon, Ford, and Carter administrations to reform the weapons acquisition process had created serious functional bottlenecks in the PPBS, especially between the planning and programming phases.

---

[163] *Report on the Commission on Government Procurement*, pp. 38–45, 60–61.

[164] U.S. Congress, Senate, testimony of Laurence E. Lynn, 21–27 October and 5 November 1981, pp. 133–35.

[165] Giles K. Smith and E. T. Friedmann, *An Analysis of Weapon System Acquisition Intervals, Past and Present*, Rand Report R-2605-DR&E (Santa Monica, Calif.: Rand Corporation, 1980), pp. 5–6.

[166] Background Information, Senior Steering Group, Office of the Secretary of Defense, DoD Acquisition Study, 7–8 November 1985.

In 1979, the Defense Resources Board completed a separate study of the acquisition process. It endorsed the use of the mission-need statement, schedule compression, multiple technologies in one weapon system, sought to improve incentives for program managers, and provide greater consideration of life-cycle costs. But the recommendations in the report were never acted on, and a new administration headed by Ronald W. Reagan was elected in November 1980.[167]

The Reagan administration would focus first on reviving the economy, controlling inflation, and strengthening U.S. defense capabilities. It would then conduct a comprehensive study and implementation of acquisition reforms described in the next chapter.

---

[167] Kosta Tsipis and Penny Janeway, eds., *Review of U.S. Military Research and Development* (Washington, D.C.: Pergamon-Brassey's, 1984), pp. 14–15; Bradburn, "Strategic Postures in the Military Aircraft Industry," pp. 45–53; U.S. Congress, Senate, testimony of Laurence E. Lynn, 21–27 October and 5 November 1981, pp. 133–35.

Chapter Three

THE 1980s: THE CARLUCCI INITIATIVES AND THE PACKARD COMMISSION

On 4 November 1980, former California Governor Ronald W. Reagan defeated incumbent Jimmy Carter to become the fortieth president of the United States. Reagan's stunning win was matched by a strong Republican win in Congress. Unlike his predecessor, Jimmy Carter, whose presidency was marred by an intractable hostage crisis in Iran, an ailing national economy, rampant inflation, soaring oil prices, and a host of other domestic problems, Reagan entered the White House in January 1981 with an election mandate to restore economic growth at home and strengthen American influence abroad. Reagan and his Republican allies in Congress cut taxes and reduced the size of the federal government while incurring huge budget deficits to help revive the economy, which was already crippled by sharp declines in industrial productivity and fierce foreign competition in key manufacturing sectors ranging from steel and automobiles to machine tools and consumer electronics.[1] The economy responded to the tax cut stimuli, and the gross national product grew at an attractive rate of 3.85 percent per year during Reagan's eight years in office. In his first inaugural address on 20 January 1981, Reagan argued: "In this present crisis, government is not the solution to our problems; government *is the problem.*" The White House moved quickly to modernize and enlarge America's military force structure, reversing the military decline of the late 1970s. During his first term in office, Reagan presided over the largest and most expensive peacetime expansion of the Army, Navy, and Air Force in American history. The budget for the Department of Defense (DoD) doubled, from $142 billion to

---

[1] On the decline of the manufacturing economy in the United States during the 1980s, see, for example, Paul R. Lawrence and Davis Dyer, *Renewing American Industry* (New York: Free Press, 1983); see also Alfred D. Chandler Jr., "The Competitive Performance of U.S. Industrial Enterprises Since the Second World War," *Business History Review* 68 (Spring 1994): 1–72; Margaret B. W. Graham, *RCA and the VideoDisc: The Business of Research* (Cambridge: Cambridge University Press, 1986); Maryann Keller, *Rude Awakening: The Rise, Fall, and Struggle for Recovery of General Motors* (New York: Morrow, 1989); Paul A. Tiffany: *The Decline of American Steel: How Management, Labor, and Government Went Wrong* (New York: Oxford University Press, 1988); and John P. Hoerr, *And the Wolf Finally Came: The Decline of the American Steel Industry* (Pittsburgh: University of Pittsburgh Press, 1988).

$286 billion, between 1980 and 1985, although inflation accounted for 30 percent or more of that increase.[2] During that period, the Defense Department acquired new weapons systems for the military services: tactical aircraft, strategic bombers, intercontinental ballistic missiles (ICBMs), nuclear submarines, tanks, and attack helicopters.

The Defense Department's acquisition of major weapons systems has always been an inherently messy process replete with political rivalries and competing institutional priorities. After World War II, the Army, Navy, and the Air Force competed intensely against one another for resources to meet new mission requirements, while the Office of the Secretary of Defense (OSD) sought to limit this behavior through centralized oversight and managerial control. Congress, meanwhile, appropriated funds to the Defense Department annually, but weapons development—from concept to production—typically required many years of effort. Throughout the Cold War, changing funding levels prompted by annual budget fluctuations often led to inefficient production rates and schedule slippages in key weapons programs contracted out to industry. Concurrently, politicians and business advocates alike hailed competition as the most effective source of weapons innovation, but defense contractors operated in an economic environment that mitigated free-market behavior. The buyer-seller relationship was dominated, not by many independent actors competing against one another, but rather by a single buying organization—the federal government. The resulting market distortions and mismatched incentives between a small number of very large firms and the Defense Department encouraged institutional rigidity in the procurement process. High barriers to entry often enabled contractors to shift the burden of cost overruns during development and production directly to the government. Cost control was, and still is, a chronic problem in the weapons acquisition process.[3]

The acquisition process has also been constrained by the decentralized and adversarial nature of representative government in the United States. Workable solutions to technological problems that appear in the process of developing new weapons systems require managerial decisiveness, flexibility, and ready access to resources. The availability of such resources, however, is limited by the necessary trade-offs between disparate political constituencies—Congress, the White House, industry, and the military

---

[2] U.S. General Accounting Office (GAO), *Major Acquisitions: Summary of Recurring Problems and Systematic Issues: 1960–1987*, GAO/NSIAD–88–135BR (Washington, D.C.: General Accounting Office, September 1988), p. 12.

[3] For an exhaustive examination of these issues, see Merton J. Peck and Frederic M. Scherer, *The Weapons Acquisition Process: An Economic Analysis* (Boston: Division of Research, Harvard University Graduate School of Business Administration, 1962).

services—who must reach agreement for acquisition programs to move forward. Decisive action in the weapons acquisition process has always been diffused to some extent by the decentralization of America's political institutions.[4]

Reagan's defense secretary, Caspar W. Weinberger (1981–1987), and his deputy secretary, Frank C. Carlucci, created an acquisition improvement program (1981) to reform the acquisition process. Whereas the predecessor secretary, Harold Brown, had sought to tighten control over key aspects of the process, Weinberger implemented what he called controlled decentralization, whereby subordinate line executives, especially program managers in the military services, were to be held accountable for executing policy decisions made by the secretary after consultation with top civilian and military advisers. Weinberger acted on the conviction that cost-overrun problems and hardware that failed to perform as planned were made worse by previous attempts at detailed, centralized control, especially by the senior civilian research and engineering advisers in the Defense Department.

The Acquisition Improvement Program (AIP) was designed to mitigate the effects of political and institutional constraints on the acquisition process. The program sought, for example, to eliminate through multiyear procurements the program instability caused by annual budget fluctuations in Congress; reduce program costs; maintain efficient production rates and delivery schedules in industry; improve the readiness, supportability and operating performance of deployed weapon systems; enhance long-range planning and establish more realistic budgeting guidelines; increase competition among contractors; and streamline acquisition management and oversight by the military services and OSD. To be sure, these goals were not new. The program was merely the latest in a long line of organizational reforms previously mandated by the Department of Defense and various independent review committees and study groups to improve the institutional mechanisms by which the government acquired weapons systems. By 1981, the concept of reform within the weapons acquisition community had become something of a litany. Recast in new terms, the program, like its predecessors, remained heavily dependent on ideas and practices dating back to the early 1960s.

The concept of centralized policy formation in the Office of the Secretary of Defense and decentralized policy execution in the military services became the centerpiece of the Weinberger AIP.

---

[4] See Thomas L. McNaugher, *New Weapons, Old Politics: America's Military Procurement Muddle* (Washington, D.C.: Brookings Institution, 1989); Laurence E. Lynn Jr. and Richard I. Smith, "Can the Defense Secretary Make a Difference," *International Security* 7 (Summer 1982): 45–69.

Using this approach, Weinberger intended to push decision-making authority on major weapons systems back down to the services, thereby ending nearly two decades of predominately top-level management of the weapons acquisition process in OSD that began in 1961 when Robert McNamara joined President Kennedy's cabinet as secretary of defense.

The recurring patterns of centralization and decentralization in the Pentagon in the two decades before Reagan entered the White House highlight the extent to which institutional pluralism—Congress, the services, industry, and OSD—frustrated Weinberger's attempts to impose order on the weapons acquisition process. The anticipated outcomes of the Acquisition Improvement Program may have looked good on paper, but the implementation at the service level was far more difficult to achieve. "As good as Weinberger makes decentralization sound," one observer wrote in *Fortune* in 1981, "it could result in wild spending and conflicting programs. . . . [C]onvinced that Weinberger intends to leave them alone, the services are updating their wish lists, thus putting themselves on collision courses with one another and with the Secretary [of Defense]."[5]

Such conflicts also had broader implications. Increased spending by the military services during the Reagan years invited more oversight from Congress, thereby imposing restrictions on the discretionary freedom originally sought by Weinberger.[6] It also prompted increased public scrutiny of the military's competence and ability to direct and oversee large engineering development programs. Media descriptions of high-priced spare parts and the ensuing scandals that followed during this period further damaged the Pentagon's image as an efficient buyer of goods and services from industry and fueled congressional criticism of the weapons acquisition process.

Setting the Stage: PPBS and the Cycles of Weapons Acquisition Reform

The massive buildup of America's conventional and nuclear forces during President Reagan's first term in office stand in marked contrast to the sharp declines in defense spending that had begun in the late 1960s and 1970s as the United States slowly extracted itself from the war in Vietnam. Expenditures for weapons procurement dropped by more than half, from $44 billion to $17 billion in constant dollars, between the late 1960s and the mid-1970s. A corresponding reduction in the size of the

---

[5] D. D. Holt, "Cap Weinberger's Pentagon Revolution," *Fortune* (18 May 1981): 79–82 (quotation).

[6] See, for example, Robert J. Art, "Congress and the Defense Budget: Enhancing Policy Oversight," *Political Science Quarterly* 100 (Summer 1985): 227–48.

defense industry accompanied this transformation as contractors cut their production rates of major weapon systems or exited the defense business altogether.[7] The soaring inflation that compounded the debilitating effects of a deepening recession begun in the late 1970s only made the prospects for improvement in the defense industry that much worse.

Early in the Reagan administration, the White House moved quickly to increase the size and strength of America's military force structure to counter the growing Soviet threat. The Pentagon, Weinberger pointed out in testimony given before the Senate Armed Services Committee in February 1982, planned to double the monthly production rate of the Army's Abrams M–1 main battle tank by the end of the year, from thirty to sixty units, and increase output another 50 percent by 1985.[8] Secretary of the Navy John F. Lehman planned an equally ambitious expansion program for the submarine and surface fleets. In 1982, Secretary Lehman secured congressional approval to float a 600-ship Navy, including 4 refurbished *Iowa*-class battleships, 15 aircraft carrier battle groups, and 100 nuclear-powered attack submarines, by the end of the decade. The Navy's annual shipbuilding budget jumped 61 percent, from $7.5 billion to $12.1 billion, between 1979 and 1986, while the size of the fleet grew from 479 ships in 1981 to nearly 580 in 1989. The Pentagon achieved similar outcomes to update America's strategic nuclear arsenal. Even before Reagan was elected president, Jimmy Carter had faced pressure to modernize the strategic nuclear triad of aging B–52 Stratofortress long-range bombers, silo-based Minuteman ICBMs, and submarine-launched ballistic missiles (SLBMs) Polaris and Poseidon. Reagan revived the previously cancelled B–1 bomber program, ordering production of 100 of the low-level manned aircraft to offset the planned retirement of older B–52s. The first production B–1 rolled off Rockwell International's assembly line in Palmdale, California, in October 1984, and entry of the B–1 into the Air Force inventory began the following year.

By the time Reagan entered the White House, the PPBS, while still functioning reasonably well, had become less efficient. Management participation by the services and zero-based budgeting had not been fully integrated into the current system. Instead, they

---

[7] Holt, "Cap Weinberger's Pentagon Revolution." See also Jacques S. Gansler, *The Defense Industry* (Cambridge, Mass.: MIT Press, 1980), pp. 4–6; Gansler, *Affording Defense* (Cambridge, Mass.: MIT Press, 1989), pp. 9–10.

[8] Testimony of Secretary of Defense Caspar W. Weinberger before the U.S. Senate, Armed Services Committee on the FY 1983 Budget, FY 1984 Authorization Request, and FY 1983–1987 Defense Programs, 2 February 1982, p. 16, Office of the Secretary of Defense (OSD) Historical Office, Puritano box 5, Folder: "DRB, February 12, 1982."

were merely layered on top of it, which resulted in excessive paperwork and cumbersome data reporting procedures, mismatched and often conflicting line and staff functions in OSD, and the reemergence of strong adversarial relations between OSD and the services.[9] According to an internal review of OSD's organization directed by Carlucci's predecessor, Deputy Secretary of Defense W. Graham Claytor, during the last months of the Carter administration, "[T]he OJCS [Office of the Joint Chiefs of Staff] and the staffs of the Military Departments and Defense Agencies that must interact with the OSD complex are often confused by it, and frequently waste time."[10] It was within this context of prior reforms and the organizational rigidities resulting from their implementation over many years that Frank Carlucci and Vincent Puritano (executive assistant to the deputy secretary of defense), acting on Defense Secretary Weinberger's behalf, undertook a major overhaul of the PPBS in 1981.

On 2 March 1981, Carlucci chartered five working groups involving all services—inviting inputs from industry—to make recommendations for improving the acquisition process. The report of the working groups was delivered on 31 March 1981. Carlucci discussed the report with the Joint Chiefs of Staff, the service secretaries, the under secretaries and assistant secretaries of defense as well as the AIP Steering Group comprised of experienced civilian and military personnel.

Carlucci expected quick results. The PPBS review should last no more than a few weeks. "I don't want a study," he insisted. "I want workable recommendations with all options considered and the major ones presented to me for decision. . . . These recommendations should be specific and provide for immediately instituting improvements without major disruptions in current operations." To meet this goal, Carlucci charged the Steering Group to meet an ambitious set of objectives:

> The overall objectives are: to use the PPBS to improve the match between capabilities and the demands of our policies and national military strategy, to streamline the DoD decision making process by avoiding unnecessary revisiting of decisions and the resulting program instability, and to improve the material acquisition

---

[9] "SECDEF Weinberger's Planning, Programming, and Budgeting System Brings Practical Management to the Defense Program," *Program Manager* 10 (May-June 1981): 14. See also Vincent Puritano, "Streamlining PPBS," *Defense '81* (August 1981): 20–23.

[10] Memo, W. Graham Claytor Jr. for the Undersecretaries and Assistant Secretaries of Defense, 4 Dec 1980, p. 3 (quotation), OSD Historical Office, box 561, Folder: "OSD/DoD 1980-81, Transition to Reagan Era."

process by assessing the interface between PPBS and the acquisition system. This will require improved long-range planning in all aspects of the PPBS process. It will also require increased participatory management involving the Joint Chiefs of Staff and all of the Military services working together with the Secretary [of Defense]'s staff.[11]

While participatory management maintained an active role in the review process and ultimately in the reformed PPBS that emerged from it, zero-based budgeting was not so fortunate. After a thorough cost-benefit analysis, OSD dropped zero-based budgeting as an independent process and incorporated some of its more useful provisions into the PPBS.[12]

In the draft report to Puritano on the proposed PPBS improvements, the Steering Group admitted that "there is an almost unlimited number of options by which the current PPBS can be improved." The members of the group reached consensus on several key points, most notably the need for greater strategic and long-range planning throughout the PPBS and the assignment of greater roles to the secretary of defense, the Joint Chiefs of Staff, and the services in the planning cycle. The group also considered specific operational problems, such as data and reporting procedures. Proposed action on these items centered on two options, but they differed more in degree than in kind. "Both options . . . have features that aim at improving front end policy and strategic planning," the report concluded. "The major difference between the two is that, while the first option streamlines the programming and budgeting phases as does the second, the second option decentralizes much more responsibility

---

[11] "DRB [Defense Resources Board] Meeting, 2 February 1981, Talking Points—Carlucci," p. 2, OSD Historical Office, Box: "Defense Resources Board, May–August 1981, Puritano-Bureau Files," Folder: "DRB, May 6, 1981." See also Memo, F. C. Carlucci for Distribution List, 13 Feb 1981, p. 1, Washington National Records Center (WNRC), National Archives and Records Administration, Suitland, Md., Series 330–83–0102, box 26/48, Folder: "100.5 (January–April 81) 1981."

[12] In a letter he wrote to Office of Management and Budget Director David A. Stockman shortly after the Steering Group completed its deliberations, Carlucci commented on the status of zero-based budgeting (ZBB): "As you know, this Department had a comprehensive PPBS in place for some time before ZBB was implemented. ZBB brought with it a useful emphasis on involvement by all managerial levels in budget formulation through basic reviews of missions and functions and explicit prioritization in support of higher level decision-making. These features should be retained in PPBS. Unfortunately, ZBB also introduced a tremendous volume of essentially nonproductive paperwork. I recommend that the revised DoD PPBS, which retains these two essential features of ZBB, be implemented as meeting the OMB ZBB requirements." Ltr, F. C. Carlucci to D. A. Stockman, 22 Apr 1981, WNRC, Series 330–83–0102, box 26/48, Folder: "100.5 (January–April 81) 1981"; "DoD Reorganizes: Greater Budget Role for the JCS," 6 April 1981, OSD Historical Office, Subject Files, box 561, Folder: "DoD Organization 1981."

to the services from OSD." Option one sought management improvements through organizational reform at the top, freeing the defense secretary to devote more time and effort to planning and policy matters, whereas option two set out to achieve the same results through administrative decentralization; that is, shifting certain management responsibilities from OSD to the services. In the case of the former, maintaining a centralized management structure preserved "a system which has served the Department [of Defense] well for twenty years and with which we are all familiar—thereby eliminating surprises." In the case of the latter, delegating responsibilities to the services promised clarification of line and staff roles and functions and less micromanagement from OSD. Perhaps most importantly, the Steering Group concluded that more participation by the services in planning and program development would guarantee a "broader level of expression, thereby promoting stability."[13]

Both options also had drawbacks. In the case of option one, the report expressed concern about the availability of "adequate time . . . for top leadership participation in planning and program review." Option two raised similar concerns at the service level. "Individual service program and budget priorities are more likely to predominate," the Steering Group noted, "possibly resulting in cross-service program mismatch and duplication."[14] Carlucci discussed the report's findings with the Steering Group; the Joint Chiefs of Staff (JCS); the secretaries of the Army, Navy, and the Air Force; Defense Secretary Weinberger; and other senior staff in OSD. After careful review, Carlucci selected the provisions of option two to guide the reform of the PPBS. OSD enhanced service participation through decentralization, but it also retained an active interest in planning and programming issues "that cut across service lines and programs and those that were of priority to Presidential and Secretary of Defense interest." The services, meanwhile, continued to have direct responsibility for the execution of programs and the day-to-day management of the resources under their control.[15]

Renewed emphasis on service participation in the PPBS signaled a sharp reversal of OSD policy. During McNamara's tenure in OSD, the programming function had experienced significant growth and influence at the expense of planning by the services.

---

[13] "PPBS Review, Draft—Internal Use Only," 19 March 1981, pp. 9–10, 12, 17, 20, 24, WNRC, Series 000-83-0102, box 26/48, Folder: "100.5 (January–April 81) 1981." See also David D. Acker, "The Maturing of the DoD Acquisition Process," *Defense Systems Management Review* (Summer 1980): 41–43.

[14] "PPBS Review, Draft—Internal Use Only," pp. 17–18 (quotation), 25.

[15] Memo, F. C. Carlucci for Distribution List, 27 March 1981, pp. 1–6, WNRC, Series 330-83-0102, box 26/48, Folder: "100.5 (January–April 81) 1981."

By the time Carlucci convened the PPBS Steering Group in the spring of 1981, OSD programming no longer functioned as an effective bridge between JCS planning and service budgeting. Carlucci resolved this organizational confusion by reforming the functions and membership of the Defense Resources Board. Established in April 1979, the board served as the principal advisory arm to OSD. The board's original membership included the OSD senior staff at the assistant and under secretary levels. Service input was initially limited to the chairman of the Joint Chiefs of Staff, but this constraint disappeared after the Steering Group issued its PPBS review report.[16] The board provided general oversight and supervision of resource allocation throughout the Defense Department, ensuring that major programs remained closely aligned to the PPBS. It also resolved problems on behalf of the secretary of defense. The board had no statutory authority, however, and its recommendations carried no weight unless specifically approved by the chairman, a position held by the deputy secretary of defense. Participation by the secretary of defense was discretionary.

Under Carlucci's guidance, the Defense Resources Board assumed a more proactive and expansive role, ensuring that major weapons acquisition programs remained closely aligned to the newly updated PPBS. No longer serving as an advisory board that provided non-binding assistance to OSD, the newly reconstituted board controlled management of the PPBS through regularly scheduled monthly meetings chaired by Carlucci. Full membership grew to include, in addition to the chairman of the Joint Chiefs of Staff, the secretaries of the Army, Navy, and Air Force, and the commanders in chief of the specified and unified commands.[17] OSD

---

[16] David D. Acker, *Acquiring Defense Systems: A Quest for the Best* (Fort Belvoir, Va.: Defense Systems Management College Press, July 1993), pp. 209–10. See also David. D. Acker and G. R. McAleer Jr., "The Acquisition Process: New Opportunities for Innovative Management," *Concepts* 5 (Summer 1982): 84; David. D. Acker, "Defense Systems Acquisition Review Process: A History and Evaluation," *Program Manager* 13 (January-February 1984): 10.

[17] Input from the commanders in chief (CINCs) comprised assessments of the weapon systems required for theater operations (e.g., Pacific Command, European Command, Strategic Air Command). CINC participation in the PPBS was streamlined in 1985, when the commanders submitted the first of a series of Integrated Priority Lists (IPLs) to the Defense Resources Board for evaluation. The CINCs compiled these lists to help the board match specific weapon systems to operational requirements. Major problem areas identified that year covered four broad areas: command, control, communication, and intelligence (C3I); mobility; readiness and sustainability; and force structure and modernization. In the last category, for example, the CINC of the Pacific Command proposed, under the category "long-range attack," development of the F–15E tactical fighter and the B–52G strategic bomber. Under "strategic programs," the chief of the Strategic Air Command advocated deployment of the new Peacekeeper (MX) ICBM and continued development of the B–1 bomber. Although they lacked sufficient cost data to assess the strengths and weaknesses of alternatives, the IPLs, as an internal OSD report confirmed, "spurred an increase in communication between

also granted de facto membership to four military service chiefs to provide input on major programs. The addition of greater service representation acknowledged a major weakness highlighted by the Steering Group in its just-completed PPBS review. "It is now generally perceived," the report concluded, "that the DRB [Defense Resources Board], having only CJCS [Chairman of the Joint Chiefs of Staff] to represent service views, tends to dampen service influence in the crucial final stages of the PPBS process."[18] Emboldened by increased service representation on the board, the Joint Chiefs of Staff, through the chairman, assumed a more active role in the planning and implementation of strategic goals. The JCS chairman also focused on the resource implications of these functions to reduce the disparity between mission requirements and budgeted funds. Guided by the decentralization of policy execution, another foundational element of the new PPBS, the defense secretary completed the process by instructing the services to recommend the most effective ways of meeting objectives within their budgets.[19]

From PPBS to the Acquisition Improvement Program

The Planning, Programming, and Budgeting System constituted only one part, albeit a significant one, at the beginning of the weapons acquisition process. The reform of the PPBS was merely the first step in what became the Acquisition Improvement Program, known informally as the Carlucci initiatives, named after the program's primary architect, Deputy Defense Secretary Frank Carlucci. Whereas the PPBS structured resources to mission requirements, the acquisition process, through various organizational units working in concert with the PPBS, dealt with the development and procurement of actual weapons systems—aircraft and missiles for the Air Force; surface ships and submarines for the Navy; and guns, artillery, and other ordnance materials for the Army. The revision of the PPBS set in motion many of the reforms that OSD subsequently institutionalized in the Acquisition Improvement Program.

---

the services, the CINCs, OSD, and the OJCS [Office of the Joint Chiefs of Staff]." See "Report to the Deputy Secretary of Defense on the Integrated Priority Lists Submitted by the Commanders-in-Chief of the Unified and Specified Commands" (n.d.), pp. 2–3, 5 (attached to Memo, M. L. Dominguez for D. S. C. Chu, 13 Feb 1985), OSD Historical Office, Puritano box 12, Folder: "DRB Wrap-Up/Offsets, 18/13/85."

[18] "PPBS Review, Draft Internal Use Only," p. 25 (quotation). See also Acker and McAleer, "The Acquisition Process," p. 84.

[19] "SECDEF Weinberger's Planning, Programming, and Budgeting System Brings Practical Management to the Defense Program," p. 14. See also "DoD Reorganizes: Greater Budget Role for the JCS," 6 April 1981, OSD Historical Office, Subject Files, box 561, Folder: "DoD Organization 1981."

Any understanding of this outcome and the concomitant effect on weapons procurement must begin with a brief delineation of the basic framework of the acquisition process as it existed in the 1980s. In addition, this section will also examine the Office of Management and Budget Circular A–109, DoD Directive 5000.1 (The Defense Acquisition System) and DoD Instruction 5000.2 (Operation of the Defense Acquisition System), the Under Secretary of Defense for Research and Engineering, the Defense Systems Acquisition Review Council (DSARC), and how their roles and functions evolved during the first half of the 1980s.

When Reagan entered the White House in 1981, the Office of the Secretary of Defense managed the acquisition of major weapon systems through the guidance of three critical documents. The first one, A–109, issued by the Office of Management and Budget five years earlier, in April 1976, recommended the appointment of a defense acquisition executive to formulate and execute acquisition policies throughout the Defense Department. Passed in 1978 by Congress, Public Law 95–140 acted on this recommendation by upgrading the existing position of director of defense research and engineering (DDR&E) to the under secretary of defense for research and engineering (USD [R&E]). The new position, now known as the defense acquisition executive, ranked third behind the secretary and deputy secretary of defense. The USD (R&E) also served as the principal adviser and staff assistant to the defense secretary on all facets of weapon systems acquisition.[20]

On the policy side, DoD Directive 5000.1 and DoD Instruction 5000.2 (described in Chapter Two) set forth the policies and procedures by which the Defense Department acquired major weapon systems. Programs with projected costs in excess of $100 million (fiscal 1980 dollars) for research, development, test, and evaluation (RDT&E) or $500 million (fiscal 1980 dollars) for procurement fell under this category. While these dollar thresholds served only as general guidelines and did not necessarily reflect the importance of any individual weapon system, major programs nevertheless accounted for approximately 30 percent of the RDT&E costs and 45 percent of the procurement costs incurred by the military services in 1981. In most cases, the Army, Navy, and Air Force initiated major weapon systems programs through their respective commodity commands: Department of the Army Readiness Command (DARCOM) (formerly the Army Materiel Command), Navy Material Command (NAVMAT), Air Force Systems Command (AFSC), and Air Force Logistics Command (AFLC). These commands performed research, development,

---

[20] Acker, *Acquiring Defense Systems*, pp. 199–200. See also Acker, "Defense Systems Acquisition Review Process," p. 8.

test, evaluation, and procurement, either in house or through contracts with private-sector organizations.[21]

The Defense Systems Acquisition Review Council (DSARC), established in 1969 by Deputy Secretary of Defense David Packard, managed the weapons acquisition process by conducting periodic milestone reviews of major programs at specified points in the acquisition program cycle (e.g., contract definition, engineering development, and production), recommending appropriate actions to the secretary of defense, and monitoring their implementation in the services.[22] The Army, Navy, and Air Force established similar councils—service systems acquisition review councils—to prepare for DSARC reviews and to correlate DSARC decisions with service-specific weapons programs. Chaired by the defense acquisition executive—in this case the under secretary of defense for research and engineering—the DSARC reflected Packard's original intention to delegate more responsibility for defense systems acquisition and management to the Army, Navy, and Air Force and, by extension, into the hands of program managers designated by the services to oversee major weapon programs. The DSARC, in Packard's mind, enabled broad but limited program oversight of the services without the burden of managing the entire acquisition process in OSD.

Carlucci instructed Puritano to organize and direct a review of the weapons acquisition process and to recommend improvements. He expected firm proposals to be submitted to his office by the end of March 1981. Puritano recruited a broad range of acquisition specialists, including experts from OSD, industry, and the military services (especially the commodity commands), and he divided them into five working groups to tackle specific problem areas: cost, acquisition time and scheduling, support and planning, DSARC, and multiyear procurement.[23]

---

[21] On the origins of the 5000-series regulations, see Acker, *Acquiring Defense Systems*, p. 169–70. On in-house and contracted research and development in the services, see also Thomas C. Lassman, *Sources of Weapons Systems Innovation in the Department of Defense: The Role of In-House Research and Development, 1945–2000* (Washington, D.C.: U.S. Army Center of Military History, 2008); Harvey M. Sapolsky, *Science and the Navy: The History of the Office of Naval Research* (Princeton: Princeton University Press, 1990); and Nick A. Komons, *Science and the Air Force: A History of the Air Force Office of Scientific Research* (Arlington, Va.: Historical Division, Office of Information, Office of Aerospace Research, 1966).

[22] At the outset, the Defense Systems Acquisition Review Council (DSARC) membership included the under secretary of defense for policy; comptroller; assistant secretary of defense for manpower, reserve affairs, and logistics; and the assistant secretary of defense for program analysis and evaluation. In special cases, others might be invited to attend a specific council meeting.

[23] Col. G. Dana Brabson, United States Air Force (USAF), "Department of Defense Acquisition Improvement Program," *Concepts: The Journal of Defense Systems Acquisition Management* 4 (Autumn 1981): 55. See also Vincent Puritano, "Getting Ourselves Together on Systems Acquisition," *Defense '81* (October 1981): 9–10.

All five groups reviewed prior studies of the acquisition process and solicited the input of key participants involved in weapons procurement. Congressional critics, for example, blasted the services for rampant cost growth and schedule slippages. Aggressively pushing the frontiers of technology prompted cost overruns, they argued, while fierce interservice competition for funds encouraged overly optimistic program cost estimates. The services, meanwhile, complained about excessive paperwork and reporting procedures required by the DSARC milestone reviews; micromanagement of weapons programs by OSD and Congress; and unrealistic demands for accurate cost estimates, especially when unknowns existed in the early stages of weapons program planning.[24] Program managers directed similar criticisms at both OSD and the services, while OSD criticized the services for failing to restrict the number of weapon systems competing for limited resources. Other service shortcomings, according to OSD, included inadequate support and readiness for fielded weapons systems and lengthy acquisition cycles. Industry directed its frustrations across the board—at OSD, Congress, and the services. Program instability—caused by sudden production starts and stops, program stretch-outs, redirections, and long decision times—threatened the bottom line and risked financial ruin, while micromanagement and excessive surveillance of programs by OSD and the services disrupted efficient contractor performance. Industry representatives also believed that OSD's emphasis on increasing price competition among contractors resulted in poor cost realism.[25]

Carlucci was well aware that throughout the 1970s similar measures had been urged—and many tried—but few significant improvements had been made. In Carlucci's view, DoD did not need another study. The time for action had arrived. This time the state-

---

[24] Observers outside the Pentagon rarely missed the opportunity to join the fray and comment on the tense relations between the major participants in the weapons acquisition process. The question of congressional oversight drew an especially acerbic, though entertaining, commentary from the editor of the journal *Government Executive* in the fall of 1981: "Congress," he wrote in the 4 October issue, "says that the [weapons acquisition] process is a mess, but when it comes time to act, all that happens is that a parade of DoD, industry, and military personnel go before Congress over and over again to make the same arguments and have the same discussions about plans to make long-lasting changes. Congress, meanwhile, does not act in any productive way." Even when Congress did act, the writer cynically pointed out, the outcome produced few beneficial results. "Its [Congress'] committee structure for coping with the broad issues of internal defense management policy and developing forces relevant to the threat estimate and support of foreign policy is an antiquated organizational sarcasm. Its penchant for micromanaging individual weapon projects, wielding authority without accepting responsibility for the result, chopping down trees with nary a pause to consider the forest, is a classic textbook example of bone-headed brainwork." C. W. Borklund, "The Carlucci Initiatives and Congress," *Government Executive* (4 October 1981): 6.

[25] Puritano, "Getting Ourselves Together on Systems Acquisition," p. 12.

ment of actions would be accompanied by a commitment to implement the actions.[26]

After careful review and evaluation of the accumulated data, the working groups, under Puritano's guidance, collectively submitted to Weinberger on 31 March 1981 a list of thirty-one actions or initiatives to improve the weapons acquisition process.[27]

Three months later, on 27 July 1981, Carlucci added the thirty-second initiative, "Increase Competition," to the original thirty-one initiatives. The primary objective of this initiative was to stimulate innovation (both in design and in manufacturing practice) and to stimulate investment. Where competition was effective, the program manager potentially could realize both cost savings and risk reduction. In addition to competition, the more significant initiatives called for more multiyear procurement contracts, stabilized programs, more realistic budgeting, and more fixed-price contracts.[28] (See Appendix C for a list of the thirty-two Carlucci initiatives.)

Carlucci's thirty-two AIP initiatives sought to streamline the process by reducing weapon program costs and shortening the acquisition cycle time, both of which had increased sharply since the 1960s. The initiatives were rooted in eight fundamental management principles. These principles were stated by Vincent Puritano in an article in the October 1981 issue of *Defense '81*:

- We must improve long-range planning to enhance acquisition program stability.
- Both OSD and the services must delegate more responsibility, authority and accountability for programs; in particular, the service program manager should have the responsibility, authority and resources adequate to execute efficiently the program for which he is responsible.
- We must examine evolutionary alternatives which use a lower risk approach to technology than solutions at the frontier of technology.
- We must achieve more economic rates of production.
- We must realistically cost, budget, and fully fund in the Five-Year Defense Plan, and Extended Planning Annex, procurement, logistics and manpower for major acquisition programs.

---

[26] Brabson, "The Department of Defense Acquisition Improvement Program," pp. 54–75, and personal discussions with Frank Carlucci in 1982.

[27] The thirty-second and last initiative, which focused on improving competition, was added to the original list of thirty-one actions later in the year.

[28] Background Information, Senior Steering Group, Office of the Secretary of Defense, DoD Acquisition Study, 7–8 November, 1985.

- Readiness and sustainability of deployed weapons are primary objectives and must be considered from the start of weapon system programs.
- A strong industrial base is necessary for a strong defense. The proper arms-length relationships with industry should not be interpreted by DoD or by industry as adversarial.
- Defense managers at all levels should expand their efforts to obtain maximum competition for their contractual requirements.[29]

Although the thirty-two initiatives did not address all the major causes of cost growth in weapon systems, many of the initiatives dealt with longstanding problems, the correction of which could do much to lower costs. Once again, however, the underlying principles were not new. For the preceding ten years, similar measures had been urged—and many tried—but few significant improvements had been made.[30]

The most significant initiatives coalesced around four broad goals: reduction of acquisition costs, shortening of acquisition times, improved support and readiness, and reorganization of the DSARC.

The first goal, reduction of acquisition costs, depended on improvements in program stability, multiyear procurement, administrative efficiency, capital investment in industry, and economic production rates. Similarly, shortening of acquisition times required more front-end planning and the introduction of a new concept—preplanned product improvement, otherwise known in shorthand as P3I. The working groups expected that weapons support and readiness would also benefit from more front-end planning during the early stages of program development, expansion of contractor incentives, and greater emphasis on the procurement of standard equipment. Finally, improvements in the operation and effectiveness of the Defense Systems Acquisition Review Council depended on a set of initiatives designed to overhaul the council's entire organization and integrate it more fully into the Planning, Programming, and Budgeting System (PPBS). In addition to these four broad goals, the AIP, like the PPBS, delegated more responsibility, authority, and accountability from OSD to the service program managers overseeing the development of major weapon systems. It also encouraged the use of evolutionary rather than radical technology alternatives during weapon systems development, preferring low-risk resolution of technical problems rather than more

---

[29] Puritano, "Getting Ourselves Together on Systems Acquisition."

[30] Robert Foelber, "Cutting the High Cost of Weapons," *Backgrounder* No. 172 (Washington, D.C.: The Heritage Foundation, 16 March 1982) pp. 5–6.

expensive and sometimes less operationally reliable state-of-the-art solutions. Moreover, given the sharp decline of the manufacturing sector as the economy entered a deep and protracted recession, the Acquisition Improvement Program sought to energize the defense industrial base by using more flexible contracting procedures and second-sourcing production of major weapons systems to more firms to enhance vendor competition.[31]

Weinberger announced the details of the Acquisition Improvement Program to the public on 30 April 1981. During the next two years, Carlucci and Puritano with the assistance of the under secretary of defense for research and engineering—the defense acquisition executive—sought to recast the institutional landscape of the weapons acquisition process.[32] From the outset, they placed major emphasis on changes to the DSARC, requiring full integration with the PPBS, accelerated centralization of policy direction in OSD, and controlled decentralization of policy execution in the services. "[W]e are not going to allow [weapons] systems to pass DSARC . . . if the money in the budget is not sufficient to support the DSARC decision," Under Secretary of Defense for Research and Engineering Richard D. DeLauer insisted late in 1981. "For years," DeLauer continued, "DSARC has approved systems that were underfunded and budgets have included systems with no [mission requirements]. We've just stopped that."[33]

Reform of the DSARC proceeded along several different but related lines. Carlucci mandated a reduction in the number of milestones required for program review in OSD, thereby delegating more responsibility to the services. He also invited the secretaries of the Army, Navy, and Air Force to sit on the DSARC as permanent members and initiated an overhaul of the 5000-series regulations governing the minimum-dollar thresholds required for DSARC reviews of major weapons systems. By raising the funding limits, he expected to reduce further OSD's role in DSARC evaluations in favor of more service participation. Finally, Carlucci planned to im-

---

[31] Brabson, "The Department of Defense Acquisition Improvement Program," pp. 54–58, 64, 67–69. See also Puritano, "Getting Ourselves Together on Systems Acquisition," pp. 16–17.

[32] News Release, 30 Apr 1981, sub: Secretary of Defense Weinberger Announces Decisions, Management Principles, to Improve Acquisition Process, p. 1, OSD Historical Office, Acquisition History File. On the AIP management structure in the Office of the Under Secretary of Defense for Research and Engineering, see Memo, J. D. Wade Jr. for the Secretary and the Deputy Secretary of Defense, 6 Apr 1981, pp. 1–3, WNRC, Series 330–83–0102, box 26/48, Folder: "100.5 (January–April 81) 1981"; and Memo, R. F. Trimble for the Deputy Secretary and Secretary of Defense, 7 Sep 1981, p. 1, WNRC, Series 330–84–0014, box 4/15, Folder: No Title.

[33] "View from the Top: Dr. Richard DeLauer, Undersecretary of Defense for Research and Engineering," *Military Electronics/Countermeasures* (November 1981): 13 (quotation).

prove efficiency by streamlining the DSARC reporting procedures and data requirements between OSD and the services.[34]

When Puritano commenced his survey of the weapons acquisition process in the spring of 1981, major programs scheduled for review by the DSARC typically had to pass four milestones: Concept Exploration (Milestone 0), Demonstration and Validation (Milestone 1), Full-Scale Development (Milestone 2), and Production (Milestone 3).[35] In an effort to execute controlled decentralization, reduce the defense secretary's direct involvement in the DSARC, and eliminate complicated reporting and data requirements, OSD cut the number of required milestones in half, from four to two. This consolidation produced two new DSARC decision points: requirements validation and full-scale development/ production—otherwise known as program initiation and program go-ahead, respectively. Both milestones, while still requiring full participation from the DSARC and the defense secretary, generalized the program approval process in OSD by delegating more management responsibility to the services. The milestone for program go-ahead, for example, provided broad oversight of service-proposed actions, including full-scale development and production and program planning for weapons testing, evaluation, support, and readiness. Under the new system, authority to approve or reject these and other actions rested squarely with the services. At the same time, the funding thresholds required for DSARC review of major weapons systems in OSD doubled from $100 to $200 million for RDT&E and from $500 million to $1 billion for production. The DSARC immediately cut ten weapons systems whose funding levels now fell below the new thresholds and transferred them to the service acquisition review councils for evaluation.[36] This reduction marked a 20-percent drop in the number of DSARC-level programs scheduled for OSD review in 1981.[37]

---

[34] Brabson, "Department of Defense Acquisition Improvement Program," pp. 59–61.

[35] Passing through all four milestones was not mandatory. In some cases where, for example, the level of technological complexity in a weapon system did not require intensive research and development, the defense secretary could bypass one or more milestones in the DSARC review.

[36] The Army, for example, assumed decision authority for two former major weapons systems that would have otherwise been evaluated by DSARC: the Force Level and Maneuver Control System, also called SIGMA, and the Infantry Manportable Antiarmor Assault Weapon System, otherwise known as the RATTLER. Moreover, the increases in the RDT&E and production thresholds for the DSARC were matched by corresponding enlargements for the same categories assigned to the Army Systems Acquisition Review Council. "Defense Acquisition Improvement Program (Weinberger/Carlucci Initiatives): Army Implementation Activities," March 1982, n.p., in "Acquisition Improvement Program: General Army Implementation," copy in David D. Acker Library, Defense Acquisition University, Fort Belvoir, Va.

[37] "DoD, Phasing in DSARC Reforms, Wants Services to Decentralize Too," *Aerospace Daily* (25 August 1981): 305; see also Puritano, "Getting Ourselves Together on Systems

Although the compressed DSARC milestone review mandated more service participation, implementation of the policies at that level proved more difficult to achieve than originally envisioned. Some programs already undergoing full DSARC review, such as the joint Navy–Air Force Advanced Medium-Range Air-to-Air Missile (AMRAAM), effectively transitioned to the new procedure, but many other weapons systems continued to abide by the old guidelines, observed Robert Trimble, DeLauer's deputy for acquisition policy, to avoid "changing horses at midstream." But Trimble also acknowledged that maximizing the effectiveness of the new DSARC would require a corresponding realignment of the decision points in the service acquisition review councils. The Army and the Air Force agreed to the mandated changes, but the Navy balked, prompting one observer who had discussed the matter with Trimble to conclude that "the Navy still believes strongly that it needs its own top-level reviews at the old (four) DSARC milestones."[38] Although he did not press the issue and agreed, in the short-term, to maintain the status quo on Navy program reviews, Trimble nevertheless cautioned that postponing full integration would complicate management and reporting procedures resulting from the overlap of the two new DSARC milestones onto those retained by the Navy. Despite the Navy's initial intransigence, however, the DSARC proceeded with plans to waive production decisions on several key weapons systems in 1981, including variants of the submarine-launched Tomahawk cruise missile manufactured under contract with the General Dynamics Corporation. The Army and Air Force, meanwhile, received the same authority from the DSARC to execute production decisions on other major systems, such as the M–1 tank (manufactured under contract with the Chrysler Corporation), Hughes Aircraft's imaging infrared Maverick missile, and the ground-launched version of the Navy's Tomahawk.[39]

Acquisition," p. 16; Acker, "Defense Systems Acquisition Review Process," p. 10; J. D. Edgar, "The New Acquisition Environment: Challenge and Opportunity," *Concepts: The Journal of Defense Systems Acquisition Management* 5 (Summer 1982): 12.

[38] Kosta Tsipis and Penny Janeway, eds., *Review of U.S. Military Research and Development* (Washington, D.C.: Pergamon-Brassey's, 1984), pp. 14-15 (quotations). See also Paul M. Bradburn, "Strategic Postures in the Military Aircraft Industry: A Comparison of Two Companies," paper prepared at Massachusetts Institute of Technology, June 1986, pp. 45–53; and U.S. Congress, Senate, Committee on Governmental Affairs, testimony of Laurence E. Lynn, Professor of Public Policy, Harvard University, 21–27 October and 5 November 1981, pp. 133–35.

[39] "DoD, Phasing in DSARC Reforms, Wants Services to Decentralize Too," pp. 305–06.

AIP IN ACTION: IMPLEMENTATION AND EXECUTION

Less then two months after the Pentagon announced the details of the Acquisition Improvement Program to the public, OSD already faced strong opposition from the services. A candid letter from Lawrence J. Korb, Assistant Secretary of Defense for Manpower, Reserve Affairs, and Logistics, clearly revealed the scope of the problem Carlucci and his staff faced. "I would like to call your attention," Korb wrote Carlucci in June, "to instances where the military departments (particularly the Air Force and Navy) appear to be resisting new initiatives by circumventing your office and trying to obtain negative reactions from congressional committees. These actions could affect your desires to achieve greater economies and efficiencies in the management of DoD."[40] Meanwhile, according to a survey of one hundred major defense firms conducted by the journal *Government Executive* one year later, the respondents generally agreed that the Carlucci initiatives constituted "an excellent package," but that "after more than a year, they're still mostly top-level talk and grass-roots inaction."[41]

Also, in 1981, Weinberger, Carlucci, Puritano, and their subordinates in OSD faced the critical problem of how to reconcile budget volatility (resulting from fluctuations in the annual appropriations authorized by Congress) and funding requirements of major weapons programs whose acquisition cycles (from concept to production) always required years to complete. Other factors contributing to program instability included technological uncertainties, changes in the priorities of competing programs within the services, and adjustments to the threat environment, all of which could—and often did—lead to sharp reductions or rapid increases in the quantities of specific weapon systems procured from industry. In cases where Congress cut the defense budget, the services typically responded by reducing production runs and spreading or stretching out the available funds over an extended period, thereby keeping the programs active, but reducing manufacturing efficiencies on the factory floor. Viewed from a long-term perspective, this tactic tended to result in high total program costs as production rates dropped and economies of scale diminished.[42]

---

[40] "Talking Notes—Carlucci, DRB Meeting, June 11, 1981, 2:00–3:00 PM," p. 1; Ltr, L. J. Korb to F. Carlucci, 1 Jun 1981, pp. 1–2 (quotation), both in OSD Historical Office, Box: "Defense Resources Board, May–August 1981, Puritano-Bureau Files," Folder: "DRB, June 11, 1981."

[41] "Why the 'Carlucci Initiatives' Aren't Working," *Government Executive* (August 1982): 30 (quotation).

[42] H. J. Schutt and David D. Acker, "Program Stability: An Essential Element in Improved Acquisition," *Concepts: The Journal of Defense Systems Acquisition Management* 5 (Summer 1982): 148, 150. Program stability also suffered from the mandatory rotation of

Because Congress, OSD, the services, and the defense industry operated interdependently, fluctuations in funding, procurement, scheduling, or the threat environment invariably produced a rippling effect that reverberated throughout the entire weapons acquisition process. Congressional budget cuts, for example, increased the likelihood of production shortfalls and schedule slippages in industry, while program cost growth in the services typically invited more scrutiny and oversight from Congress. OSD sought to mitigate this problem—and hence lower weapon systems costs—by encouraging the services to prioritize their major programs, cancel marginal ones before they grew too large to stop, and restrict the number of new program starts still on the drawing board. Program cancellations, if they occurred, also had the added benefit, at least on paper, of releasing additional resources to fund higher priority programs in their entirety. The services, however, opposed this strategy, because, in their view, it required trade-offs that reduced managerial control and operational flexibility in their own backyards and reduced the number of acquisition programs under way. Rather than cut programs outright, the Army, Navy, and Air Force favored maintaining the same number of programs but proceeding at a lower rate, increasing unit cost, and placing much of the blame for structural problems in the weapons acquisition process on OSD and Congress.

Despite sharply rising defense budgets in the early 1980s, the services often resisted multiyear procurement because they believed requirements for heavy up-front funding to keep major programs on track would likely limit managerial flexibility even further and leave fewer resources available for other programs deemed worthy of support.[43] Notes Carlucci wrote to himself for upcoming meetings of the Defense Resources Board in the fall of 1981, just a few months before his appearance before the Senate Armed Services Committee, highlight the extent to which he felt pressure to obtain cooperation from the services. "We have to show some program kills <u>now</u>, next year will be too late, <u>and</u> we have to signal that the 32 points [initiatives], on program stability and efficient production rates particularly, are real," he wrote in November. "These are <u>two major issues</u> which will not only

---

program managers through the military ranks. Military officers typically held these positions, and short tours of duty resulted in a recurring brain drain within the weapons acquisition process. See also W. D. Brown, "Program Instability: Fighting Goliath," *Program Manager* 12 (November-December 1983): 32; and J. Ronald Fox, *Arming America: How the U.S. Buys Weapons* (Boston: Division of Research, Graduate School of Business Administration, Harvard University, 1974), ch. 9.

[43] Memo, W. A. Long for the Under Secretary of Defense for Research and Engineering (n.d.), p. 8, WNRC, Series 330–84–0035, Box 10, Folder: "1305—July 1–30."

affect the budget internally but also the DoD image externally [emphasis in original]."⁴⁴ While he understood that the services "feel that OSD is about to do business the old way . . . and drive unwanted decisions down their throat," Carlucci nevertheless refused to back off his agenda. He wanted to reassure the services and encourage their participation, but, at the same time, he strongly reaffirmed OSD's commitment to reductions in cost, schedule slippages, and stretch-outs in major weapons programs. "Tell the services this is real," Carlucci reminded himself. "They have to do better and find [program] cancellations, or [I] will find them for [the] services."⁴⁵

In the summer of 1982, while the services labored to improve the support and standardization of weapons systems operating in the field, Carlucci assessed the AIP's progress in a brief foreword written for a special edition of *Concepts* (a Defense Systems Management College publication) that focused on the status of weapons acquisition reform in the early 1980s. His discussion exuded much enthusiasm:

> As I reflect over the past year, I am pleased to report significant progress toward our objective of improving the acquisition process. We have decreased the number of programs over which the Secretary of Defense retains decision-making authority; the principle of controlled decentralization is being embraced by the services. We have achieved economies in the acquisition process; major multi-year procurements are in place, and selected programs have been restored to economic production rates. We have begun to make the defense marketplace more attractive to industry; flexible process payments are easing cash-flow problems, and increased investments in manufacturing technology are accelerating the pace of modernization. We have increased the readiness of our systems in the field; supportability and maintainability are being accorded the same emphasis as cost, schedule, and performance, and recent budget decisions provided additional resources to support the readiness of key systems.⁴⁶

Behind the scenes, however, the results had been more sobering. Four years later, the General Accounting Office (GAO) issued

---

⁴⁴ "Carlucci Talking Notes, DRB Meeting, Monday, November 23, 1981, 2:00 to 4:00 PM," (n.d.), p. 2 (quotation), OSD Historical Office, Puritano Box 4, Folder: "DRB, November 23, 1981."

⁴⁵ "Frank Carlucci, DRB Talking Notes, Wednesday, October 14, 1981," (n.d.), pp. 1–2 (quotation), OSD Historical Office, Puritano Box 4, Folder: "DRB, October 14, 1981."

⁴⁶ Frank C. Carlucci, "Foreword to Special Edition," *Concepts: The Journal of Defense Systems Acquisition Management* 5 (Summer 1982): n.p.

a report claiming that only eight of the original thirty-two Carlucci initiatives had been fully implemented. Displeased with the GAO's conclusions, OSD responded sharply, "This is a highly subjective finding. Even reasonable men will never see eye-to-eye on the degree of monitoring required to conclude that a management initiative is fully implemented."[47] Though defensive in tone, this statement, in effect, captured what turned out to be the central problem in weapons acquisition reform during the first half of the 1980s: a broadly conceived but locally contingent disjunction between policy formulation in the Office of the Secretary of Defense and policy execution in the military services. The competing motives and organizational rivalries among the major participants—OSD, Congress, the Army, Navy, and the Air Force, and myriad industrial contractors—continuously recast the institutional landscape of the weapons acquisition process, thereby complicating the efforts undertaken by Carlucci and his staff to impose clear direction and broad oversight from the top.

While it is true that Congress had authorized successively lower defense budgets below approved planned levels each year since 1981, an outcome that frustrated OSD and the services, it is also true, as the GAO concluded in 1986, that Congress "approved what amounts to nearly a 100 percent increase in DoD's procurement budget from fiscal years 1980 to 1985"[48] Predictably—at least in part because of the disparity between planned and actual budgeted funds—major programs destabilized, costs rose, and schedules slipped. While critics outside the Pentagon often placed blame on what they considered to be a poorly planned and executed weapons procurement system, the Acquisition Improvement Program nevertheless did record, as Carlucci pointed out in 1982, a number of significant successes, ranging from reform of the Defense Systems Acquisition Review Council to closer, if often strained, relations between OSD and the services.

In retrospect, it is clear that DoD experienced a number of problems implementing the Carlucci initiatives. In July 1986, five years after their introduction, more than half of a GAO sample of fifty-four program managers (who had been in their jobs more than two years) thought that the initiatives had made little or no difference in the acquisition process. The GAO survey suggested that

---

[47] General Accounting Office (GAO) Report, *Status of the Defense Acquisition Improvement Program's 33 Initiatives*, GAO/NSIAD 86–178BR (Washington, D.C.: General Accounting Office, September 1986), p. 62 (quotation).

[48] GAO Report, *DoD's Defense Acquisition Improvement Program: A Status Report*, GAO/NSIAD–86–148 (Washington, D.C.: General Accounting Office, July 1986), pp. 11–12 (quotation).

THE 1980s: THE CARLUCCI INITIATIVES AND THE PACKARD COMMISSION

the senior-level commitment to change had not filtered down to the program management level.[49]

The GAO study concluded that DoD had once again "not carried through with its action plans on most of the Carlucci initiatives" and was "not monitoring actions to ensure that results were being achieved." It added that although DoD had made some progress in implementing the program, implementation had not been completed, and consequently, results had not been fully achieved.[50]

The core idea of the Carlucci initiatives was that overregulation thwarts efficiency and increases costs. The principle is sound to a certain point, after which problems arise, according to critics. Some decentralization may increase efficiency—assuming government program managers and their superiors are properly trained and can be held responsible for their program's performance. But initiatives such as reduced oversight of fixed-price contracts make industry less accountable to senior DoD management and less accountable to Congress and the public.[51]

Defense analyst Gordon Adams pointed out that the defense initiatives of the early 1980s, which collectively sought increased "up-front" spending and more "realistic" budgeting, were reforms that attempted to streamline an inefficient procurement system without attacking the real sources of cost overruns. For example, if the cost data from industry are not strictly and independently verified by DoD program managers or auditors, many of the Carlucci initiatives could have precisely the opposite result from the one intended. Specifically, "more realistic" (i.e., higher) estimates of costs and inflation, longer-term contracts, greater reliability, and more test items could result in large budget increases. These reforms, by themselves, could provide contractors with less incentive to control and to minimize costs while providing DoD with a rationale to accept rising costs as "more realistic." In short, the Carlucci initiatives would have made a great deal of sense, but only if the Defense Department had created incentives for cost reduction and had sufficient numbers of skilled personnel assigned to manage large industrial programs.[52]

In 1982, Senator Sam Nunn (D-Ga.) and Senator Dave McCurdy (D-Okla.) introduced an amendment in the 1982 Defense Authorization Act, made permanent in 1983, to curtail cost growth in weapons acquisition programs. Known as the Nunn-McCurdy Amendment, it required notification of Congress of cost growth of more than 15 percent

---

[49] Ibid., pp. 5, 14.
[50] Ibid., pp. 12–13 (quotation).
[51] Gordon Adams, Paul Murphy, and William Grey Rosenau, *Controlling Weapons Costs: Can the Pentagon Reforms Work?* (New York: Council on Economic Priorities, 1983), p. 36.
[52] Ibid., pp. 32–33 (quoted words).

and called for the termination of acquisition programs whose total cost grew by more than 25 percent above the original estimate, unless the secretary of defense submitted a detailed explanation certifying that the program was essential to national security, that no suitable alternative of lesser cost was available, that new estimates of total program costs were reasonable, and that the management structure was (or had been made) adequate to control costs.

While this amendment rarely led to the cancellation of an acquisition program, it led to frequent changes in programs. For example, the meteorological satellite program NPOESS (National Polar-Orbiting Operational Environmental Satellite System) was redesigned with lesser capability after being affected by the amendment, as were a number of subsequent programs.

By the mid-1980s, OSD oversight of the Defense Acquisition Improvement Program had begun to fade. OSD continued to monitor selected initiatives internally, but, as a GAO study concluded in the summer of 1986, "OSD has not formally reported on the program's status since June 1984, and does not plan to issue any further reports." Service reporting to OSD on the status of program implementation had also stopped.[53] Moreover, both Carlucci and Puritano—the program's major architects and advocates—left OSD in 1983 and 1984, respectively, to pursue careers in industry. By 1985, damaging reports of overpriced spare parts and other forms of alleged waste and fraud sensationalized by the media drew widespread attention and scrutiny from Congress. Prompted by these and other crises, Caspar Weinberger reorganized OSD's executive leadership, while President Reagan, bowing in part to public pressure, appointed the Blue Ribbon Commission on Defense— headed by Hewlett-Packard cofounder and former Deputy Secretary of Defense David Packard—to review the entire weapons acquisition process and recommend reforms for improvement.

Responding to Charges of Fraud, Waste, and Mismanagement

Even though he won a landslide victory against democratic opponent Walter Mondale in the 1984 presidential election, Ronald Reagan began his second term in the White House under a cloud of controversy. Charges of fraud, waste, and mismanagement in the Department of Defense had been circulating in the media for several years, but by the beginning of 1985 following the defense buildup, some of those charges had already led to formal government investigations of major defense contractors, and in some cases, criminal charges and convictions. Allegations of fraud and corruption at the Electric Boat Division of the General Dynam-

---

[53] GAO Report, *DoD's Defense Acquisition Improvement Program*, GAO/NSIAD–86–148, Jul 1986, pp. 12–13 (quotation).

ics Corporation, builder of the Navy's nuclear-powered attack and ballistic missile submarines, prompted a major investigation by the Defense Department and Congress. The Pentagon also threatened to seek punitive damages against Texas Instruments, one of the military's largest suppliers of precision electronic components, for delivery of improperly tested computer chips to other defense contractors. Although the government took appropriate action in many instances, these and other embarrassing problems drew sharp criticism from the general public. Some observers demanded more congressional oversight of major weapon programs and increased regulation of defense contractors. Republican Senator Alan Simpson of Wyoming blasted the Pentagon for using "bookkeeping gimmickry" to conceal what he believed to be outright incompetence in the Defense Department's management of weapons procurement.[54]

On 5 July 1985, ten days before the president issued Executive Order 12526 establishing the Packard Commission, Deputy Secretary of Defense William H. Taft IV activated the new position of assistant secretary of defense for acquisition and logistics, also commonly referred to as the defense acquisition executive (DAE).[55] Taft and other top officials in the Pentagon openly acknowledged in the press that this move had been taken, as the *Washington Post* reported in January, "to help Weinberger fend off expected prodding from Congress this year for more far-reaching changes."[56] Those changes would come in the form of the Packard Commission six month later. In the meantime, however, Weinberger, who had officially announced his plans to set up the new post in January 1985, assigned the assistant secretary of defense for acquisition and logistics (ASD [A&L]) responsibility for managing weapon sys-

---

[54] J. F. Fitzgerald, "Pentagon to Create Procurement Chief Post," *Hartford Courant,* 30 January 1985, p. 5. For other examples of contractor misconduct, see also "Former Defense Official Sentenced for Fraud," *Aviation Week and Space Technology* 121 (26 November 1984): 59–60; C. P. Alexander, "Scandal Rocks General Electric," *Time* 125 (27 May 1985): 60; T. Morgenthau, "Waste, Fraud, and Abuse?" *Newsweek* 105 (3 June 1985): 22–23; J. Nielsen, "The Party's Over for Arms Makers," *Fortune* 112 (5 August 1985): 88–92; J. K. Gordon, "House Subcommittee Charges Overpricing by F-16 Contractors," *Aviation Week and Space Technology* 123 (30 September 1985): 26–28; "Defense Department Suspends Litton from Receiving New Contracts," *Aviation Week and Space Technology* 125 (21 July 1986): 22; J. K. Gordon, "Defense Department Has Debarred 322 Contractors for Fiscal 1986," *Aviation Week and Space Technology* 125 (6 October 1986): 69; "Sunstrand Admits Guilt: Fines Total $128 Million," *Aviation Week and Space Technology* 129 (17 October 1988): 37; and P. Mann, "GE Charged with $21 Million Fraud Scheme Against Army," *Aviation Week and Space Technology* 129 (5 December 1988): 33.

[55] News Release, 5 Jul 1985, sub: Assistant Secretary of Defense (Acquisition and Logistics) Established, OSD Historical Office.

[56] M. Struck and F. Hiatt, "Defense Post to Be Added," *Washington Post,* 29 January 1985.

tems acquisition. In addition to reporting directly to the secretary of defense, the assistant secretary would, according to a Pentagon news release, "strengthen controls, clarify responsibilities and provide emphasis for certain programs requiring additional management attention."[57] Weinberger also charged the ASD (A&L) with monitoring suspected fraud and abuse and preventing purchases of overpriced spare parts and substandard weapon systems.[58] While the reorganization of acquisition management in OSD may have looked good on paper, effective implementation at the working level proved far more difficult to achieve. Even without resistance from the military services, a problem that had impeded progress of the Acquisition Improvement Program earlier in the decade, effective policy formation and execution in the Office of the Assistant Secretary of Defense for Acquisition and Logistics was often sidetracked by conflicting personalities in OSD.

Prior to the establishment of the Office of the Assistant Secretary of Defense for Acquisition and Logistics, management of weapons acquisition—from initial concept to operation in the field—had been split between two organizations: the Office of the Assistant Secretary of Defense for Manpower, Installations, and Logistics (ASD [MI&L]) occupied since 1981 by Lawrence Korb, and the Office of the Under Secretary of Defense for Research and Engineering (USD [R&E]) headed by Richard DeLauer. Korb managed weapons operation and maintenance (logistics), while DeLauer controlled research and development (R&D) and the purchase of weapon systems (procurement). The new ASD (A&L) absorbed the acquisition management and policy functions from the USD (R&E) and the logistics and spare parts procurement functions from the ASD (MI&L). The ASD (A&L) also took over management of the Defense Logistics Agency.[59]

Korb and DeLauer lost some managerial authority when Weinberger restructured OSD's acquisition management functions. An article in *Defense Week* suggested that Weinberger had been displeased with Korb's performance as a consequence of reports published in the press that the Pentagon had paid unreasonably high prices for spare parts. Korb dismissed this explanation, but doubts apparently lingered. Similar rumors circulated about DeLauer, who also stood to lose power with the appointment of the

---

[57] News Release, 29 Jan 1985, sub: Secretary of Defense Weinberger Announces Management Streamlining, OSD Historical Office, p. 1 (quoted words).

[58] P. Bedard, "Pentagon Acquisition Czar," *Defense Week* 7 (4 February 1985): 13.

[59] Struck and Hiatt, "Defense Post to Be Added," p. 17. See also News Release, 29 Jan 1985, sub: Secretary of Defense Weinberger Announces Management Streamlining, p. 1.

first ASD (A&L). He opposed Weinberger's plan to shift control of weapons acquisition from his office to the new position, which may have prompted his resignation from the Defense Department in December 1984 near the end of Reagan's first term.

When Taft activated the Office of the Assistant Secretary of Defense for Acquisition and Logistics in the summer of 1985, the Office of the Under Secretary of Defense for Research and Engineering had already been vacant for more than six months. To fill the position, Weinberger next turned to James P. Wade Jr., a graduate of the United States Military Academy at West Point and a Ph.D. physicist who had spent nearly twenty years working in the Pentagon and who had also helped implement the Acquisition Improvement Program earlier in the decade. At the time, Wade was serving simultaneously in two senior OSD positions—acting under secretary of defense for research and engineering, DeLauer's old post, and assistant secretary of defense for development and support (ASD [D&S]). The ASD (D&S) disappeared when Wade accepted appointment as the first defense acquisition executive.[60]

Wade initially had to wear two hats as the assistant secretary of defense for acquisition and logistics. First, he had to define the operating parameters of his new position, which translated into convincing other senior policymakers and acquisition organizations—such as the USD (R&E), the secretary of defense, and the military services—to fall in line behind his strategies for acquisition management. Second, Wade had to regain the public's confidence in the weapons acquisition process, which had already been badly damaged by the procurement scandals that seemed to appear in the press and other media outlets on a daily basis. One day after Wade took office, the *Washington Post* reported that "administration supporters believe the procurement scandals have undercut the president's political consensus for a strong defense and given congressional doves ammunition in their fight for deep cuts in military spending."[61]

While Wade brought considerable experience to the Office of the Assistant Secretary of Defense for Acquisition and Logistics, he did not inspire confidence among some Pentagon associates who believed that his preference for consensus building would not suffice in a position where hard and decisive choices had to be made concerning the distribution of limited resources among competing weapon systems in the military services. Nonetheless, Wade set

---

[60] M. Weisskopf, "Defense 'Procurement Czar' Named," *Washington Post*, 6 July 1985. See also News Release, 5 Jul 1985, sub: Assistant Secretary of Defense (Acquisition and Logistics) Named, OSD Historical Office; Struck and Hiatt, "Defense Post to Be Added."

[61] Weisskopf, "Defense 'Procurement Czar' Named."

out to achieve a broad range of goals. He intended to emphasize what he called "front-end" planning in the acquisition process, using standard commercial components rather than specialized parts produced in small quantities and at high cost.[62] "That's how you end up with $600 ashtrays," he said. Wade also planned to improve training programs for acquisition officers and promote greater cooperation among the services to streamline purchasing.[63] Ambitious as these goals may have been, however, Wade never came close to achieving them. He had fallen out of favor as the defense acquisition executive before the year was out.

Wade's troubles began before Weinberger appointed him ASD (A&L). Preliminary evidence suggests that he initially opposed Weinberger's plans to create the office, hoping that he would be elevated to DeLauer's old and more senior post as USD (R&E). The appointment went to Donald Hicks instead. Hicks was an experienced industrial physicist and senior vice president at the Northrop Corporation who had worked previously at the Boeing Company and the Lawrence Berkeley National Laboratory.[64] When Hicks left the aircraft industry for a job in the Pentagon, he soon found himself in conflict with Wade concerning the separation of management functions between their two offices. Deputy Secretary of Defense Taft, *Defense Week* reported in December 1985, "never really spelled out the lines of authority between Hicks and Wade, and confusion arose as to areas of responsibility." Since nearly a year had passed following DeLauer's departure from the Office of the Under Secretary of Defense for Research and Engineering, Wade had taken over many of its functions by default while serving as ASD (A&L), thereby handling management of most acquisition functions. Taft apparently disapproved of this outcome, while Hicks sought to consolidate his authority as the new research and engineering chief. Tensions rose over an acceptable division of labor between Wade and Hicks until Taft took over the functions of the ASD (A&L) and designated himself defense acquisition executive. Wade and Hicks retained their official titles and posts, until the spring of 1986, when, with the Packard Commission's interim report in hand, Reagan announced plans to establish a new Office of the Under Secretary of Defense for Acquisition (USD [A]).

---

[62] The Packard Commission had also recommended the use of off-the-shelf commercial parts.

[63] M. Weisskopf, "Pentagon's New Troubleshooter," *Washington Post*, 16 July 1985.

[64] The Lawrence Berkeley National Laboratory was one the leading centers for high-energy physics research in the United States. See Robert W. Seidel, "Accelerating Science: The Postwar Transformation of the Lawrence Radiation Laboratory," *Historical Studies in the Physical Sciences* 13(2) (1983): 375–400.

Within a few months, the Office of the Assistant Secretary of Defense for Acquisition and Logistics had been downgraded to a subordinate position under the new Office of the USD (A), a move that prompted Wade to leave the Pentagon and seek employment elsewhere. Similarly, Hicks left the Pentagon in October 1986 as the Office of the Under Secretary for Research and Engineering was downgraded to Office of the Director of Defense Research and Engineering under the USD (A).[65]

THE PACKARD COMMISSION, 1985–1989

In 1985, Senator Goldwater (R-Ariz.), along with Senator Nunn (D-Ga.), then one of the most knowledgeable and respected defense experts in the Senate, issued a lengthy report critical of the Defense Department. The report highlighted the problems of cost increases and cost mischarges and concluded that DoD was in a mess, that U.S. combat readiness was in a lamentable state, and that the correlation between spending a lot of money and acquiring better defense did not exist. The report also blamed Congress for meddling with the defense budget and thereby contributing heavily to waste and inefficiency.[66]

In mid-1985, Senator Charles E. Grassley (R-Iowa) expressed similar criticism of the acquisition process: "I and others here in Congress have charged that the defense industry is fat, wasteful, poorly managed, and consequently contributes to an erosion of our national defense. Now I plead guilty to having called the defense industry the new generation of welfare queens, and I intend to verify this, right or wrong, through strictly empirical data and analysis."[67]

Again in 1985, House Armed Services Committee Chairman Leslie "Les" Aspin (D-Wisc.) launched a series of hearings addressing the question: What have we received for a trillion dollars? He was referring to the trillion-dollar defense spending total for the first half of the 1980s. Aspin's answer: Not enough. In a twenty-five-page report, the Wisconsin Democrat cited "skimpy improvements in the U.S. defense posture despite the huge increases in defense spending over the years."

---

[65] "Taft Tightens His Grip," *Defense Week* 9 (December 1985): 15 (quotation). See also "Who's in Charge?" *Washington Post,* 4 April 1986, and "The Roles and Authorities of the Director of Defense Research and Engineering," Office of the Under Secretary of Defense for Acquisition, Technology, and Logistics, October 2005, p. 27.

[66] "Don't Ignore These Pentagon Critics," *Business Week* (28 October 1985): 130.

[67] U.S. Congress, Senate, statement of Senator Charles E. Grassley before the Subcommittee on Administrative Practice and Procedure of the Committee on Armed Services, *Agency Flow of Information*, 23–24 July 1985, p. 2.

The Pentagon dismissed Aspin's charges as "uninformed and inaccurate," and Defense Secretary Weinberger continued to assert that there was nothing basically wrong with the military establishment. "If a thing ain't broke," he repeatedly argued, "don't fix it."

Not surprisingly, the dissatisfaction in Congress with defense spending and management mirrored the increasingly vocal dissatisfaction among the general public. In March 1985, a Business Week/Harris survey revealed that 70 percent of Americans were convinced that defense contractors routinely overcharge the Pentagon. The respondents also thought, by a three-to-one margin, that the congressional committees in charge of military programs "are so influenced by defense contractors that they won't crack down on wasteful spending." And 56 percent thought that Defense Secretary Weinberger was doing at best a "fair" and at worst a "poor" job of managing the Pentagon's budget. Only 4 percent gave him an "excellent" rating.[68]

In analyzing the poll, Business Week concluded that the public was unhappy enough to want dramatic action. By a margin of 57 percent to 36 percent, those surveyed would bar any company found to have overcharged the Pentagon from receiving any new defense contracts. Approximately 60 percent would cancel "some or all" of the offending company's existing contracts. Respondents would also like to see anyone found guilty of fraud go to jail, "no matter how important they are." Most of the respondents thought that the costs of defense programs were inflated because of design changes to defense systems while they were being developed and produced.

In the summer of 1985, President Reagan established the Blue Ribbon Commission (the Packard Commission) on Defense Management, marking the culmination of numerous related and sometimes conflicting reform initiatives that had been under way in Washington since the early 1980s.[69] Representative examples include the President's Private Sector Survey on Cost Control (the Grace Commission), established by the White House in 1982 as part of a larger effort to reduce the size of the government and streamline federal operations; and the Military Reform Caucus, a congressional bipartisan group founded by Colorado Senator Gary Hart, that questioned the anticipated outcomes of Reagan's defense buildup and sought alternatives to existing weapons pro-

---

[68] Business Week/Harris Poll reported in *Business Week*, 25 March 1985.

[69] The Packard Commission continued a long tradition of Defense Department reviews that had been conducted by various study groups and panels since the end of World War II. See, for example, *Defense Acquisition: Major U.S. Commission Reports (1949–1988)*, vol. 1, prepared for the use of the Defense Policy Panel and Acquisition Policy Panel of the Committee on Armed Services, House of Representatives, 100th Cong., 2d sess., 1 November 1988.

curement procedures.[70] Congress also assumed a more active and direct role in the oversight of weapons acquisition that went beyond control of defense appropriations. In the Senate, for example, the Armed Services Committee established the Defense Acquisition Policy Subcommittee, chaired by Indiana Senator James Danforth "Dan" Quayle. Meanwhile, Pentagon whistleblowers and grass roots organizations, such as Dina Rasor's Project on Military Procurement, further inflamed public outrage with allegations of widespread criminal misconduct and mismanagement in the military services and the defense industry that quickly put the White House on the defensive and threatened to undermine political support for the president's rearmament program.[71] Regardless of the veracity of these charges, Reagan established the Packard Commission in part as a preemptive measure to deflect the litany of growing criticism leveled against his administration and the Pentagon by external pressure groups, Congress, and the media.

The Packard Commission comprised a group of distinguished defense experts who, among other things, recommended a sweeping reorganization of the weapon systems acquisition process—centralization of all management functions under civilian authority in OSD. The following year, Congress, which had closely followed the commission's deliberations, enacted legislation establishing the position of USD (A) recommended by the commission. Ranking third behind the defense secretary and the deputy secretary of defense, this new post expanded OSD control of weapons procurement at the expense of weakened acquisition organizations in the Army, Navy, and Air Force. Though controversial and often criticized by the services, the Office of the Under Secretary of Defense

---

[70] On the recommendations of the Grace Commission, see President's Private Sector Survey on Cost Control, *A Report to the President* (Washington, D.C.: U.S. Government Printing Office, 1983). The Military Reform Caucus is discussed in Daniel Wirls, *Buildup: The Politics of Defense in the Reagan Era* (Ithaca: Cornell University Press, 1992). See also D. M. Alpern and J. J. Lindsay, "Fighting to Win the War," *Newsweek* 98 (14 September 1981): 27; G. Hart, "What's Wrong with the Military?" *New York Times Magazine,* 14 February 1982, 16–19; Hart, "The Need for Military Reform," *Air University Review* 36 (September-October 1985): 41–46; A. K. Marsh, "Military Reform Caucus Seeks Targets," *Aviation Week and Space Technology* 116 (29 March 1982): 55–56; D. Griffiths, "An Unlikely Alliance Takes on the Pentagon," *Business Week,* 5 August 1985, 54–55; S. Crock, "Military Reform: Congress May Steal Reagan's Thunder," *Business Week* (14 October 1985): 53; and P. Mann, "Congress Continues Drive for Procurement Reform," *Aviation Week and Space Technology* 125 (3 November 1986): 36–37.

[71] See Dina Rasor, ed., *More Bucks, Less Bang: How the Pentagon Buys Ineffective Weapons* (Washington, D.C.: Fund for a Constitutional Government, 1983). See also Rasor, *The Pentagon Underground: Hidden Patriots Fighting Against Deceit and Fraud in America's Defense Program* (New York: Basic Books, 1985); A. Ernest Fitzgerald, *The Pentagonists: An Insider's View of Waste, Mismanagement, and Fraud in Defense Spending* (Boston: Houghton-Mifflin, 1989).

for Acquisition nevertheless served as the focal point of weapons acquisition reform during the second half of the 1980s.

The Packard Commission characterized the defense acquisition process as expensive, inefficient, and cumbersome. It observed that "the increasing complexity of the process meant unnecessary delays occur in acquiring needed goods and supplies and that higher costs were paid for what was acquired." In brief, the Packard Commission concluded that "the defense acquisition process is not being operated and managed effectively, and that this is having a disastrous effect on the cost and efficiency of the system."[72]

The lengthy acquisition process (seven to ten years or longer) for major weapon systems was a central problem and produced other acquisition problems. The Packard Commission pointed out three typical hazards:

- It leads to unnecessarily high costs of development. Time is money, and experience argues that a ten-year acquisition cycle is clearly more expensive than a five-year cycle.
- It leads to obsolete technology at the time of deployment.
- It aggravates the concern that is one of its causes. Users, knowing that the equipment designed to meet their requirements is fifteen years away, make extremely conservative (i.e., high) threat estimates. Because long-term forecasts are uncertain at best, users tend to err on the side of overstating the threat.[73]

The 1986 Packard Commission also found that the general public held "professional military personnel" in very high esteem. The public placed the military, on a scale of zero to one hundred, in the range of eighty, along with doctors, ministers, and other professional people with high status and recognition. On the other hand, "the defense industry was down at 25 percent, and in some of the detailed questions the public indicated that they thought half the defense budget was being wasted by the defense industry."[74]

In response to the reported cost problems, congressional members adopted a fragmented approach to reform, introducing a large number of bills designed to impose new requirements on DoD and

---

[72] President's Blue Ribbon Commission on Defense Management, *A Quest for Excellence*, June 1986, cited in John C. Yoder and Jan Horbaly, "Department of Defense Procurement Alternatives," paper prepared for the Defense Acquisition Study, Center for Strategic and International Studies, Georgetown University, 17 March 1986, pp. 7–10 (quotation).

[73] President's Blue Ribbon Commission on Defense Management, *A Quest for Excellence: Final Report to the President* (Washington, D.C.: U.S. Government Printing Office, June 1986), p. 47.

[74] David Packard press conference on *A Quest for Excellence*, 2 July 1986.

THE 1980s: THE CARLUCCI INITIATIVES AND
THE PACKARD COMMISSION

the defense industry. In 1985, members of Congress introduced more than one-hundred-forty bills related to improving the defense acquisition process, many of which were accompanied by numerous press conferences, public expressions of outrage, and assertions that the new legislation would plug a few more holes in the dike. In 1986, once again, members of Congress introduced more than one hundred bills concerning defense acquisition.[75]

As a result of the paperwork required by the various defense acquisition initiatives of the past, the program management task of researching, interpreting, and applying the various rules and regulations to the numerous contracts issued each year required large government and contractor staffs. The problem, as the Packard Commission observed, was that much of the work performed by those who reviewed the proposals, plans, contracts, reports, and legal documents was now unproductive and costly. To address this and other major problems, the Packard Commission made four major recommendations:[76]

- Create a new Under Secretary of Defense for Acquisition, who would "set overall policy for procurement and research and development (R&D), supervise the performance of the entire acquisition system, and establish policy for administrative oversight and auditing of defense contractors.
- Create the senior position of Service Acquisition Executive (SAE) in each service, who would be a civilian presidential appointee reporting to the new DoD Under Secretary, as well as to the service secretary.
- Create Program Executive Officers (PEOs) appointed by the SAEs. Each PEO would oversee a group of program managers in charge of major acquisition programs reporting up this civilian chain of command from the Program Executive Officers to the Service Acquisition Executives to the Under Secretary of Defense for Acquisition.
- Give the chairman of the Joint Chiefs of Staff more authority and create a vice chairman, who, along with the new Under Secretary, will be part of a Joint Requirements Management Board, which will establish requirements for new weapons and approve or reject them at each step along the path to production.[77]

---

[75] Yoder and Horbaly, "Department of Defense Procurement Alternatives," pp. 11–12.

[76] President's Blue Ribbon Commission on Defense Management, *An Interim Report to the President* (Washington, D.C.: U.S. Government Printing Office, 28 February 1986), p. 16.

[77] Ibid. The commission also recommended other reforms, including recruitment of more qualified acquisition personnel; elimination of "goldplating" (overstated requirements, leading to unrealistic specifications and higher costs); more frequent

These recommendations were subsequently implemented throughout DoD. Since the late 1980s, defense program managers have reported to program executive officers. Program executive officers can have many program managers reporting to them. Program executive officers can also be military officers or federal civil servants and report to a service acquisition executive in a military service.[78] The service acquisition executive is a political appointee and is usually an assistant secretary of a service, responsible for all acquisition and acquisition programs within the service. Service acquisition executives report to a service secretary and to the under secretary of defense for acquisition, technology, and logistics (USD [AT&L]), who also serves as the defense acquisition executive.[79]

In 1986, the Packard Commission released its final report focusing on four broad subject areas: national security planning and budgeting; military organization and command; acquisition organization and procedures; and government-industry accountability.[80] All four areas touched on the organization of the military services and weapon systems acquisition. In the case of national security planning and budgeting, for example, the commission extended a programming element of the Acquisition Improvement Program—

---

use of commercial parts rather than specially designed components based on military specifications; expanded testing of prototype weapons systems prior to production (fly-before-buy); and multiyear procurement and base-lining (establishment of firm internal agreement on system requirements, design, production, and cost) to improve program stability. The report also dismissed claims that fraud and waste were rampant in the Defense Department. The commission argued instead that the acquisition system suffered from managerial and operational inefficiencies in OSD and in the services. Rather than recommend more external oversight and regulation (from Congress, for example), the commission believed that "meaningful change will come ... only with major institutional change." This interpretation of the problem of weapons acquisition reform prompted the establishment of the USD (A) and the new acquisition management positions in the services.

[78] A service acquisition executive is the component acquisition executive for a military department.

[79] Congressional Research Service Report for Congress, "Defense Acquisition: Overview, Issues, and Options for Congress," RL34026, 20 Jun 2007. DoD Instruction 5000.1 states that the defense acquisition executive takes precedence on all acquisition matters after the secretary and the deputy secretary of defense.

[80] The commission submitted the full report, which elaborated on the recommendations in the interim report, in June. See President's Blue Ribbon Commission on Defense Management, *A Quest for Excellence: Final Report to the President*. The commission also issued supplemental reports on specific topics: John Norton Moore and Robert F. Turner, *The Legal Structure of Defense Organization: Memorandum Prepared for the President's Blue Ribbon Commission on Defense Management* (Washington, D.C.: 15 January 1986); President's Blue Ribbon Commission on Defense Management, *A Formula for Action* (Washington, D.C.: April 1986); *National Security Planning and Budgeting* (Washington, D.C.: June 1986); and *Conduct and Accountability* (Washington, D.C.: June 1986), all copies in OSD Historical Office.

reform of the annual budget process to avoid funding fluctuations in major weapons programs. Suggested alternatives proposed by the commission included biennial budgeting and authorizations of appropriations for programs at key development milestones.

In addition to calling for a new under secretary of defense for acquisition, the Packard Commission also favored the extension of civilian management and coordination of procurement functions in each of the military services. It also encouraged greater use of off-the-shelf commercial products rather than components designed to rigid military specifications; rigorous testing of prototypes prior to production (a concept typically known as fly-before-buy); and a more active role for the Defense Advanced Research Projects Agency (DARPA) in weapon systems prototyping and other development work not sufficiently emphasized in the services.[81]

The Packard Commission report also contained strong recommendations for improving the training and experience of government personnel assigned to defense acquisition, citing the need to "enhance the quality of [government] acquisition personnel." It stated that "significant improvements should be made in the senior-level appointment system" and cited a GAO report confirming the central importance of "improving the quality of training for program managers and contracting officers." The Packard report continued, "We support recent legislation that has further defined career paths for all program managers." In 1984, Congress established a minimum four-year tenure for program manager assignments.

The 1986 Defense Authorization Act prescribed requisite qualifications and training, including at least eight years of acquisition-related experience and appropriate instruction at the Defense Systems Management College (or equivalent training). The Packard report highlighted in particular the need for business-related education and experience.[82]

Even though many of the Packard Commission recommendations became law, they did not all bring about significant procedural changes in the weapons acquisition process or in the training, assignments, or tenure of program managers. Waivers were frequently granted to program manager candidates (as continued to be the practice in 2009). Congress enacted reform legislation that simply overlaid new

---

[81] President's Blue Ribbon Commission on Defense Management, *An Interim Report to the President*, pp. 5, 9–10, 14–18, copy in OSD Historical Office. The concept of fly-before-buy was not new. Packard had implemented the same policy into the weapons acquisition system during his three-year tenure as deputy secretary of defense, from 1969 to 1971.

[82] President's Blue Ribbon Commission on Defense Management, *A Quest for Excellence: Final Report to the President*, pp. 65–70 and GAO Report, *DoD Acquisition: Strengthening Capabilities of Key DoD Personnel in Systems Acquisition*, GAO/NSIAD–86–45 (Washington, D.C.: U.S. General Accounting Office, May 1986).

institutional mechanisms, such as the USD (A), on existing acquisition organizations in the Office of the Secretary of Defense and the military services. This outcome created serious management bottlenecks and conflicting priorities, as evidenced, for example, by rapid turnover of occupants in the Office of the Under Secretary of Defense for Acquisition described later in this chapter. Moreover, the resulting organizational ambiguity enabled the Army, the Navy, and the Air Force to maintain considerable control over weapons acquisition.

Under Secretary of Defense for Acquisition

The Packard Commission's recommendation that the White House set up the Office of the Under Secretary of Defense for Acquisition was a continuation of policies and procedures favoring the centralization of weapons acquisition management in OSD, a process that had begun when Weinberger merged the functions of the ASD (MI&L) and part of the USD (R&E) into the Office of the Assistant Secretary of Defense for Acquisition and Logistics in 1985. But the commission also recommended more sweeping reforms that called for major changes to the acquisition organizations in the military services and more involvement in weapons acquisition by the Joint Chiefs of Staff and the commanders in chief of the unified and specified commands. Congress institutionalized these reforms in the authorization legislation for fiscal years 1986 and 1987, the Military Retirement Reform Act of 1986, and the Goldwater-Nichols Department of Defense Reorganization Act, which President Reagan signed into law on 1 October 1986.

The authority embodied in the legislation enacted by Congress in 1986 to reform acquisition management in the Defense Department did not immediately translate into effective compliance at the working level. Conflicts about organizational efficiency, military career paths, and jurisdictional authority persisted in OSD and the military services long after Congress completed its task. The legislative reforms endorsed by the White House and enacted by Congress in 1986 transferred and centralized the management of weapons acquisition to a high-ranking civilian presidential appointee—USD (A)—in OSD. Perhaps not surprisingly and with some justification, the services resisted the Packard Commission's recommendations and the provisions of the enabling legislation. In many cases, the service chiefs initially bypassed or ignored the measures taken by the USD (A) to impose new management strategies on major weapons programs. Moreover, the limits of oversight acceptable to the services differed substantially from the expectations advocated by reformers in Congress who favored the assignment of broad regulatory authority to the USD (A). This tension between service autonomy and greater oversight pushed by reformers in Congress, in combination with Defense Secretary Weinberger's initial opposition to the Packard Commission's recommendations, helped to create a hostile working environment for the USD (A) during the second half of the 1980s.

In its interim report to the president, the Packard Commission had identified the lack of coordination between the Office of the Secretary of Defense and the military services as the major problem in acquisition management:

> Responsibility for acquisition policy has become fragmented. There is today no single senior official in [OSD] working full-time to provide overall supervision of the acquisition system.... In the absence of such a senior OSD official, policy responsibility has tended to devolve to the services, where at times it has been exercised without the necessary coordination or uniformity. Authority for acquisition execution, and accountability for its results, have [sic] become vastly diluted.[83]

Without calling attention to the Acquisition Improvement Program, perhaps an odd omission given that the program deliberately encouraged greater service autonomy in the acquisition process, the commission proposed the establishment of the Office of the Under Secretary of Defense for Acquisition to deal with the lack of coordination and uniformity. This office, which replaced the current Office of the Assistant Secretary of Defense for Acquisition and Logistics, would "set overall policy for procurement and research and development (R&D), supervise the performance of the entire acquisition system, and establish policy for administrative oversight and auditing of defense contractors."[84]

As part of its overall plan to improve the acquisition management organization, the Packard Commission also recommended sweeping changes to the military command structure, a process that had already been under way before the commission convened. The commission identified a lack of integration between the commanders in chief of the unified and specified commands, who managed combat operations, and the service chiefs, whose procurement organizations determined weapon system requirements and carried out logistics functions. At the time, the chairman of the Joint Chiefs of Staff served as the primary communications link between the secretary of defense and the commanders in chief. The JCS chairman, defense secretary, and the commanders in

---

[83] President's Blue Ribbon Commission on Defense Management, *An Interim Report to the President,* p. 14.
[84] Ibid., p. 16.

chief, for example, all sat on the Defense Resources Board. This advisory unit assigned to OSD provided management oversight of the PPBS, which matched available resources to weapons requirements. Pointing out the growing emphasis on joint combat operations, the commission intended to cement this relationship even further along two separate but related lines. The new position of vice chairman of the Joint Chiefs of Staff would represent the views of the commanders in chief. In this way, the commanders in chief, through the vice chairman, would have the opportunity to participate directly in acquisition planning and resource allocation and be assured that the strategies and tactics of the unified and specified commands received full support.[85]

These functions would be executed by a newly reconstituted Joint Requirements Management Board (JRMB) headed by the vice chairman of the Joint Chiefs of Staff and the Under Secretary of Defense for Acquisition. Established in 1984, the JRMB (renamed two years later as the Joint Requirements Oversight Council [JROC]) had been modeled on the Defense Systems Acquisition Review Council (DSARC), set up by then-Deputy Defense Secretary Packard in 1969 to help manage the acquisition process by conducting periodic milestone reviews of major weapons programs at specified points in the procurement cycle.[86] Under these guidelines, the JROC defined and validated new weapon systems requirements; trade-offs between cost and performance; alternatives to the initiation of new programs at the research and development stage; and the development and production recommendations for joint programs.[87] In 1987, the Defense Acquisition Board (DAB) was created, replacing the Defense Acquisition Review Council as the senior-level forum for advising the under secretary of defense for acquisition on critical decisions concerning major acquisition category (ACAT) 1D programs. The under secretary of defense for acquisition (later expanded to acquisition, technology, and logistics) chaired the DAB, and the vice chairman of the Joint Chiefs of Staff served as vice chairman. Other DAB members included the service secretaries and several DoD acquisition officials.

---

[85] Ibid., pp. 9–12. See also Gordon Nathaniel Lederman, *Reorganizing the Joint Chiefs of Staff: The Goldwater-Nichols Act of 1986* (Westport, Conn.: Greenwood Press, 1999); James R. Locher III, *Victory on the Potomac: The Goldwater-Nichols Act Unifies the Pentagon* (College Station: Texas A&M University Press, 2002).

[86] The Defense Systems Acquisition Review Council (DSARC) was created by the deputy secretary of defense to achieve better coordination in the major weapons acquisition process.

[87] A. F. Klick, "The Newly Created Office of the Under Secretary of Defense, Acquisition," *National Defense* (January 1987): 34–36.

Even before the Packard Commission issued its final report on acquisition reform, the president and Congress moved quickly on the legislative front. On 1 April 1986, Reagan issued National Security Decision Directive (NSDD) 219, Implementation of Recommendations of President's Commission on Defense Management. "This directive," Reagan wrote, "outlines the steps I have approved for the implementation of the initial recommendations of the [Packard] Commission on Defense Management. . . . We must . . . be especially mindful of the need to move quickly and decisively to implement those changes." Anticipating legislative approval by Congress, Reagan endorsed establishing the Office of the Under Secretary of Defense for Acquisition and implementing a three-tiered acquisition management chain of command within each service consisting of a service acquisition executive, program executive officer, and program manager. He also endorsed restructuring the Joint Requirements Management Board cochaired by the USD (A) and the new vice chairman of the Joint Chiefs of Staff, to define weapons requirements, select programs and provide alternatives, streamline the program review process, and strengthen the acquisition workforce. The directive also authorized the Packard Commission's other recommendations concerning national security planning and budgeting and government-industry accountability.[88]

In mid-November 1986, shortly after Reagan signed the Goldwater-Nichols Defense Reorganization Act into law, Congress passed the National Defense Authorization Act for Fiscal Year 1987 (Public Law 99–661; Title XI of the Defense Acquisition Improvement Act of 1986). The National Defense Authorization Act and the Military Retirement Reform Act of 1986 created and authorized the responsibilities of the Office of the Under Secretary of Defense for Acquisition; set baseline descriptions for each of the Defense Department's major weapons acquisition programs; expanded multiyear procurement; increased the authority of program managers; and required prototype competitions (fly-before-buy) to identify among several alternatives the most suitable and cost-effective weapon systems.[89]

---

[88] Memo, John M. Poindexter for Distribution List, 1 Apr 1986; National Security Decision Directive (NSDD) 219, Implementation of the Recommendations of the President's Commission on Defense Management, 1 April 1986, (Reagan, quotation p. 1); copies of memo and directive in OSD Historical Office.

[89] Klick, "The Newly Created Office of the Under Secretary of Defense, Acquisition," pp. 33, 37. See also William E. Kovacic, "Blue Ribbon Defense Commissions: The Acquisition of Major Weapon Systems," in *Arms, Politics, and the Economy: Historical and Contemporary Perspectives*, ed. Robert Higgs (New York: Holmes and Meier, 1990), pp. 82–83. When Congress passed the National Defense Authorization Act for Fiscal Year 1987, the Pentagon had already

In February 1987, several months after it had filled the USD (A) position, the Office of the Secretary of Defense issued DoD Directive 5134.1, which outlined the functions of the USD (A). The holder of this position, the directive stated, would serve as "the principal staff assistant and adviser to the Secretary of Defense for all matters relating to the acquisition system; research and development; production; logistics; command, control, communications, and intelligence activities related to acquisition; military construction; and procurement."[90]

Title V of the Goldwater-Nichols Act, which Reagan had signed into law less than two months before Congress passed the fiscal year 1986 authorization legislation, established the legal guidelines used by the military services to restructure their acquisition organizations based on the Packard Commission's recommendations. To create the commission's three-tiered military and civilian acquisition management structure—service acquisition executive, program executive officer, program manager—the Army, Navy, and Air Force each merged the separate acquisition organizations previously assigned to each service secretary's office and the corresponding office of the service chief of staff. The creation of the newly combined acquisition organizations in the offices of the secretary of the Army, Navy, and Air Force apparently expanded civilian authority of the acquisition process. But as William W. Thurman, the GAO's deputy director for planning and reporting (National Security and International Affairs Division), observed during his testimony before the Subcommittee on Investigations of the House Armed Services Committee in April 1988, "the consolidation . . . was not intended to exclude the service chiefs from participating in these functions. . . . Title V specifies that in the acquisition area the service secretary *may* [emphasis added] assign responsibility for military requirements and test and evaluation to the service chiefs, thus allowing responsibility for these functions to remain in the service Chiefs' organizations."[91]

---

selected Northrop Grumman's B–2 stealth bomber program as the leading test case for fly-before-buy competition. The company's B–2 prototype completed its maiden test flight in the summer of 1989. On the development of the B–2, see Michael E. Brown, *Flying Blind: The Politics of the U.S. Strategic Bomber Program* (Ithaca, N.Y.: Cornell University Press, 1992), pp. 294–304.

[90] DoD Directive 5134.1 quoted in GAO, *Status of Recommendations by Blue Ribbon Commission on Defense Management*, GAO/NSIAD-89-19FS (Washington, D.C.: General Accounting Office, November 1988), p. 30 (quotation).

[91] U.S. Congress, House, statement of William W. Thurman, Deputy Director for Planning and Reporting (National Security and International Affairs Division, GAO), before the Subcommittee on Investigations, Committee on Armed Services, *Reorganization of the Military Departments' Acquisition Management Structures*, GAO/T–NSIAD–88–28, 20 April 1988, pp. 2–3 (quotation).

The Army began reorganizing its internal acquisition functions in March 1987. At the time, acquisition policy, management, and oversight resided in the Office of the Assistant Secretary of the Army for Research, Development, and Acquisition (ASA [RD&A]), who reported directly to the Under Secretary of the Army. The Office of the Deputy Chief of Staff for Research, Development, and Acquisition (DCS [RD&A]) reported to the Vice Chief of Staff and handled the execution of all of the Army's acquisition functions through the major commands. After Congress enacted Goldwater-Nichols, both offices combined to form a new acquisition organization headed by the ASA (RD&A), also known as the Army acquisition executive. The DCS (RD&A), a position previously held by a lieutenant general, became the principal deputy to the ASA (RD&A) responsible for overseeing day-to-day execution of operations and providing general staff support. Goldwater-Nichols prompted a similar reorganization of acquisition management functions in the Air Force. Acquisition responsibilities at Air Force headquarters had been divided between the assistant secretary of the Air Force for acquisition and logistics (ASAF [A&L]) and the deputy chief of staff for research, development, and acquisition (DCS [RD&A]). Like the Army, the Air Force merged the offices of the ASAF (A&L) and the DCS (RD&A). The civilian ASAF (A&L) served as the Air Force acquisition executive. "This integration [in the Army and the Air Force]," Thurman told the House Committee, "is designed to provide [the] assistant secretaries with authority and direct control over the people directing, managing, and executing acquisition activities."

The realignment of management authority for weapon systems acquisition from the deputy chief of staff of the Army and the Air Force to the corresponding assistant secretaries extended all the way down to the major commands. Before 1987, the Army Materiel Command directed the management and execution of weapons acquisition programs in its subordinate commodity commands. Under the new organizational structure, the weapon system program offices shifted to the three-tiered chain of command, leaving the Army Materiel Command to provide staff support. The program managers and program executive officers, for example, maintained small staffs but received functional support from Army Materiel Command's commodity commands. Essentially, the Army had split its acquisition management functions along two separate lines: one functional and under the direction of the Army Materiel Command, the other programmatic and controlled at the top by the assistant secretary of the Army for research, development, and acquisition—the Army acquisition executive. The provisions of Title V of Goldwater-Nichols prompted a similar division of labor between the acquisition management and support functions at the command level in the Air Force and the Navy.[92]

When he issued NSDD 219 in the spring of 1986, Reagan specified, as the Packard Commission had, that the proposed under secretary of defense for acquisition "should have a solid industrial background."[93] Ever since he had entered the White House, Reagan had sought to apply the lessons of efficient business management to government operations, and it is likely that the same concept guided his approach to weapons acquisition reform.[94] Packard had also adopted a business model to solve the same problem on two separate occasions, first as deputy secretary of defense from 1969 to 1971 and then as chairman of the President's Blue Ribbon Commission on Defense Management in 1985 to 1986.[95] To be sure, Packard's preference for a business solution to resolve the difficulties of acquisition reform seemed consistent with his background and experience as cofounder and head of Hewlett-Packard, one of the largest and most successful diversified electronics industrial firms in the United States conducting engineering development and production programs. It was also consistent with the industrial tasks of engineering development and production inherent in major acquisition programs. Guided by this experience, the Packard Commission concluded that unlike an industrial firm in which managers at the headquarters office maintained clear lines of authority to and from the manufacturing divisions, the Pentagon's acquisition organization lacked an equivalent centralized mechanism to regulate weapons acquisition from OSD to the services. The proposed under secretary of defense for acquisition would fill the need for centralization at the top, whereas the Army, Navy, and Air Force acquisition executives, like the general managers in charge of a firm's manufactu-

---

[92] Ibid., pp. 5–14. For a more detailed discussion of the organizational changes in the U.S. Army Materiel Command, see *U.S. Army Materiel Command Annual Historical Review, Fiscal Year 1987* (Fort Belvoir, Va.: Headquarters, U.S. Army Materiel Command Historical Office, August 1989).

[93] NSDD 219, Implementation of the Recommendations of the President's Commission on Defense Management, p. 1. See also President's Blue Ribbon Commission on Defense Management, *An Interim Report to the President,* p. 16 (quotation).

[94] Reagan's views on business management and government operations are discussed in his autobiography, *An American Life* (New York: Simon and Schuster, 1990).

[95] Fox, *Arming America*. See also J. Ronald Fox, *The Defense Management Challenge: Weapons Acquisition* (Boston: Harvard Business School Press), 1988, pp. 322–23.

ring divisions, would oversee—through their program executive officers—acquisition projects in the services.[96]

Not all observers, however, agreed with Reagan, Packard, and other like-minded officials in OSD that employing a business model promised the quickest route to a more efficient weapons acquisition management organization. Some critics charged that drawing on contemporary corporate management practices ignored the unique institutional structure of the defense establishment. Perhaps the strongest opposition to the under secretary of defense for acquisition came from the military services, the leaders of which saw the new position and its first occupant—Richard P. Godwin— as a direct assault on their autonomy to manage major weapons programs.[97]

Weinberger handpicked Richard Godwin to fill the position of under secretary of defense for acquisition. Even before Godwin set foot in Washington, however, his appointment had created controversy in the Pentagon, Congress, and the press. Since 1961, Godwin had been employed at the Bechtel Group, a huge engineering and construction firm headquartered in San Francisco. By the mid-1970s, he had worked his way up through the corporate ranks to become vice chairman of the company and a member of the board of directors. During the same period, Godwin had worked with Weinberger, at the time vice president and general counsel of the company, and also with George P. Shultz, who left Bechtel in 1982, a year after Weinberger departed for the Defense Department, to join Reagan's cabinet as secretary of state. Godwin's previous ties to Weinberger and Shultz, what the press often referred to as the "Bechtel Mafia," served as the basis for some of the discontent with Godwin.

When Weinberger announced in the spring of 1986 that Godwin would be the first under secretary of defense for acquisition, some critics in Congress immediately expressed their dissatisfaction with the appointment. Several Republican senators, including

---

[96] S. Eisenstadt, "The Packard Reforms: A Year Later," *Military Logistics Forum* 3 (May 1987): 40, 42. See also on the history of business organization and management at large firms such as Hewlett-Packard, Alfred D. Chandler Jr., *Strategy and Structure: Chapters in the History of the American Industrial Enterprise* (Cambridge, Mass.: MIT Press, 1962); Chandler, *Scale and Scope: The Dynamics of Industrial Capitalism* (Cambridge, Mass.: Belknap Press of Harvard University Press, 1990); and Chandler, "The Competitive Performance of U.S. Industrial Enterprises since the Second World War," *Business History Review* 68 (Spring 1994): 1–72.

[97] Harold J. Brumm Jr., an economist at the General Accounting Office writing for the *Defense Management Journal*, also questioned the wisdom of centralizing acquisition management in OSD. He argued that such an outcome would reduce competition between the services, inhibit technological innovation, and lower operating efficiencies. See H. J. Brumm Jr., "Bureaucratic Competition and Weapon System Procurement," *Defense Management Journal* 22 (Third Quarter 1986): 13–17.

Barry Goldwater (Arizona), Pete Wilson (California), Dan Quayle (Indiana), and William Philip "Phil" Gramm (Texas) preferred Donald Hicks, under secretary of defense for research and engineering (USD [R&E]), instead. Quayle, for example, disliked Godwin's ties to Bechtel and his association with Weinberger and Secretary of State Shultz. Unlike Hicks, Godwin had no experience working in the Department of Defense, and Bechtel operated almost exclusively in the civilian sector. The company had very little experience working in the defense business.[98] Support from the Senate, especially members of the Armed Services Committee (whose members included Goldwater, Wilson, and Quayle) was not enough to put Hicks in a favorable position to be the first USD (A).

When it became clear that the White House would not budge on Godwin's appointment, the Senate Armed Services Committee backed off and, in September, confirmed him as the first USD (A). Meanwhile, Hicks prepared to leave OSD. Under the new acquisition management structure, Weinberger eliminated the Office of the USD (R&E) and downgraded the Pentagon's research and development management function to the position—director of defense research and engineering (DDR&E)—reporting directly to Godwin.[99] "I didn't come to the Pentagon to be a director instead of an under secretary," Hicks reportedly confided to his colleagues in OSD.[100] He announced his resignation as USD (R&E) shortly after Godwin's Senate confirmation. So did James Wade, who still served as ASD (A&L). "I do not want to be a professional second-tier bureaucrat," Wade told *Defense News*. Godwin's appointment as the USD (A), he continued, "is an example [of] the system picking its top guys from outside" even though, as *Defense News* later paraphrased in its write-up of an interview with Wade, "capable people are already working within the [Pentagon] bureaucracy."[101]

---

[98] C. W. Coddry, "Weinberger's Support of Bechtel Official for Acquisition Post Angers Senators," *Baltimore Sun*, 23 May 1986; see also S. Eisenstadt, "Godwin Opposition May Be on the Wane," *Defense News*, 8 September 1986; J. Kitfield, "'Acquisition Czar' Gains Supporters," *Military Logistics Forum* (October 1986): 13.

[99] OSD established the Office of the Director of Defense Research and Engineering (DDR&E) in 1958. In 1977, Secretary of Defense Harold Brown abolished the DDR&E position and elevated its functions to the new Office of Under Secretary of Defense Research and Engineering. See Appendix D, "A Brief History of the Office of the Director of Defense Research and Engineering," in *Defense Science Board Task Force on the Roles and Authorities of the Director of Defense Research and Engineering* (Washington, D.C.: Office of the Under Secretary of Defense for Acquisition, Technology, and Logistics, October 2005).

[100] Donald Hicks quoted in Marjorie Williams, "Insult and Injury as 'Weapons Czar' Assumes New Post," *Washington Post*, 6 October 1986.

[101] "Godwin Proposes to Abolish Hicks' Job in New 'USDA' Reorganization," *Inside the Pentagon*, 26 September 1986; see also James Wade quoted in S. Eisenstadt, "Wade to Close Curtain on Career in Pentagon," *Defense News*, 22 September 1986; Eisenstadt, "Officials Do the Procurement Post Shuffle," *Defense News*, 13 October 1986.

By the time Godwin entered office, the Army, Navy, and Air Force had assumed significant management control over the development and procurement of major weapon systems. To be sure, Godwin faced a steep learning curve when he entered office. One industry observer who had worked in the Pentagon pointed out that "Godwin will basically have only two years left in this administration in which to organize a whole new office."[102] Thomas L. McNaugher, a defense analyst at the Brookings Institution, a think tank in Washington, D.C., offered a more pessimistic assessment of Godwin's prospects for success. "It's an incredible act of faith to think that one man is now going to come fresh into an intricate organization of thousands of people and make a real difference."[103] Confirming McNaugher's opinion of the difficulties the new USD (A) would likely face—though perhaps unknowingly—Secretary of the Navy John Lehman acknowledged that he would appeal directly to Weinberger if he and Godwin failed to reach agreement on any acquisition issue.[104]

A clear indication of the resistance that Godwin would face as "acquisition czar" first appeared during conferences held in the Senate and the House of Representatives to iron out differences in the proposed fiscal year 1987 defense bill, which authorized the position of the USD (A). The House version of the bill stipulated that the new position would "direct" all functions of the weapons acquisition procurement process, which were at the time managed by the services. The Senate bill, by contrast, stipulated that the USD (A) would only "supervise" weapon systems purchased by the services. Although all three services "strongly opposed the more intrusive role the [USD (A)] would have in their affairs under the House language," reported the *Congressional Quarterly,* "the House conferees dug in and the conference accepted the House position."[105] The authority of the under secretary to "direct" remained in the bill. Backed by legislative authority from Congress, Godwin, in one of his first actions as USD (A), reorganized OSD's civilian acquisition command structure, as planned, into five subordinate offices that reported directly to him: Assistant Secretary of Defense for Acquisition and Logistics, Wade's old post; Assistant Secretary of Defense for Command, Control, Communications, and Intelligence (C3I); Assistant Secretary of Defense for Research and Technol-

---

[102] Kitfield, "'Acquisition Czar' Gains Supporters," p. 13 (quotation).

[103] Thomas McNaugher quoted in J. Kitfield, "Sizing Up Godwin," *Military Logistics Forum* 3 (March 1987): 11.

[104] Ibid., p. 14.

[105] P. Towell, "Pentagon Gets a New Procurement 'Czar,'" *Congressional Quarterly* (25 October 1986): 32 (quotation).

ogy; Assistant Secretary of Defense for Atomic Energy; and Director of Defense Research and Engineering, previously occupied by Hicks.[106]

Even after he had made these organizational changes, however, Godwin's position as USD (A) had still not completely stabilized within OSD. In March 1987, for example, Weinberger received a letter signed by Congressman Les Aspin (D-Wisc.), Congressman William Dickinson (R-Ala.), Senator Sam Nunn (D-Ga.), and Senator John Warner (R-Va.) demanding that Godwin only report directly to him on matters of acquisition, bypassing Deputy Secretary of Defense Taft's office.[107] Preliminary evidence suggests that the letter had been prompted by congressional concern over Godwin's ability to "wield true authority in [Defense Department] acquisition" and Weinberger's detached management style, which had also led some defense experts to conclude that the USD (A) did not have sufficient support from OSD to enforce critical acquisition decisions. It is likely that conflicting expectations for acquisition reform coming from different constituencies—Congress, the military services, industry, and OSD—manifested themselves in the managerial difficulties that Godwin experienced. Commenting on this problem of mismatched priorities, R. James Woolsey, a lawyer, consultant, and former under secretary of the Navy who had served on the Packard Commission, pointed out that legislators in Congress who sought improvements in the Defense Department's acquisition process had, to some extent, misunderstood the commission's original expectations for the USD (A). The position had not been conceived to consolidate full authority over the entire acquisition process in an all-powerful acquisition czar. Rather, Woolsey argued, it had been set up to manage the acquisition process on behalf of OSD and the military services. "I had conceived of the under secretary [of defense] for acquisition to be an extremely important person for policy and procedures," he recalled in a story about the status of the Packard Commission reforms published in *Military Logistics Forum* shortly after Weinberger had received the letter about Godwin's role as USD (A) from Aspin, Dickinson, Nunn, and Warner.[108]

THE BATTLE FOR CONTROL OF WEAPONS SYSTEMS ACQUISITION

Whether or not Woolsey's recollection about the Packard Commission's stated intentions for the Office of the Under Secretary

---

[106] Williams, "Insult and Injury as 'Weapons Czar' Assumes New Post."

[107] Congressman William Dickinson and Senator John Warner also served as the ranking members and chairmen of the House and Senate Armed Services Committees, respectively. J. Kitfield, "Godwin: Battling the Powers That Be," *Military Logistics Forum* 4 (July-August 1987): 56.

[108] Eisenstadt, "The Packard Reforms," p. 43 (quotation).

of Defense for Acquisition had an impact on reformers in Congress, evidence suggested that the leaders of the military services did not assign much significance to his clarification of Godwin's expected role in OSD. It is likely that the services interpreted Godwin's actions as an all-out assault on their prerogatives to control weapon systems acquisition. According to press coverage and several reports issued by the GAO, the sharpest opposition came from the Navy and the Air Force, both of which bypassed the new civilian management functions Godwin assigned to their acquisition organizations and appealed directly to Deputy Secretary Taft to resolve conflicts. Frustrated and without sufficient support from Weinberger and Taft to execute the functions of the USD (A), Godwin abruptly resigned from the Pentagon in September 1987, less than a year-and-a-half after his appointment. Evidence suggests that his replacement as USD (A)—Robert Costello—fared better, despite continued resistance from the services.

Godwin began experiencing major problems with the service acquisition organizations almost as soon as he set foot inside the Pentagon. More than six months after he had entered office with a mandate from the Packard Commission and the White House to reform the weapons acquisition process, *Military Logistics Forum* reported that "working the changes into the Pentagon system has been slow. Not until March 1987, a year after Godwin had been named under secretary, did the services put into effect the alterations in their acquisition hierarchies." Several months earlier, Godwin had clashed with Secretary of the Navy John Lehman, the architect of President Reagan's ambitious plan to expand the Navy's surface and submarine fleets to a combined total of six hundred ships by the end of the decade. Godwin, believing he had the authority to overrule the service secretaries, reversed Lehman's prior decision to cancel development of the Deadeye, a five-inch laser-guided projectile designed for use in amphibious assault missions. Lehman bypassed Godwin and appealed directly to Taft, complaining that the USD (A) did not have the authority to reactivate the Deadeye program. Taft agreed, and in February, he issued a directive that the USD (A) could not overrule service secretaries in cases, such as the Deadeye program, in which disputes arose over program execution. Only the deputy secretary of defense—Taft or whoever held the office at the time—could make that decision.[109]

Taft, prompted by Secretary of the Air Force Edward "Pete" Aldridge, also weakened the civilian acquisition management structure that OSD had set up in the Navy and the other services. Guided by the recommendations of the Packard Commission

---

[109] Ibid., pp. 40, 42 (quotation).

for a single, unified acquisition, Godwin wanted each of the newly appointed service acquisition executives to report directly to him rather than through Lehman, Aldridge, and Secretary of the Army John Marsh. This adjustment, he concluded, would eliminate a bureaucratic layer from the reporting structure and put him in a more effective position to manage weapons acquisition. Lehman and Aldridge flatly rejected the proposed reorganization. So did Donald Hicks, former under secretary of defense for research and engineering, who observed, "If they [the service acquisition executives] report directly to the under secretary [Godwin], I am not sure I understand why they [the Army, the Navy, and the Air Force] have service secretaries," implying oddly that the policy, personnel, logistics, financial management, and advocacy roles of the service secretaries were insignificant. Meanwhile, Aldridge suggested that Godwin's new reporting arrangement would "separate those people that have acquisition responsibility from those people who have the responsibility for operating the forces once they are fully developed and deployed. It's like the White House directing an assistant secretary of defense without telling Weinberger . . . and that wouldn't fly more than about two seconds."[110] Godwin shot back by pointing out that he did not want to control individual weapon programs. To the contrary, his intent all along had been to streamline the management structure to ensure accurate and timely reporting of data to avoid problems in major programs. Perhaps troubled by Aldridge's comment, Godwin replied more directly in the *Washington Post,* "[W]e can't have a decision based simply on how glib a service secretary is or how good his slide presentation is."[111]

As he had done for Lehman during the Deadeye controversy, Taft sided with Aldridge. After consulting Pentagon lawyers, and receiving tacit approval from Weinberger, Taft concluded that Godwin's reorganization plan illegally appropriated the power of the service secretaries and would have to be altered. While Godwin retained management control over acquisition functions, the service acquisition executives reported directly to the service secretaries, who then reported to the USD (A).[112] But Godwin's authority also suffered from service opposition to the management hierarchy at the working level. Here too, the Air Force proved to be a formidable adversary.

While Aldridge opposed Godwin's policies at the senior management level, evidence suggests that ongoing efforts to integrate

---

[110] Donald Hicks and Edward Aldridge quoted in R. J. Smith and M. Moore, "Pentagon Purchasing Chief to Quit," *Washington Post,* 14 September 1987.

[111] Richard Godwin quoted in Smith and Moore, "Pentagon Purchasing Chief to Quit."

[112] Kitfield, "Godwin: Battling the Powers That Be," p. 61.

the new three-tiered acquisition management organization into the Air Force's existing procurement structure proceeded slowly and showed mixed results. "Although there have been some organizational changes in the Air Force's combined [military-civilian] acquisition organization[s]," the GAO's Thurman told the House Subcommittee on Investigations in the spring of 1988, "there appears to be little integration of the previous secretariat and military staffs." Thurman elaborated:

> Acquisition personnel previously assigned to the Deputy Chief of Staff for Research, Development, and Acquisition continue to function much as they did before the reorganization—formulating acquisition policy, reviewing procurement documents, performing day-to-day acquisition program integration functions with other secretariat and military staff organizations, developing acquisition budget estimates, and responding to congressional and other external requests for Air Force acquisition information. The most significant change in these organizations is that they now report to the Assistant Secretary [of Defense] for Acquisition, and he appears to be much more involved in the day-to-day activities of managing Air Force acquisition programs.[113]

Thurman also explained that the Air Force's progress lagged behind that of the other services, especially the Army: "The Air Force Chief of Staff continues to play an active role in the acquisition process. Documents are routinely routed to the chief of staff's office for approval or coordination. In the Army, officials characterize the chief's involvement as significantly reduced. The Army Staff no longer routinely reviews the paperwork supporting many acquisition-related actions."[114]

The following year, Frank C. Conahan, the GAO's assistant comptroller general (National Security and International Affairs Division), confirmed that all three of the services had merely overlaid the three-tiered acquisition structure onto their existing management organizations. Even the Army, which the GAO had credited with integrating the Packard Commission reforms more completely than the Air Force and Navy, did not escape criticism. "The Army's [new civilian] acquisition chain is dependent upon resources of the existing [military] command chain to manage and

---

[113] U.S. Congress, House, statement of William W. Thurman before the Subcommittee on Investigations, Committee on Armed Services, *Reorganization of the Military Departments' Acquisition Management Structures*, 20 April 1988, pp. 18–19.

[114] Ibid., pp. 19–20.

execute programs," Conahan reported in testimony given before Senator Gary Hart's Congressional Military Reform Caucus in August 1989.[115]

The GAO found much to criticize in service efforts to implement the acquisition reforms recommended by the Packard Commission and required by law in the Goldwater-Nichols Act. Indeed, the seemingly intractable conflicts between Richard Godwin and Secretaries Lehman and Aldridge corroborate some of what the GAO had to say about the level of service compliance. By late summer 1987, two years before the GAO's Conahan testified before the Military Reform Caucus, rumors abounded in Washington that Godwin, frustrated by his dealings with Lehman and Aldridge and the general slow pace of organizational reform in the services, had decided to leave the Pentagon. Perhaps in response to these problems, Packard told Reagan directly that the USD (A) had not been given sufficient authority to manage the weapons acquisition process.[116] Commenting on his brief tenure as USD (A), Godwin acknowledged, "When we brought in a new system and superimposed it on top of the current one we came down on everyone's toes." In mid-September 1987, Godwin told the *Baltimore Sun*, "I haven't been able to carry out the recommendations of the Packard Commission."[117] Later that year, after Godwin resigned, Weinberger, in one of his last acts before stepping down as defense secretary, appointed Robert Costello, assistant secretary of defense for acquisition and logistics and previously the head of materials procurement at the General Motors Corporation, as under secretary of defense for acquisition.[118]

THE LEGACY OF 1980S WEAPONS ACQUISITION REFORM

In 1992, former Deputy Secretary of Defense Frank Carlucci reflected on the significance and impact of weapons acquisition reform during the 1980s. Given his role as one of the major architects

---

[115] Statement of Frank C. Conahan, Assistant Comptroller General (National Security and International Affairs Division, GAO) before the Congressional Military Reform Caucus, *Defense Management: Streamlining the Acquisition Process*, 2 August 1989, p. 2.

[116] GAO Report, *Status of Recommendations by Blue Ribbon Commission on Defense Management*, GAO/NSIAD–89–19FS, Nov 1988, pp. 30–31.

[117] Richard Godwin quoted in Smith and Moore, "Pentagon Purchasing Chief to Quit."

[118] V. A. Guidry Jr., "Pentagon Procurement Chief Quits, Says 'Business as Usual' Foiled Reforms," *Baltimore Sun*, 0 September 1987, p. 6 (quotation). On Robert Costello and his policies, see, for example, "Acquisition Reform Under Costello," *National Security Record* (March 1989): 2–3; News Release, 9 Mar 1989, sub: Improving the Acquisition Process, OSD Historical Office; Memo, R. Costello for Distribution List, 15 Feb 1989, OSD Historical Office. Costello's tenure as USD (A) is also discussed in Philip L. Shiman's Volume V of the Defense Acquisition History series, currently in draft.

of the Defense Department's Acquisition Improvement Program earlier in the decade, it is perhaps not surprising that he leveled the sharpest criticism at those would-be reformers in Congress who attempted to change the weapons acquisition system from the outside in response to widespread allegations of waste, fraud, and mismanagement in the Pentagon:

> The magic isn't in reform. People like to talk about reform. If you reform the Pentagon every year, it will never function properly. The proper words are stability, consistency, long-range planning and buying on the basis of quality, not just price. . . . It is not a problem of overpricing or spare parts. That takes pieces of the problem instead of standing back and looking at the forest. . . . Everybody wants to grab a chunk. [Senator] Barbara Boxer wants to create a separate procurement agency; [Senator Charles] Grassley wants to strengthen the whistle-blowers. The more you chip away at the pieces, the more complex and cumbersome the system becomes, and the more abuses you are going to have in it. You need to simplify the system, put it on a stable course, and express some confidence in it. . . . You will find that costs will go down enormously.[119]

While perhaps overly optimistic about the anticipated cost reductions for weapon systems and no doubt benefiting from hindsight, Carlucci nevertheless had a point. Greater oversight of weapons programs and monitoring of contractor compliance did expose cases of fraud, waste, and mismanagement, but increased scrutiny also introduced institutional rigidity and instability into the acquisition process, typically leading to higher unit costs and extended production schedules. The conflicting motivations, mismatched priorities, and institutional rivalries behind the actions of Congress, the White House, and the Pentagon also constrained the acquisition system's flexibility.[120] The establishment of the Office of the Under Secretary of Defense for Acquisition may have made lasting reform possible, but only to the extent that these three constituencies were able to work together to change the incentives reinforcing the behavior patterns long established in contractor plants and in the government acquisition workforce. The long-term backing required to improve the chances of a positive outcome for

---

[119] Frank C. Carlucci, "Looking Back: Reflections by Former Secretaries of Defense," December 1992, OSD Historical Office, p. 32.

[120] David D. Acker, "Issues and Actions Affecting the Systems Acquisition Process (July 1983–July 1984)," *Program Manager* 13 (September-October 1984): 36. See also William E. Kovacic, "The Sorcerer's Apprentice: Public Regulation of the Weapons Acquisition Process," in *Arms, Politics, and the Economy: Historical and Contemporary Perspectives*, ed. Robert Higgs (New York: Holms and Meier, 1990).

acquisition reform, for example, might exceed the short-term political compromises required by legislators to remain in office.[121]

During Ronald Reagan's first term in the White House, the Weinberger team had transformed the internal mechanisms of the weapon system acquisition process to handle more efficiently the rapid growth in defense spending, only to see the results of their efforts—decentralized execution of acquisition policy in the military services—assaulted from all sides by Congress, the Military Reform Caucus, and other reformers after the president won re-election in 1984. Clearly, the demands for change in the way the Pentagon did business proved exceedingly difficult to implement at the working level in the services where the acquisition workforce had limited training and few incentives to change their way of operating.

In its interim progress report to President Reagan, the Packard Commission acknowledged the central premise of the Acquisition Improvement Program. "In general," the report concluded, "Congress should permit the Secretary [of Defense] to organize his Office as he chooses to accomplish centralized policy formulation and decentralized implementation within the Department."[122] Putting aside his initial hostility to the commission's deliberations as a corrective action for what some observers interpreted as his own managerial shortcomings, Weinberger did not enjoy the discretionary freedom suggested in the report. Congress' expectations for acquisition reform turned out to be very different from his own. Pentagon critics wanted the under secretary of defense for acquisition to have broad powers of authority over weapons procurement, whereas Weinberger, his subordinates in OSD, and especially the secretaries and chiefs of staff of the services favored the status quo or at least a far more circumscribed role for the USD (A). Richard Godwin's brief and tumultuous tenure as the USD (A) illustrates the extent to which these differences manifested themselves and complicated relations between his office and the services. But perhaps nowhere were the mismatched priorities between Congress and the Pentagon more evident than in the caustic reactions of the Army, Navy, and Air Force to the three-tiered acquisition organization recommended by the Packard Commission. They strongly opposed constraints on their own acquisition decisions and the imposition of a new management structure that transferred weapons acquisition authority to a civilian executive in OSD. It also shifted

---

[121] On this point, see Kovacic, "Blue Ribbon Defense Commissions: The Acquisition of Major Weapon Systems."

[122] President's Blue Ribbon Commission on Defense Management, *An Interim Report to the President,* p. 6 (quotation). See also Ltr, D. Packard to the President, 28 Feb 1986, copy in OSD Historical Office.

line management of weapons acquisition from the offices of the chiefs of staff to civilian managers—headed by the service acquisition executives—outside the military chain of command.

1980s RETROSPECTIVE

Few people have been as dedicated to improving the acquisition process as David Packard. Although he did not forget what had proved successful for him at Hewlett-Packard, there were crucial differences between that company and the government. At Hewlett-Packard, large numbers of career professionals were skilled in managing development and production programs and highly motivated to reduce costs to produce profits. In the Defense Department, acquisition managers normally incur penalties, not rewards, for failing to expend at least their entire budget. At Hewlett-Packard, there were strong incentives for performing work at or below budget. In government, a successful agency is usually expected to increase, not decrease, its budget year after year. Therefore, positive evaluations go to acquisition managers in the military service who achieve their technical performance objectives, spend the money allotted in one year and can justify an increase for the next year, while incurring the least amount of opposition.[123]

In 1986, the Packard Commission characterized the defense acquisition process as expensive, inefficient, and cumbersome. It observed that "the increasing complexity of the process means unnecessary delays are incurred in acquiring needed goods and supplies and that higher costs are paid for what is acquired." In brief, the Packard Commission concluded that "the defense acquisition process is not being operated and managed effectively, and that this is having a disastrous effect on the cost and efficiency of the system."[124]

As noted earlier, the problem with any reform recommendation that rests on DoD reorganization is that the underlying counterproductive incentives usually remain unchanged. The Defense Department has grown accustomed to reorganizations; they occur at least once every four years. A DoD acquisition manual stated:

> The central cry heard in the halls of the Pentagon when things go wrong is reorganize, restructure the management system. Some think that if enough organizational boxes or enough people are moved, the problem will go away. Of course, it doesn't, yet those responsible for creating the organizational mess think so. Consequently, we are left with a legacy that only grows worse with time.

---

[123] "The Pentagon: Waste Probers Faulted," *Boston Globe*, 27 July 1986.
[124] President's Blue Ribbon Commission on Defense Management, *A Quest for Excellence*, June 1986, cited in Yoder and Horbaly, pp. 7–10.

Why is this the case? Most probably because it is the path of least resistance.[125]

In considering improvements to the acquisition process, one may do well to remember that there is no sovereign power in Washington; instead, there are many independent powers. It is easier to block the policy initiatives of others than to translate one's own initiatives into action.[126]

Acquisition reforms up to 1987 tended to attack the symptoms of cost increases, not their causes, and at best have been only partially implemented. They have left the basic negative incentives for government and industry personnel largely undisturbed.

---

[125] U.S. Department of Defense (DoD) Manual 4245.7-M, *Transition from Development to Production*, Assistant Secretary of Defense for Acquisition and Logistics, September 1985, p. 1-3.

[126] Robert J. Art, "Bureaucratic Politics and American Foreign Policy: A Critique," *Policy Sciences*, December 1973, cited by Bradburn, "Strategic Postures in the Military Aircraft Industry," p. 8.

CHAPTER FOUR

ACQUISITION REFORM FROM 1990 TO 2000

Significant cost growth and schedule slippages on major defense acquisition programs continued to occur during the two decades from 1990 to 2009, although this chapter will focus on 1990 to 2000. In 1993, the administration of William J. "Bill" Clinton came into office with high hopes for reforming the defense acquisition process, and though it left an uncertain legacy, it was a sustained eight-year effort to achieve that goal.

Inspired by new ideas in management, the Clinton administration adopted "reinventing government" as its mantra and called for the improvement of government processes, including procurement, through streamlining and the application of technologies such as computers and data networks. Secretary of Defense Leslie "Les" Aspin came to the Pentagon from the U.S. House of Representatives with concerns that acquisition cost and schedule problems would threaten the ability of the military services to continue to acquire the latest high technology of the kind that had performed so impressively during the Persian Gulf War. He brought with him from the House Armed Services Committee his "resource strategy," which proposed ways that DoD might afford such technology in an era of lean budgets and reduced force structure.

Yet it was William J. Perry in 1993 who, as deputy secretary and later as secretary of defense, would become the driving force behind the acquisition reform program that marked DoD during the Clinton years. Perry came to office from the defense industry with many fully formed ideas about what needed to be done to reform the acquisition process. These stemmed from his long and impressive experience with defense acquisition, as a DoD official, an industrialist, and as a member of the Packard Commission. When Perry left the Pentagon in 1981 as under secretary of defense for research and engineering, he was proud of his role in promoting the development of more sophisticated weapon systems, but he also regretted his failure to tackle the problem of acquisition reform.[1] Reforming the acquisition process subsequently became one of his primary concerns. His next opportunity came a few years later when David Packard, chairman of the President's Blue Ribbon Commission on Defense

---

[1] Ashton B. Carter and William J. Perry, *Preventive Defense: A New Security Strategy for America* (Washington, D.C.: Brookings Institution Press, 1999), p. 181.

Management, asked him to lead the acquisition task force. Perry seized that opportunity, and under his leadership, the acquisition portions of the Packard Commission report became one of the more influential acquisition reform documents ever published. Perry called the report a "blueprint for transforming the acquisition system." Some of his recommendations were implemented—the creation of an "acquisition czar," the adoption of a streamlined acquisition organization, and improvement in workforce training, standards, and career management—but implementing these and other recommendations proved to be a difficult challenge. Most notably, the Pentagon had made little progress in expanding its use of commercial products and practices—the fundamental theme of the report.[2]

Perry was determined to see acquisition reform carried through. "[M]y passion for this goal was my principle reason for returning to DoD," he explained in 1984 to the Business Executives for National Security (BENS), an industry group.[3] He told a colleague at the time that he wanted to leave a legacy of change, especially tearing down the "Chinese firewall" between civilian and defense procurement processes.[4] When he recruited John M. Deutch in 1993 to be the under secretary for acquisition, the first thing they talked about was acquisition reform.[5] Perry's first action after being confirmed as deputy secretary of defense, he later recalled, "was to pull this blueprint (Chinese firewall) off the shelf and use it to lay out the department's plan of action for acquisition reform."[6]

Perry started the program cautiously, initially focusing the department's efforts on concrete steps and near-term measures. He spoke of his goals freely and earnestly and did not downplay the obstacles. "[T]he acquisition reform agenda I described to you will be very difficult to implement. I have no illusions on that point," he explained to the House Armed Services Committee in June 1993.[7] He

---

[2] Ibid., pp. 180–83. See also the President's Blue Ribbon Commission on Defense Management, *A Quest for Excellence: Final Report to the President,* June 1986, pp. 52–71; idem, *National Security Planning and Budgeting: A Report to the President,* June 1986, pp. 20–21. For more on the Blue Ribbon Panel's recommendations, see Chapter 3, above.

[3] Ltr, Secretary of Defense [William J.] Perry to Friends [Business Executives for National Security], 12 Apr 1994, William J. Perry Papers, Disk 2, Office of the Secretary of Defense (OSD) Historical Office, Washington, D.C.

[4] "Running the Pentagon—Aspin Style," *Navy News & Undersea Technology* (27 September 1993).

[5] U.S. Congress, Senate, Committee on Governmental Affairs and Committee on Armed Services, *Federal Acquisition Streamlining Act of 1993: Joint Hearings on S. 1587,* 103d Cong., 2d sess., 1994, p. 19.

[6] Carter and Perry, *Preventive Defense,* pp. 183–84 (quotation).

[7] U.S. Congress, House, Committee on Armed Services, *Acquisition Reform: Fact or Fiction,* 103d Cong., 1st sess., HASC No. 103-26, 1994, Hearing before the Military Acquisition Subcommittee, 15 June 1993, pp. 6–7, 12–13.

rejected suggestions that he convene a blue ribbon panel to launch the program. "I agree with you that the opposition to reform is entrenched and powerful," he told BENS. "But I am skeptical that an independent commission, like the Base Realignment and Closure Commission, is the best way to overcome this resistance . . . [w]e certainly don't need another commission to study the problem yet again."[8] Perry received much support in Congress, which had long been prodding DoD to pursue reforms. But not unexpectedly, there was skepticism as well—the hearing at which Perry testified in June was entitled *Acquisition Reform: Fact or Fiction.*

A Mandate for Change

Perry finally answered that question on 9 February 1994, in the form of a white paper he delivered to the House Armed Services Committee at a hearing on acquisition reform. He had been secretary of defense for only six days. (As secretary, Perry succeeded Les Aspin, who left office on 3 February 1994 for health reasons.) Seated next to Perry was a member of his staff, Colleen A. Preston, making her first appearance on Capitol Hill as the deputy under secretary of defense for acquisition reform. Aspin and Perry created this new position to provide a full-time focus for their acquisition reform efforts and, perhaps, to underscore their serious commitment to change.

The eighteen-page paper, entitled "Acquisition Reform: A Mandate for Change," laid out the themes that by now were familiar to those who had been listening to Perry. Referring to the Bottom-Up Review, DoD's vision for the U.S. armed services announced the previous fall, Perry stated flatly, "DoD will not be able to carry out this blueprint, without dramatic changes in its acquisition processes—from determining what the Department needs, to logistics support and reutilization requirements." Change, he declared, "is imperative." DoD was losing access to state-of-the-art technology, it could not buy from commercial companies, and its costs of doing business were just too high. To fulfill its mission, DoD needed to be able to maintain its technological edge while reducing its costs. Maintaining that edge required breaking down the barriers that deterred or prevented commercial firms from selling the latest technologies to the government and promoting the integration of the civilian and military industrial sectors. Costs were to be reduced by modernizing the Pentagon's business practices and reducing the unnecessary costs imposed on contractors by government-unique contract terms, burdensome oversight, and arcane (and archaic) military specifications and

---

[8] Ltr, Perry to Friends [Business Executives for National Security], 12 Apr 1994.

standards that encouraged inefficient business practices. To address these problems, DoD must reengineer its acquisition system in three crucial areas: requirements determination and resource allocation (i.e., what to buy); the acquisition process (i.e., how to buy); and contract terms and conditions.[9]

"A Mandate for Change" was little more than a statement of principles, but it had a significant effect. It impressed many in the defense community—the uniformed services, the civilian workforce, and industry—that the DoD leadership was serious about the subject and was giving it high-level attention. Perry, an effective business manager, who knew exactly what he wanted if not yet how to get it, was firmly committed to acquisition reform. Perry, along with Colleen Preston and others worked tirelessly—persuading, cajoling, teaching—to instill their vision in others. The intricacies of Perry's plans were unclear to many in the acquisition workforce, but the message they heard was to perform acquisition "faster, better, cheaper": products must be acquired faster, they must be better quality, and they must become cheaper. The major challenge was finding ways to achieve those goals. Implicit in this mantra was the philosophy of Total Quality Management: the process can *always* be improved. "Faster, better, cheaper" became the unofficial vision for acquisition reform, first in parts of the services, later in parts of OSD itself.[10]

ORGANIZING THE REFORM PROCESS

Possibly the two most important actions that Perry chose to launch the acquisition reform program were to create the position of deputy under secretary for acquisition reform and to appoint Colleen Preston to it. Preston was a long-time staff member of the House Armed Services Committee (HASC) who came to the Pentagon with her HASC boss, Congressman Les Aspin. Preston seemed ideal for the job. She had both Pentagon and congressional experience and a strong background in acquisition and acquisition reform issues. A lawyer by training, she had spent four years in the Department of the Air Force, where she advised the secretariat and the Air Staff on contracting and other acquisition matters. In 1983, she joined the HASC staff, rising to general counsel. During her ten years with the HASC, she had a hand in many of the key acquisition reform studies and legislation, including the Competi-

---

[9] Paper, Secretary of Defense William J. Perry, "Acquisition Reform: A Mandate for Change," n.p., 9 February 1994.

[10] Charles L. Beck Jr., Nina Lyn Brokaw, and Brian A. Kelmar, *A Model for Leading Change: Making Acquisition Reform Work*, Report of the DSMC [Defense Systems Management College] Military Research Fellows, 1996–1997 (Fort Belvoir, Va.: Defense Systems Management College Press, December 1997), ch. 5, p. 10.

tion in Contracting Act, the Defense Procurement Act of 1984, the Defense Procurement Improvement Acts of 1985 and 1986, and the Defense Acquisition Workforce Improvement Act. She was a leading proponent of the effort to catalog and overhaul the acquisition statutes, culminating in the establishment of the Section 800 Panel for which she served as an adviser and liaison with the HASC.[11] One of her first tasks on coming to the Pentagon was to plan the organization of the new acquisition reform office. Perry and Deutch chose her to be the deputy under secretary because, Perry would write, she is "one of the toughest, most informed, and most committed professionals we know."[12] She was officially confirmed in that position on 24 June 1993.[13] She later described her activities in *Program Manager* magazine:

> We started off initially with following up on the Section 800 Panel recommendations because we believed that we had a one-time opportunity to take advantage of what the panel recommended and we had a receptive Congress. For the first year we practically did nothing but focus on that legislative effort day-to-day. . . . Then we started working the Process Action Teams [PATs], and we worked the ones that we believed were most critical. We started with electronic commerce because that was critical to our ability to get the simplified acquisition threshold increase. And we had to know what we were capable of doing within the Department in terms of electronic commerce before we could make commitments that Congress wanted us to make in return for increasing that threshold.
>
> Then, of course, one of Dr. Perry's (Secretary of Defense February 1994–January 1997) primary objectives was to deal with the Specifications and Standards issue, which we took on as our second Process Action Team.
>
> And then in terms of priorities, we looked at contract administration, the procurement process, and oversight and review of the systems acquisition process. That particular PAT process was very difficult because it focused on the relationship between OSD and the services in terms of oversight. It's a lot easier to talk about our oversight of industry, but when you get into the inter-

---

[11] The Section 800 Panel was chartered by Section 800 of the National Defense Authorization Act for fiscal year 1991 to assess laws affecting defense procurement, to encourage the use of commercial and non-developmental items, and to expand the exemption for "adequate price competition" in the Truth in Negotiations Act.

[12] Ltr, Perry to Friends [Business Executives for National Security], 12 Apr 1994.

[13] Colleen A. Preston biographical data. Files are in the office of Philip Shiman, OSD Historical Office, Washington, D.C.

personal reviews that occur within the Pentagon, it's much more challenging.[14]

Preston would be responsible for laying out the broad reform program, establishing the short- and long-term priorities and goals, formulating specific initiatives, planning for executing them, and then overseeing the implementation. To accomplish this mission, the deputy under secretary would direct or work with the various responsible offices in the Pentagon, from the secretary of defense down to the military departments where acquisition programs were conducted. She would also coordinate with the White House and other executive departments and agencies, an essential job given that reform was to span the executive branch and that many of the relevant regulations originated from outside DoD, especially in the Office of Federal Procurement Policy, a part of the Office of Management and Budget in the Office of the President. And, of course, she would work with Congress to formulate the necessary legislation and see it enacted into law. Finally, the deputy under secretary was given oversight of the Defense Acquisition University and the Defense Systems Management College, reflecting the new administration's view of the importance of training and education in changing the acquisition culture. The job was part planner, part manager, part salesperson, and part cheerleader.

Preston was responsible for "directing the conception, development, adoption, implementation, and institutionalization of new and innovative acquisition policies and processes." She was not burdened with the day-to-day problems of acquisition management and contracting, which continued to be conducted and controlled by the military services.[15]

Preston's office was deliberately small, only about twenty-two people, including the president of the Defense Acquisition University and the commandant of the Defense Systems Management College. She received assistance from several groups. At the highest level, an Acquisition Reform Senior Steering Group, which she chaired, was to advise her in planning and implementing the reform agenda. The group nominally comprised fourteen senior OSD and service officials, although in practice it was made up of staff at

---

[14] Brig. Gen. Richard A. Black, "Colleen Preston on Acquisition Reform," *Program Manager* (Special Issue, January-February 1997): 22–31.

[15] Draft Memo, Deputy Secretary of Defense for Secretaries of the Military Departments, et al., n.d., sub: Strategic Plan for Acquisition Reform, attached to Memo, Colleen Preston, Deputy Under Secretary of Defense for Acquisition Reform (DUSD [AR]), to Deputy Secretary of Defense, 27 May 1993, sub: Proposed Strategic Plan to Pursue Acquisition Reform, with attached draft memo, Washington National Records Center (WNRC) 330–97–0030, USD (A) Chronological Files, 1993, filed under 28 May 1993 (hereafter cited as DUSD [AR], Proposed Strategic Plan).

the principal deputy level, and it acted more to disseminate information and speed up interoffice coordination than to make high-level decisions on its own. It met biweekly.[16] Most of the work of formulating the initiatives and devising specific proposals would fall to ad hoc process action teams (PATs) and working groups comprising members from throughout DoD. These PATs were intended to bring together workers with a range of experience and working-level expertise to plan the practical details of the reforms. PATs varied in size from roughly 25 to 50 members, with further assistance from research and support staff. The members represented a wide variety of line and staff organizations in the military services, defense agencies, and OSD. Most had working experience in the acquisition policy under consideration. They could also call on experts and officials from within and outside DoD. The work of each PAT was overseen by a board of advisers or "directors" comprising senior DoD officials. The experience of working on such a study with other practitioners was educational for the members. "As the PAT members shared their insights and experiences with each other, substantial differences emerged," the Procurement Process Reform PAT observed in its report. "Many PAT members with 15, 20, or more years of experience on the front lines of procurement who thought they had pretty much done it all or at least mostly seen it all had their eyes opened by the experiences of others."[17]

The PATs were not intended to perform their studies *de novo*. They were not to revisit the issues and draw new conclusions. Their focus was to find ways to implement policies that had largely been predetermined by the leadership. For example, the PAT studying specifications and standards was told in its charter exactly what the secretary wanted to accomplish and told in detail what was expected of it.[18] Each PAT was to follow a fifteen-step process

---

[16] Beck et al., *A Model for Leading Change*, ch. 5, pp. 3–5. The Acquisition Reform Senior Steering Group officially included the Vice Chairman of the Joint Chiefs of Staff; the DoD General Counsel; the DoD Comptroller; the DoD Inspector General; the Director of Defense Research and Engineering; the Director of Program Analysis and Evaluation; the Assistant Secretary for Command, Control, Communications, and Intelligence; the Director of the Defense Contract Audit Agency; the Directors of Defense Procurement and Acquisition Program Integration; the Service Acquisition Executives; and the Director of the Defense Logistics Agency.

[17] The report of the Contract Administration Reform Process Action Team listed almost two hundred individuals from DoD and industry as "contributors." See *Final Report of the Contract Administration Reform Process Action Team to the Under Secretary of Defense for Acquisition and Technology*, February 1995, pp. xi–xv (quotation).

[18] Memo, Preston for Perry (through USD [A]), 1 Sep 1993, sub: Process Action Team on Military Specifications and Standards—Information Memorandum, WNRC 330–97–0030, USD (A) Chronological File, 1993 (filed under 1 September 1993); *Blueprint for Change: Report of the Process Action Team on Military Specifications and Standards* (Washington, D.C.: Office of the Under Secretary of Defense for Acquisition and Technology, April 1994), app. A.

for analyzing the issue, deciding on the actions to be taken, and preparing a proposal for approval and implementation. It was given sixty or ninety days to complete its work and submit a report. The emphasis was on practical plans and concrete actions. PAT reports were to discuss the actions required to implement the policies, designate the agency or office that should be responsible for those actions, establish a timetable for implementation, and identify the expected resources and costs. In the case of specifications and standards, a second panel reviewed the PAT's report and prepared a new implementation plan that accepted most—but not all—of the PAT's recommendations.[19] If the Office of the Secretary of Defense (OSD) accepted a PAT report and plan, the secretary or the under secretary issued a memorandum explaining the policy and ordering its implementation in accordance with the plan. PATs dealt with program management, the procurement process, cost estimating, electronic commerce, specifications and standards, contract administration, and the use of commercial practices and components.

Finally, the task of implementing the reform program fell to the services. They developed their own acquisition reform organizations that worked closely with Preston's office. These offices were responsible for relaying the directives issued by OSD and translating them into initiatives to be applied by the service. Each service had its own set of initiatives: the Air Force had its "Lightning Bolts," the Navy had its "Cardinal Points," and the Army had its "Thrust Areas." The establishment of the reform offices, and the selection of pro-reform acquisition officials in the military departments, provided some measure of uniformity within the services and OSD, and minimized official resistance to their reform programs.

Tools for Reform

To conduct the acquisition reform program, Aspin, Perry, and Preston needed to accomplish several tasks: they had to test their ideas, measure and evaluate the results, and then disseminate the lessons learned to the entire acquisition community. To accomplish these tasks, the leaders had a variety of tools at their disposal. To try out their ideas, they had the Defense Acquisition Pilot Programs, which were similar in concept to the Defense Enterprise Programs established by Congress in 1986 to implement the Pack-

---

[19] *Implementation Plan for the Process Action Team Report on Specifications and Standards* (Washington, D.C.: Office of the Assistant Secretary of Defense for Economic Security, 23 June 1994).

ard Commission recommendations. Although the enterprise programs were offered relief from DoD regulations, policies, directives, and administrative rules, they were still required to follow the Federal Acquisition Regulation (FAR), the Defense FAR Supplement (DFARS), and existing procurement statutes. Believing that the enterprise programs were more trouble than they were worth and that ongoing reforms were providing the same regulatory relief, DoD showed little enthusiasm for the initiative and allowed it to lapse by 1990.

After urging from DoD, Congress passed the pilot program legislation, requiring DoD to collect and analyze data on contractor performance in the pilot programs. The law also specified some of the reforms that should be applied to one or more of the pilot programs, in the realm of contracting, program management, and workforce incentives. It called for DoD to use the lessons from the pilot programs to reduce the acquisition systems management and administrative costs by at least 25 percent by October 1998. These provisions, included as suggestions, were not binding on DoD. The Defense Department was largely given a free hand in managing the pilot programs, but it had to obtain approval not only for the selected programs but also for waiving applicable statutes for each program.[20]

Perry wanted the pilot programs approved and launched as quickly as possible, so choosing the candidate programs, submitting the nomination packages for submission to Congress, and suggesting legislation to the White House's Office of Management and Budget became one of Preston's top priorities.[21] Preston was looking for programs that were still early in their cycle, were assured of relatively stable funding, had an approved requirement, and had low technological risk. Of course, the prospective pilot programs had to be conducive to some aspect of acquisition reform; those that could satisfy their military requirement using commercial or non-developmental items were preferred.[22] Finding and selecting the programs proved difficult. Program managers of prospective pilot programs had to go to considerable effort to prepare a pilot program acquisition strategy, identify the laws and regulations to be waived, and justify the waivers (usually in terms of dollars saved)—all while preparing a standard acquisition strategy in the

---

[20] Public Law 103–160, *National Defense Authorization Act for Fiscal Year 1994*, secs. 831–39.

[21] Memo, DUSD (AR) Preston for Deputy Secretary of Defense Perry, 16 Jul 1993, sub: Status Report on Short Term Acquisition Reforms, WNRC 330–97–0030, USD (A) Chronological File (filed under 19 July 1993).

[22] Memo, USD (A) [John M.] Deutch for Secretaries of the Military Departments, et al., 21 Jul 1993, sub: Defense Acquisition Pilot Programs, WNRC 330–97–0030, USD (A) Chronological File.

event the application for pilot program status was rejected.[23] Ultimately, OSD selected six programs. The Joint Primary Aircraft Training System (JPATS), for example, was to demonstrate DoD's ability to procure a non-developmental aircraft using extensive commercial components. The Joint Direct Attack Munition (JDAM) would demonstrate the value of regulatory relief as well as a new approach to engineering called the integrated product and process development (IPPD).[24]

Preston hoped to have the nomination packages ready for Congress by the summer of 1993, but the selected programs were not submitted until October, the day the Federal Acquisition Streamlining Act was introduced.[25] Congress folded the pilot programs into the bill, which then took another year to pass. In the meantime, DoD began the pilot programs but could waive only internal regulations, not statutory or FAR requirements.

The DoD reformers wanted more than just surveys and anecdotal evidence on the success of the reform program. They devoted considerable attention to the development of metrics, objective yardsticks with which to track and judge the progress of reform initiatives.[26] Critical to the acquisition reform effort, the use of metrics would demonstrate to Congress and (no less importantly) to the workforce that the reform effort could achieve results. Furthermore, OSD needed to know as early as possible how the effort to streamline its processes to save time, money, and personnel, largely driven by the relentless pressure of the declining defense budget, was affecting the ability of the acquisition system to fulfill

---

[23] U.S. Congress, House, Committee on Government Reform and Oversight, *Oversight of Implementation of Federal Acquisition Streamlining Act of 1994*, 104th Cong., 1st sess., 1995, p. 53.

[24] Memo, Preston for Perry, 16 Jul 1993.

[25] DUSD (AR), Proposed Strategic Plan; U.S. Congress, Senate, Armed Services Committee, Subcommittee on Defense Technology, Acquisition, and Industrial Base, *Department of Defense Authorization . . . National Defense Authorization Act, Fiscal Year 1994*, p. 449.

[26] A metric was any concrete measurement that could be compared to a standard or starting point (a benchmark) and with other data over time, to indicate a trend. Examples of metrics include unit procurement or life-cycle costs, the length of the acquisition cycle from program start to production, contractor overhead, production lead time from contract award to delivery. Any statistic that could be calculated, input into a database, and displayed on a spreadsheet or chart could conceivably be used as a metric. There were essentially three kinds of metrics: (1) "go/no-go" metrics that simply recorded whether an event had occurred—whether a report had been issued, for example, or a particular developmental milestone was passed; (2) "activity" metrics that determined the extent to which an activity was taking place, such as the use of commercial or non-developmental items in the development of a given system; and (3) "effectiveness" metrics that measured whether the actions being taken were leading to the desired results. See *Final Report of the Contract Administration Reform Process Action Team to the Under Secretary of Defense for Acquisition and Technology*, February 1995, ch. 3, p. 21.

its mission.[27] Finally, a set of suitable metrics was mandated by the Government Performance and Results Act of 1993, the first in a series of landmark measures to promote efficiency and accountability in government.[28] The act required federal agencies to prepare strategic plans identifying long-term goals, link those long-term goals to short-term goals in annual performance plans, and issue annual reports on their success at meeting those goals. Although most agencies, including DoD, were not required to present their strategic plans until September 1997 and their performance plans until 2000, the deadlines provided added pressure to devise a set of suitable metrics for measuring the progress of acquisition reform programs and to ensure that the means were in place to collect and evaluate the necessary data.[29]

The development of accurate and meaningful metrics was challenging. It was often difficult to connect goals with statistics that were easily collected and calculated, especially if the goal was unclear and subjective, or if it involved improving a process. Furthermore, the complexity and varied nature of acquisition programs made it difficult to find standard metrics for them. Ideally, metrics would be tailored for each program to be meaningful. Yet how would DoD devise metrics at the enterprise level—that is, giving trends for the entire acquisition system—when the "subordinate metrics" varied from program to program and from activity to activity? Finally, the metrics had to measure the progress of a program or initiative while it was still under way, which was far more difficult to do than analyzing the results after the fact. One could never be quite certain that a measurement of progress was in fact showing any progress.[30]

The first attempts to devise metrics for the early reforms demonstrated these problems. Preston directed that the process action teams must identify the metrics for any reforms they proposed. Most suggested some objective measures such as statistics on the number of users of a new technique or system, or the number of entries in a database, or the number of design specifications converted to

---

[27] "AR's Benchmarking Initiative," *Acquisition Reform Today* 3, no. 1 (Jan/Feb 1998): 1.

[28] Public Law 103–62, *Government Performance and Results Act of 1993*, enacted 3 August 1993.

[29] U.S. Congress, Senate, Committee on Governmental Affairs, *Government Performance and Results Act* [GPRA] *of 1993*, 103d Cong., 1st sess., 16 June 1993, S. Rpt 103–58, pp. 28–29; "GPRA Spurs Efforts to Measure Results," *Acquisition Reform Today* 2, no. 4 (July/August 1997): 1, 7.

[30] Aron Pinker, Charles G. Smith, and Jack Booher, "Selecting Effective Acquisition Process Metrics," *Acquisition Review Quarterly* 4 (Spring 1997): 189–91. See also Joseph Kevin Pope, "Measuring the Effect of the Defense Acquisition Workforce Improvement Act" (Master's thesis: Naval Postgraduate School, June 1997), p. 25.

performance specifications. The metrics could be dollars saved (which were difficult to determine, given the other possible variables) or positions eliminated (probably not a happy idea for the front-line workers participating in the PATs). Furthermore, the relationship between the metrics and the ultimate goals they were measuring were frequently unclear. Some PATs responded to the task vaguely—even the practitioners sometimes did not know what to look for. Customer satisfaction was indeed a key element of many of these reforms, to end the longstanding hostility between line commands and procurement offices. But customer satisfaction was a subjective and even nebulous yardstick that might give little indication of what was actually being measured, especially if the customers did not fully understand the goals of a given reform. In general, the identification of useful and appropriate metrics proved to be an ongoing problem. Indeed, the effort revealed a weakness in the process of implementing any acquisition initiatives, for without good metrics of some sort, failure was likely.[31]

A more organized approach to developing metrics began in April 1995 when the Defense Standards Improvement Council formed the Tiger Team on Metrics. The tiger team proposed a set of twenty-three strategic outcome metrics for measuring the impact of acquisition reform.[32] The metrics were divided into four general categories relating to cost, acquisition technical performance, schedule, and training, and included algorithms for calculating them. The team evidently chose these particular metrics because they were easy to collect.[33]

Preston established the Acquisition Reform Benchmarking Initiative in September 1995 to finalize and track metrics related to progress in achieving acquisition reform. This effort was the responsibility of the Acquisition Reform Benchmarking Group, which superseded the tiger team. After reviewing the metrics efforts within DoD, in other federal agencies, and in the commercial sector, the group devised its own hierarchy of metrics. This framework included

---

[31] Pinker, Smith, and Booher, "Selecting Effective Acquisition Process Metrics," p. 191.

[32] The term *tiger team* originally referred to an ad hoc group of experts who tested the security of facilities or computer systems by trying to break in. More recently, and in the sense used here, it refers to a group called in to provide expert analysis of a particular problem or system design.

[33] Briefing, "Acquisition Reform: Tiger Team on Metrics, April 1995-August 1995," 19 Sep 1996, copy in the files of Philip Shiman, OSD Historical Office. See also Pinker, Smith, and Booher, "Selecting Effective Acquisition Process Metrics," pp. 191–92, 206. In 1996, the tiger team won the Heroes of Reinvention Hammer Award from the National Performance Review for its metrics work ("Acquisition Reform Efforts Win Hammer Award," DoD News Release No. 542-96, 20 September 1996).

three levels: enterprise metrics, used to assess the efficiency gains of the total acquisition process; subordinate or "process" metrics, used to measure the subordinate tasks or elements that contributed to enterprise metrics; and program metrics, used to measure factors relating to specific acquisition programs. The enterprise metrics were further subdivided into cost metrics, schedule metrics, training metrics, and technical performance metrics.[34]

The quest for useful metrics remained a problem throughout the 1990s. In December 1996, during the waning days of the first Clinton administration, Under Secretary Paul Kaminski worried that "while we are making good progress with our acquisition reform initiatives, there are few good measures of that progress." He solicited suggestions from senior DoD acquisition officials for metrics, focusing on two areas: cycle-time reduction and program stability. In 1999 even the Defense Science Board was called in to study the problem. The DoD leadership understood that the reform program had to show results and that in order to do that, it needed a yardstick.[35] Metrics were adopted but the acquisition problems of schedule slippage, cost growth and technical performance shortfalls persisted.

Finally, Preston and her staff organized a "communications program" to publicize the results of acquisition reform and disseminate the lessons to the workforce.[36] This was a key part of the acquisition reform effort because the reformers believed that its success or failure depended on the attitude and actions of the workers. "I am firmly convinced that fundamental reform will not occur unless those who are part of the existing system participate in developing and implementing the changes," Perry wrote in the memorandum announcing the acquisition reform program to DoD. "DoD will not succeed in fundamentally re-engineering the acquisition system unless those 'on the front line' of the acquisition

---

[34] Memo, DUSD (AR) Preston, 3 Sep 1996 [misfiled under 18 Sep 1995], sub: Acquisition Reform Benchmarking Initiative Charter; Acquisition Reform Benchmarking Group, *1997 Final Report*, 30 June 1997, ch. 1, copy in the files of Philip Shiman, OSD Historical Office. See also Pinker, Smith, and Booher, "Selecting Effective Acquisition Process Metrics," p. 192; Pope, "Measuring the Effect of the Defense Acquisition Workforce Improvement Act," pp. 35–56; Curtis K. Munechika, "Acquisition Reform: 'This, Too, Shall Pass...?' " (Research paper, Air Command and Staff College, March 1997), pp. 55–60.

[35] Munechika, "Acquisition Reform," p. 55; Memo, USD (A&T) [Under Secretary of Defense for Acquisition and Technology] Kaminski for PDUSD (A&T) [Principal Deputy Under Secretary of Defense for Acquisition and Technology] et al., 3 Dec 1996, sub: Metrics for Measuring Acquisition Reform, copy in the files of Philip Shiman, OSD Historical Office; Defense Science Board, *Report of the Defense Science Board Task Force on Acquisition Reform Phase IV* (Washington, D.C.: Office of the Under Secretary of Defense for Acquisition and Technology, July 1999).

[36] "E-Mail Bulletin Added to Effort for AR Info," *Acquisition Reform Today* 1 (March-April 1996): 4.

process embrace this effort. I know they are the experts, not those of us sitting in the Pentagon."³⁷

One approach to engaging the workforce was through the publication of periodicals. For discussion of broader acquisition issues, including reform, the *Acquisition Review Quarterly* was founded in 1994; the lead article in its first issue was a piece by Preston entitled "Acquisition Reform: Making It a Reality."³⁸ In early 1996, Preston's office began publication of a bimonthly newsletter, *Acquisition Reform Today*. Yet Preston also made use of the new media that were becoming more widespread. A month after *Acquisition Reform Today* appeared, Preston's office began emailing bulletins called *Acquisition Reform Now*, with brief notices on key reform news, events, and links to relevant World Wide Web pages.

The most significant of these communications projects was the Defense Acquisition Deskbook, a digital compendium of reference materials and how-to guides. First released in July 1996, the Deskbook was distributed on a CD-ROM, by download from the Internet, and via the World Wide Web. Instead of fishing through endless volumes of bulky binders for critical information, acquisition workers could now search and read up-to-date information in a user-friendly format on their desktop workstations. The Deskbook, which was updated quarterly, applied to all DoD components. It included mandatory guidelines, lessons learned, tips and hints about successful business practices, a reference library, and a feature called "Ask a Professor," in which workers could ask Defense Acquisition University professors about current acquisition policies and procedures.³⁹

Preston relied on more than passive means of communication. She and her staff tirelessly disseminated the message of reform through speeches, traveling "road shows," and other events. She spent increasing amounts of time visiting front-line workers in various offices. Under Secretary Kaminski designated 31 May 1996 as Acquisition Reform Acceleration Day. The workforce was expected to spend the day listening to lectures and participating in training exercises, workshops, and roundtable discussions. (The workers'

---

[37] Memo, Secretary of Defense Perry for Distribution, 15 Mar 1994, sub: Acquisition Reform, Defense Systems Management College, Acker Library, Vertical File: "Defense Acquisition—Reform."

[38] *Acquisition Review Quarterly* 1 (Winter 1994): 6–11. See also documents relating to "Acquisition Reform Day #1–May 31, 1996" on the Web site of Office of the Deputy Under Secretary of Defense for Acquisition Reform (ODUSD [AR]), archived at http://web.archive.org/web/19970605161357/www.acq.osd.mil/ar/arday1.htm.

[39] "Deskbook: New Info Source Looms at AR 'Best Seller,'" *Acquisition Reform Today* 1 (Aug/Sep 1996): 1. See also U.S. Congress, House, Committee on Government Reform and Oversight, *Implementation of Federal Acquisition Streamlining Act*, 104th Cong., 1 sess., 1995, p. 18.

feedback from these discussions was carefully studied by Kaminski and Preston.)[40] This was followed by another Acquisition Reform Day, 19 March 1997, which expanded into Acquisition Reform Week. The theme was "Sustaining the Momentum." Every government-industry team was expected to take a day to focus on learning about acquisition reform initiatives. Activities included speeches, workshops, roundtable discussions, and various training exercises, all of which were broadcast live via television and the Internet and later made available on videotape. The military services, defense agencies, and OSD all organized events. Program offices and teams were to develop their own specially tailored local activities.[41] Another Acquisition Reform Week was held in 1998 with the theme, "Leading and Embracing Change: Institutionalizing and Accelerating Acquisition Reform."[42] While the communication problems were successful, aligning individual and contractor incentives with the desired reform goals remained difficult to attain.

THE BROAD REACH OF REFORM

The reform impulse extended beyond the executive branch to Congress, which had long been prodding DoD to streamline its procedures and adopt commercial procurement practices. With DoD struggling to put its leadership team in place and slow to submit its own proposed bill, the legislators put forward several of their own.[43] The most important of these measures was H.R. 2238, the Federal Acquisition Improvement Act (FAIA), introduced in May 1993 by Congressmen John Conyers Jr. of Michigan and Ronald Dellums of California, the respective chairmen of the Government Operations Committee and the House Armed Services Committee. The bill encouraged commercial product acquisition,

---

[40] See documents relating to "Acquisition Reform Day #1–May 31, 1996," archived at http://web.archive.org/web/19970605161357/www.acq.osd.mil/ar/arday1.htm.

[41] Memo, USD (A&T) Kaminski, 20 Dec 1996, sub: Planning Guidance for Acquisition Reform Day 2, March 19, 1997, copy in the files of Philip Shiman, OSD Historical Office. Web pages for Acquisition Reform Week on the ODUSD (AR) Web site, archived at http://web.archive.org/web/19970605143530/http://www.acq.osd.mil/ar/#arweek; "AR Week: March 17-21 Theme 'Sustaining the Momentum,' " *Acquisition Reform Today* 2 (Jan/Feb 1997): 1, 7; "AR Week Wrap-Up," *Acquisition Reform Today* 2 (Mar/Apr 1997): 4–5.

[42] "AR Week '98 Embraces Change," *Acquisition Reform Today* 3 (Mar/Apr 1998): 1, 3. See also "AR Week III Kickoff Ceremony," *Acquisition Reform Today* 3 (Jul/Aug 1998): 1, 3–4; Web pages for "AcqReform Week III" on the Web site of USD (A&T), archived at http://web.archive.org/web/19980425053420/www.acq.osd.mil/arweekIII/.

[43] U.S. Congress, Senate, 103d Cong., 1st sess., *Hearing on S. 554, Solicitation Enhancement Act of 1993*; S. 555, *Procurement Protest Clarification Act of 1993*, and S. 556, *A Bill to Amend Chapter 35 of Title 31, United States Code, to Improve the Procurement Protest System*.

enhanced competition, strengthened the bid protest process, and streamlined small purchases. It also reserved $3 billion in additional business for small firms.[44] The original bill was not comprehensive, however; it contained little of substance regarding the acquisition of commercial products and left out most of the Section 800 Panel recommendations. Perry described the bill as "a modest, useful step," but he told HASC it was only "a small step in the direction we want to go."[45]

However, at this point neither DoD, the White House, nor the Senate were interested in small steps. They were looking for a broader reform package that would apply to the entire federal government. The Section 800 Panel report, though directed at defense acquisition laws, became the basis of the broader reform legislation. Immediately after receiving the report in January 1993, a bipartisan group of reform-minded senators and their staffs from the three committees launched an intensive effort on a comprehensive reform package, meeting weekly for nine months. The resulting bill, S.1587, the Federal Acquisition Streamlining Act or FASA, was largely completed by September and unveiled late the following month.[46]

The procurement reform bill (FASA) followed the structure of the Section 800 Panel's report and accepted the bulk of its recommendations, supplemented by a few reform proposals from the vice president's National Performance Review and some congressional ideas left over from the previous term. It emphasized commercial acquisition, a threshold of $100,000 for simplified acquisition procedures, and various changes in defense acquisition, including statutes covering major systems. However, being the product of three distinct committees, each with its own traditional concerns and constituencies, the bill hedged on some key issues. For example, instead of giving procuring offices the freedom to use innovative methods and their own judgment to obtain the "best value" for their organizations, the bill included new restrictions and oversight, a nod to the powerful old-line Democratic committee chairmen who were strongly attached to the old regulatory laws that not infrequently bore their names. It provided no simplification or streamlining at all for contracts valued over $100,000. The bill also showed particular sensitivity to the interests of small business-

---

[44] U.S. Congress, House, *Congressional Record*, 103d Cong. 1st sess., *The Federal Acquisition Improvement Act of 1993*, Congressman John Conyers, Extension of Remarks, 24 May 1993, p. E1337.

[45] U.S. Congress, House, Committee on Armed Services, *Acquisition Reform: Fact or Fiction*, 103d Cong., 1st sess., S. 11547, testimony of William J. Perry, 15 June 1993, p. 14.

[46] For a time the Federal Acquisition Streamlining Act (FASA) was often called FAStA or FASTA, but that usage eventually disappeared.

es, which had a powerful hold on the Small Business Committee. Nonetheless, FASA represented a considerable compromise among the various participants, each of whom acknowledged the need for a major overhaul of the acquisition system.[47]

Some members of the acquisition workforce believed the bill went too far in relaxing restrictions and oversight of contractors. Their experiences on large acquisition programs led them to believe that rigorous government oversight of contractors was necessary on programs where engineering and design changes occurred with high frequency. Senator William V. Roth Jr. (R-Del.) bolted from the bill when the eleventh-hour compromises threatened the monetary savings it was supposed to offer. Two days later, Roth and two other reform-minded Republican senators, Charles Grassley and William Cohen, introduced a more comprehensive bill (S. 1587) calling for overhaul of DoD acquisition that included a single DoD acquisition agency, a simplified acquisition program cycle, and streamlined procedures, though not the broad deregulation that DoD wanted.[48] But the problems of cost growth and schedule slippages continued.

Controversy continued to rage within the administration over the Senate's procurement reform bill. In the working group assembled to formulate the administration's position on FASA, DoD squared off against the vice president's office. The latter was not particularly happy with the Senate bill but was anxious for a legislative victory—or even just the appearance of victory—for the National Performance Review, to maintain the momentum of the reform effort. Vice President Al Gore's staff favored accepting the bill whether or not the administration obtained the changes it wanted. Their primary concern was to pass the bill—*any* bill—before the end of the congressional session in December.[49] DoD strenuously opposed this approach. The refusal of the White House to accept DoD's draft bill, and its endorsement of FASA S. 1587 instead, was a sharp blow to Colleen Preston and the acquisition reform office, which believed the Senate bill did not go far enough. DoD refused to abandon its own stillborn proposals and assumed what one

---

[47] S. 1587, *Federal Acquisition Streamlining Act of 1993*, version as introduced, 103d Cong., 1st sess., 26 October 1993.

[48] U.S. Congress, Senate, *Congressional Record*, 103d Cong., 1st sess., S. 14376, statement of Senator William V. Roth Jr., 26 October 1993; and S. 1598, *The Department of Defense Acquisition Management Reform Act of 1993*, introduced 28 October 1993.

[49] Steven Kelman, *Implementing Federal Procurement Reform*, Ash Institute for Democratic Governance and Innovation, John F. Kennedy School of Government, Harvard University, Spring 1998, p. 11. See also U.S. Congress, Senate, *Congressional Record*, 103d Cong., 2d sess., S. 6491, statement of Senator Roth, and S. 6493, statement of Senator John H. Glenn, both statements on 7 June 1994.

observer described as a "passive-aggressive" stance: it did not openly disagree with the vice president's support for FASA, but it aggressively promoted all of the revisions it sought.[50]

After long discussions with the executive branch and three hearings on the subject, the Governmental Affairs and Senate Armed Services committees released on 26 April a new bill. This bill, which included many of the provisions proposed by Roth, Grassley, and Cohen, pleased many of the DoD reformers. "Over the last six months," Senator Roth told his colleagues, "the reforms that we are making have grown from Tonka toys to a full-blown paving crew that can pave the way to significant savings."[51] The administration offered strong support for S. 1587. DoD, too, "wholeheartedly" backed the bill, even though it did not get everything it wanted.[52] The Senate's version of FASA passed on 8 June 1994, the House version (H.R. 2238) on the twenty-sixth. After two more months of wrangling, the Senate approved the compromise bill in August and the House two months later. President Clinton signed it into law on 13 October 1994.

FASA's primary thrusts sought to promote the use of commercial products and simplify the process of awarding and managing contracts in the hopes of luring more commercial firms into the defense market. For example, it broadened the definition of commercial items and reduced the requirements placed on offerors of such items. One of the most important changes amended the Truth in Negotiations Act to relax the requirement for bidders to reveal cost and pricing data, a major deterrent for commercial firms. The law also required the government to increase its use of electronic commerce and electronic data interchange and created the Federal Acquisition Network (FACNET), which would ease public access to the acquisition system.

While DoD was pleased with most of these provisions—Preston later told the Congress that FASA gave DoD 95 percent of what it needed to reengineer its business processes—it did not get everything it wanted. It did not, for example, receive blanket waivers of some existing statutes, including the Davis-Bacon Act and the Walsh-Healy Act.[53] It also failed to obtain changes regarding operational testing and evaluation. The Pentagon had long sought to weaken the

---

[50] Kelman, *Implementing Federal Procurement Reform*, p. 11.

[51] U.S. Congress, *Congressional Record*, 103d Cong., 2d sess., S 1587, statement of Senator Roth, 7 June 1994.

[52] Ibid.

[53] U.S. Congress, House, Committee on Government Reform and Oversight, *Implementation of Federal Acquisition Streamlining Act*, 104th Cong., 1st sess., 1995, pp. 36–37, requiring all government contracts over $10,000 to pay employees at or above the federal minimum wage and time-and-a-half pay for work over forty hours.

independence of the director of operational test and evaluation and to dilute the rigorous testing requirements imposed by Congress. The original Senate bill would have given the Pentagon the right to waive existing statutory testing requirements if the secretary of defense certified "that such testing would be unreasonably expensive and impracticable, cause unwarranted delay, or be unnecessary because of the acquisition strategy for that system." The reformers in the Senate, who dubbed this provision the "Mack-truck loophole" because "it would have opened a loophole large enough to drive a Mack truck through," rebelled.[54] Although the final bill allowed the secretary to waive full live-fire testing under certain circumstances, it reaffirmed the independence of the director of operational test and evaluation and left the operational testing requirements largely intact.[55]

FASA was a landmark piece of legislation. Some in Congress called it the most important acquisition legislation since the Competition in Contracting Act in 1983, and Chairman Sam Nunn of the Senate Armed Services Committee described it as the second installment on major changes in the Department of Defense begun by the Goldwater-Nichols Act in 1987.[56] It was a bipartisan effort; while the two parties haggled over such issues as the Davis-Bacon Act, they broadly agreed on FASA's goals and methods. Indeed, acquisition reform was one of the few issues on which Republicans and Democrats did agree—FASA passed the House by a unanimous vote of 425 to 0— and the preparation and passage of reform legislation continued after Congress came under the control of the Republicans in early 1995.

Of primary significance, FASA demonstrated to acquisition managers and workers the commitment of Congress and the executive branch leadership to modernizing the government's business practices. It helped fuel a spirit of reform; as a result of FASA, agencies began making changes not covered by the act at all! The reform measures in the act itself were actually relatively modest and incomplete. Steven Kelman, the director of the Office of Federal Procurement Policy, later reflected that FASA "accomplished less than some of the rhetoric suggested."[57] In February 1995, after a bitter battle between reformers and traditionalists, Congress passed

---

[54] U.S. Congress, Senate, *Congressional Record*, 103d Cong., 2d sess., S. 6587, statement of Senator David Pryor, 8 June 1994; S. 1597, *Federal Acquisition Streamlining Act*, introduced 26 October 1993, sec. 3013.

[55] FASA, Title III, secs. 3011–15.

[56] U.S. Congress, Senate, Committee on Governmental Affairs and Committee on Armed Services, *Federal Acquisition Streamlining Act of 1993: Joint Hearings on S. 1587,* 103d Cong., 2d sess., S. Hearing 103-849, 1994, p. 6.

[57] Steven Kelman, *Unleashing Change: A Study of Organizational Renewal in Government* (Washington, D.C.: Brookings Institution Press, 2005), pp. 136–37. See also Kelman, *Implementing Federal Procurement Reform*, p. 12.

a new act, the Federal Acquisition Reform Act (FARA), which together with the Information Technology Management Reform Act (ITMRA) became known as the Clinger-Cohen Act.[58] More radical than FASA, the act included changes intended to promote commercial purchasing and it overhauled the procurement integrity laws governing post-employment restrictions. It eliminated the General Services Board of Contract Appeals, which heard bid protests in computer procurements. Ultimately, FARA, too, passed unanimously in the House.[59] FASA and FARA moved the defense acquisition behemoth in the right direction but left most DoD and contractor activities largely unchanged.

Unlike the Defense Management Report of the previous administration, there was no single road map for acquisition reform during the Clinton administration. Perry's white paper, "The Mandate for Change," presented a broad statement of principles and overall goals. The program that flowed out of this document, still ill-defined and unfocused, would evolve over the next seven years, during which time OSD issued a blizzard of memorandums, directives, and instructions. There never has been an official count of the various Clinton-era acquisition reform initiatives. A 1997 Coopers & Lybrand study identified fifty-two initiatives that it called change elements.[60] In 2005, a careful review by the Arroyo Center of the Rand Corporation (described later in this chapter) identified sixty-three initiatives, a list Rand acknowledged was "not exhaustive." Three of these initiatives predated the Clinton administration and one followed it.[61] Among the rest, the large majority, forty-nine, came during Clinton's first term, almost half of them in 1995 alone; only ten were begun during the second administration. They ranged in importance from high priority areas such as military specifications and standards to small, incremental reforms such as allowing oral presentations of industry proposals.[62]

---

[58] *Federal Acquisition Reform Act of 1996*, Division D of the National Defense Authorization Act of 1996 (Public Law 104–106), approved 10 February 1996.

[59] Kelman, *Unleashing Change*, p. 137. See also Kathleen Day, "Streamlining Procurement Begins Phase 2," *Washington Post*, 9 February 1996.

[60] Coopers & Lybrand, "Acquisition Reform Implementation: An Industry Survey," Exhibit 1, October 1997.

[61] Competitive sourcing, DoD purchase card, and performance-based service acquisition were three initiatives that predated the Clinton administration, and contractor cost sharing was an initiative that followed it.

[62] Christopher H. Hanks, et al., *Reexamining Military Acquisition Reform: Are We There Yet?* (Santa Monica, Calif.: Rand Arroyo Center, 2005), pp. 5–17, 97–99. For a description of each initiative, see pages 81 to 96. Rand grouped these initiatives into four primary categories (some appear in more than one): (1) Rationalizing and Improving the Industrial Base–18 initiatives, (2) Streamlining–40 initiatives, (3) Civilian-Military Integration–27 initiatives, and (4) Logistics Transformation and Total Life-cycle System Management–6 initiatives.

The assault on the requirements generation process began by focusing on the problem of military specifications and standards, usually known collectively as "milspecs." Changing the nature and application of milspecs had long been a key goal of military reformers. Many studies had examined the problem over the years, and Congress had weighed in from time to time. DoD sought to reduce its reliance on milspecs, but its efforts achieved only modest results. The detailed specifications for fruitcakes, chocolate syrup, and dog combs became the subject of much public amusement and ridicule, yet by 1993 many serious analysts believed that the overuse of milspecs was strangling the acquisition system by adding significantly to the cost of products ranging from commodities to major systems and preventing commercial firms from offering innovative technology to the Pentagon.[63]

As noted earlier, milspec reform constituted "an area of intense interest" for Perry because he believed it was critical to achieving civil-military integration.[64] In August 1993, Preston chartered a process action team to prepare a milspec reform plan. In March 1994, the PAT released its report, *Blueprint for Change*, proposing a broad range of changes, including sharp restrictions on the use of milspecs in favor of commercial specifications and performance-based specifications.[65] The analyses and recommendations were not new; the PAT's analysis was limited to the review of previous studies. However, *Blueprint for Change* went into much more de-

---

[63] U.S. Government Accounting Office (GAO) Report, *Acquisition Reform: DoD Begins Program to Reform Specifications and Standards*, GAO/NSIAD-95-14, Oct 1994, pp. 4–5, 21; Jacques S. Gansler, "How the Pentagon Buys Fruitcake," *Air Force Magazine* (June 1989): 94; House Committee on Armed Services, Investigations Subcommittee, *DoD Military Specifications and Standards*, Hearing, 102d Cong., 2d sess., HASC No. 102-75, 1993, pp. 1–29, 106–11, 206–23; Steering Committee on Security and Technology, *Integrating Commercial and Military Technologies for National Strength: An Agenda for Change* (Washington, D.C.: Center for Strategic and International Studies, March 1991), pp. 41–52; Working Group on Military Specifications and Standards, *Road Map for Milspec Reform* (Washington, D.C.: Center for Strategic and International Studies, 1993).

[64] Memo, Deputy Secretary of Defense Perry to Jacques Gansler, 17 Sep 1993, attached to Memo, ASD (ES) [Assistant Secretary of Defense for Economic Security] Walter B. Bergman for Perry, 1 Sep 1993, sub: Report on Military Specifications and Standards, WNRC 330-97-0030, USD (A) Chronological File, 1993, box 7 (filed under 13 Sep 1993).

[65] Performance specifications told contractors what performance was required but not how to achieve it. According to the Defense Standards Improvement Council, a performance specification states requirements in terms of the required results with criteria for verifying compliance but without stating the methods for achieving the required results. A performance specification defines the functional requirements for the item, the environment in which it must operate, and the interface and interchangeability characteristics. See Defense Standardization Program Standardization Document (SD)-15, *Performance Specification Guide* (Washington, D.C.: Office of the Assistant Secretary of Defense for Economic Security, 29 June 1995), p. 6.

tail than previous plans.⁶⁶ Another PAT followed this report with an implementation plan.⁶⁷

On 29 June 1994, in his first major acquisition reform memorandum, Perry "wholeheartedly" accepted the PAT's recommendations and ordered that they be implemented. He prohibited the use of military specifications and standards in any acquisitions except as "a last resort," and even then required a waiver for their use. Otherwise, performance specifications were to be preferred, with non-governmental specifications as second choice. Whereas previously program managers were required to seek permission to use commercial standards, now they were required to obtain permission not to use them. "[W]e are . . . turning the present system upside down," Perry commented.⁶⁸

As some observers noted at the time, a few of these policies were hardly new. For example, DoD had preferred performance specifications for several years. Yet, as Perry himself recognized, cultural change was required. The PAT's plan largely focused on changing DoD's culture through training and education, incentives, and leadership initiative. Perry wanted to shock the system and get its attention. Severely restricting the use of milspecs got people's attention. The idea seems to have spread that Perry was abolishing their use altogether, which was not the case.⁶⁹ But it was still a bold and challenging move difficult to implement. Perry noted: "[T]he problem of unique military systems did not begin with the standards. The problem was rooted in the requirements determination phase of the cycle."⁷⁰

---

⁶⁶ Memo, DUSD (AR) Preston for Deputy Secretary of Defense Perry, 1 Sep 1993, sub: PAT on Mil Specs and Standards—Information Memorandum, WNRC 330–97–0030, USD (A) Chronological File, 1993, box 7; Process Action Team on Military Specifications and Standards, *Blueprint for Change: Report of the Process Action Team on Military Specifications and Standards* (Washington, D.C.: Office of the Under Secretary of Defense for Acquisition and Technology, April 1994); GAO Report, *Acquisition Reform*, GAO/NSIAD–95–14, Oct 1994, pp. 4–5

⁶⁷ *Implementation Plan for the Process Action Team Report on Specifications and Standards*, version 1.0 (Washington, D.C.: Office of the Assistant Secretary of Defense for Economic Security, 23 June 1994).

⁶⁸ Memo, Secretary of Defense Perry for Distribution, 29 Jun 1994, sub: Specifications & Standards—A New Way of Doing Business, Perry Papers, Disk 2, OSD Historical Office; Thomas E. Ricks, "Pentagon, in Streamlining Effort, Plans to Revamp Its Purchasing Procedures," *Wall Street Journal*, 30 June 1994.

⁶⁹ Walter D. Bergmann, "Message from Chairman, Defense Standards Improvement Council," DoD Standardization Newsletter (Special Edition, October 1994): 1; "Chairman's Message: Waiver Requests—A Matter of Balance," *Standardization Newsletter* (October 1995): 2.

⁷⁰ Memo, Perry for Distribution, 29 Jun 1994, p. 4. See also GAO Report, *Acquisition Reform*, GAO/NSAID–95–14, Oct 1994, pp. 4–11.

Perry considered his document, "A Mandate for Change," to be the effective start of the acquisition reform program. Five years later he would write:

> A far-reaching reform was stated in a single sentence, clear and direct; the idea thus expressed was, in Victor Hugo's words, "more powerful than the tread of mighty armies." It read: "The use of military specifications and standards is authorized as a last resort, with an appropriate waiver." The time had come; acquisition reform was launched.[71]

By the end of 1995, it became apparent that milspec reform had hit a serious snag. The restrictions on the use of military specifications and standards applied only to new contracts. Existing programs were exempted. This meant that a company performing both old and new contracts might have to use multiple manufacturing and management processes in one facility. At one factory, for example, a defense contractor was forced to use eight different soldering specifications, including five for the government and three for commercial clients. The workers had to be trained on all eight soldering and inspection techniques and the company had to maintain eight different types of production documentation. Needless to say, this drove up costs; it also made plant managers reluctant to adopt new processes while still committed to the old.[72]

Therefore, in December 1995 DoD established the Single Process Initiative (SPI), which allowed companies to make "block changes" to its contracts, shifting all of them over to a single process at each facility. Contractors were encouraged to submit proposals that would be reviewed and approved by the onsite administrative contracting officer (ACO) assigned to the facility. The government would even pay for the changes if the contractor could demonstrate that they would produce significant long-term savings.[73]

The first two block change agreements were with Texas Instruments Defense Systems and Electronics. Within nine months, 103

---

[71] Carter and Perry, *Preventive Defense*, p. 185.

[72] Speech, USD (A&T) Kaminski to the Lockheed-Martin Common Processes Conference, Arlington, Va., 18 Jan 1996, copy in the files of Philip Shiman, OSD Historical Office.

[73] Memo, Secretary of Defense Perry for Distribution, 6 Dec 1995, sub: Common Systems/ISO-9000/Expedited Block Changes, Perry Papers, Disk 2, OSD Historical Office. See also Memo, USD (A&T) Kaminski for Distribution, 8 Dec 1995, sub: Single Process Initiative, copy in the files of Philip Shiman, OSD Historical Office; and "Department of Defense Announces Policy on Single Process Initiative," Office of the Secretary of Defense for Public Affairs (OASD [PA]), News Release No. 647–95, 8 Dec 1995.

contractors submitted 341 proposals covering 426 process changes, of which 349 process changes were accepted.[74] OSD believed this approach was critical to the success of milspec reform and ultimately civil-military integration; it came to see the initiative as a primary vehicle for introducing best business and manufacturing practices among its contractors. DoD maintained the Single Process Initiative through the rest of the decade, periodically tweaking and reinforcing it.[75]

After restricting the use of milspecs in favor of commercial standards and performance specifications, a logical next step was to mandate the use of open systems. The open systems approach, a design and business philosophy, emphasized common, non-proprietary standards, especially for interfaces and operating systems. The use of such standards was expected to expand DoD's supplier base, because any company could apply them to its products to sell to the government. When used in conjunction with such concepts as modularity and functional partitioning—the use of self-contained functional components to build systems—the open systems approach was also expected to reduce costs, make technology upgrades easier, and lessen the reliance on military-unique systems. The goal was to promote "plug-and-play" (or, at the level of operating forces, "plug-and-fight"): different products, including technology upgrades and modular technological add-ons, that could be swapped in and out of the larger system with no delay and no degradation of performance.[76]

Five months after Perry issued his memorandum, "Specifications and Standards—A New Way of Doing Business," Under Secretary Kaminski took the first steps toward adopting the open systems approach by ordering that it be applied to the acquisition of weapon system electronics. He also established the Open Systems Joint Task Force "to promote and oversee the enactment of this policy, identify opportunities for implementing open systems architectures, develop training and education programs, and coordinate the identification and selection of open systems specifications and standards."[77] In March 1996, the newly revised DoD 5000-series

---

[74] Robert W. Drewes, "SPI—Progress Made and Lessons Learned," *Program Manager* (Special Issue, January-February 1997): 37.

[75] See especially Memo, USD (A&T) Jacques Gansler for Distribution, 3 Jun 1998, sub: The Single Process Initiative—A Long Term Perspective, copy in the files of Philip Shiman, OSD Historical Office.

[76] For descriptions of the open systems approach, see Matt Gillis, "Open Systems Joint Task Force Gets the Word Out," *Program Manager* (July-August 1999): 44–47. See also Michael Hanratty, Robert H. Lightsey, and Arvid G. Larson, "Open Systems and the Systems Engineering Process, *Acquisition Review Quarterly* (Winter 1999): 47–58.

[77] Memo, USD (A&T) Kaminski for Distribution, 29 Nov 1994, sub: Acquisition of Weapons Systems Electronics Using Open Systems Specifications and Standards, copy in the files of Philip Shiman, OSD Historical Office.

regulations expanded this order to cover all weapon system components. After a workshop late that spring studied the practical aspects of implementing the policy, Kaminski ordered the component acquisition executives to implement the policy and report their progress regularly. DoD Regulation 5000.2-R was revised periodically to clarify and strengthen the mandate to apply the open systems approach.[78]

CHANGING THE ACQUISITION PROCESS

Although Perry's highest priorities were to change the system of specifications and standards, begin procurement reform, and launch the pilot programs, he did not wait long to begin the overhaul of the acquisition process. At the end of August 1994, Perry chartered a process action team on acquisition oversight and review, giving it ninety days to produce "a comprehensive plan to reengineer the oversight and review process for systems acquisition, in the services and OSD, to make it more effective and efficient, while maintaining an appropriate level of oversight." The PAT had a mandate to suggest radical changes; it did not disappoint. Its report, issued in December, made thirty-three recommendations covering the milestone process, oversight organization and documentation, management of joint programs, and workforce issues. The report included a separate volume with detailed plans for implementing its recommendations.[79]

With regard to the DAB (Defense Acquisition Board) process, the PAT sought to reduce the number of expensive and disruptive reviews and rely more heavily on continuous oversight based on improved flows of information to the decision makers. The PAT recommended reducing the number of milestone reviews to three: the Need Validation Decision, the Program Initiation Decision, and the Production Decision. Likewise, there would be three phases:

---

[78] DoD Regulation 5000.2-R, "Mandatory Procedures for Major Defense Acquisition Programs (MDAPs) and Major Automated Information System (MAIS) Acquisition Programs," sec. 4.3.4. See also Memo, Kaminski for DoD Component Acquisition Executives, 10 Jul 1996, sub: Open Systems Acquisition of Weapons Systems; Paper, Chien Huo, "Open Systems Policy Directions: The DoD 5000.2-R, Change 3," 11 April 1998; and Paper, "Open Systems Policy in the DoD 5000.2-R," 24 May 1999. Copies of memo and papers in the files of Philip Shiman, OSD Historical Office.

[79] Memo, Secretary of Defense Perry for Distribution, 6 Sep 1994, sub: Process Action Team on Oversight and Review, Perry Papers, Disk 2, OSD Historical Office. See also Acquisition Reform Process Action Team, *Reengineering the Acquisition Oversight and Review Process: Final Report to the Secretary of Defense* (Washington, D.C.: Department of Defense, 9 December 1994), p. 1; and John S. Caldwell Jr., "Reengineering the Oversight and Review Process for Systems Acquisition," *Program Manager* (May-June 1995): 3–5.

Concept Exploration, Development, and Production. The number of pre-DAB reviews would be reduced to no more than one, and the subsequent DAB meetings might be done away with in the absence of outstanding issues. This would be made possible by replacing the traditional DAB committee structure with integrated product teams (IPTs).[80] IPTs would include representatives of OSD and the military services who would work with the program manager throughout the life of the program. Every program would have a top-level IPT (called an Overarching IPT, or OIPT) that would shepherd it through the development process, providing strategic guidance, assessing the program, and resolving issues; and one or more Working IPTs (WIPTs) that would have more of a hands-on role. Because these IPTs would include personnel from the various organization and management layers, they would obviate the need for multiple, serial committee meetings. They were expected to address problems as they arose instead of allowing them to fester until the next review.[81]

The PAT also recommended reducing the oversight burden in other ways. Whereas the 5000-series revision released by the previous administration included an extensive compilation of documents required of every program, the PAT proposed reducing the documentation by making the smallest number mandatory, then adding documents only as required. The PAT wanted to weaken the influence of the Defense Contract Management Command by prohibiting the Defense Plant Representative Offices from conducting independent investigations of contractors. It would reduce the frequency of routine DoD Inspector General audits. It even suggested reducing the oversight on well-performing contractors by allowing them to be self-governing.[82] The PAT report reflected the popular emphasis on employee empowerment and teamwork, as well as a modest faith in both the government workforce and the contractors to function well with minimum oversight. While contractors were generally enthusiastic about the reduced oversight, the modest faith was shared by some members of the DoD acquisition workforce and not by others.

Kaminski accepted most, although not all, of the recommendations. He maintained the milestones and phases as they were, except for eliminating Milestone IV (Major Modification Approval), but he adopted the integrated product teams. "Rather than checking the work of the program office beginning six months prior to

---

[80] An integrated product team (IPT) is a multidisciplinary group of people who are collectively responsible for delivering a defined product or process. IPTs are used in complex development programs/projects for review and decision making.

[81] "Acquisition Reform PAT," *Reengineering*, 1: 8–9, 24–38.

[82] Ibid., pp. 38–44, 47–48, 51–52.

a milestone decision point, as is often the case today," he directed, "the OSD and Component staffs shall participate early and on an on-going basis with the program office teams, resolving issues as they arise, rather than during the final decision review." The Overarching IPT for each program would decide which subordinate teams to establish. Prior to a review, the Overarching IPT would meet to determine if all issues had been resolved and the program was ready to move forward. When the program was deemed ready to move forward, a DAB readiness meeting would be held to advise the under secretary before the DAB. If no problems were anticipated, an Acquisition Decision Memorandum might be prepared and signed without holding a DAB meeting at all, an action known as a paper DAB. There should be no surprises, Kaminski noted, because the Overarching IPT would have been closely involved with the program from the start. He described this new policy as a shift from "after-the-fact oversight" to "early-and-continuous insight."[83]

Kaminski also accepted the PAT's approach to contractor oversight: "Once a contractor has demonstrated a system of stable, compliant processes leading to performance as contracted, the Defense Contract Management Command (DCMC) shall rely almost exclusively on contractor self-governance, rather than Government inspectors, auditors, and compliance monitors." This reduction in oversight was of particular concern to the DoD Inspector General. However, the under secretary did not approve the recommendations to weaken DCMC oversight, for example, and he made clear that DCMC onsite personnel could continue to make independent investigations, although the program managers would have access to their reports.[84]

IPTs by themselves represented an important change, but they also provided the foundation for another change of equal significance, integrated product and process development (IPPD), "a management process that integrated all activities from product concept through production/field support" using multifunctional IPTs. Instead of proceeding through the development process in a strictly serial manner, with participants performing their parts in strict sequence, in IPPD the participants worked together in an IPT from the start. Early on, in the design phase, at which point changes were much easier and less costly, potential problems that

---

[83] "Paul Kaminski on Acquisition Reform," *Program Manager* (Special Issue, January-February 1997): 7. See also Memo, USD (A&T) Kaminski for Distribution, 28 Apr 1995, sub: Reengineering the Acquisition Oversight and Review Process, copy in the files of Philip Shiman, OSD Historical Office; and U.S. Congress, Senate, statement of Paul Kaminski before the Subcommittee on Acquisition and Technology of the Senate Committee on Armed Services on FY 1997 DoD Acquisition and Technology Program, 20 March 1996, p. 31.

[84] "Paul Kaminski on Acquisition Reform," p. 7.

could arise in the manufacturing or production phases were identified and resolved.

IPPD grew out of an industry concept called concurrent engineering, a component of Total Quality Management (TQM) that called for a systematic approach to integrated design of products taking into consideration all elements of the system life cycle. By the late 1980s, at least nine major defense contractors were using concurrent engineering on weapon system programs, and reports by the Institute for Defense Analyses (IDA) and the Defense Science Board (DSB) recommended that DoD adopt the approach as policy.[85] Under Secretary of Defense for Acquisition Robert Costello, a TQM advocate, did so, but he left office soon after and the idea was largely forgotten. Meanwhile, the Air Force had also been studying the concept, which it expanded from a technical design approach into a broader management philosophy called Integrated Product Development (IPD). IPD became a key element of the service's Integrated Weapon System Management (IWSM), adopted officially in 1992. Because IPD (like concurrent engineering) involved the integrated design of products and processes, it came to be called integrated product and process development by 1993, when a Defense Science Board report strongly promoted the concept.[86] On 10 May 1995, Secretary Perry ordered that the IPPD and IPT concepts be applied throughout the acquisition process. His memorandum and that of Kaminski accepting the Acquisition Oversight and Review PAT's report were publicly announced together on 16 May.[87]

---

[85] The Defense Acquisition University Glossary of Defense Acquisition Terms (September 2003) defines *concurrent engineering* as a systematic approach to the integrated, concurrent design of products and processes considering all elements of the system life cycle from requirements development through disposal, including cost, schedule, and technical performance.

[86] Robert I. Winner, et al., *The Role of Concurrent Engineering in Weapons System Acquisition*, IDA Report R–338 (Alexandria, Va.: Institute for Defense Analyses, December 1988), pp. 1–49. See also Memo, USD (A) Costello for Secretaries of the Military Departments, 9 Mar 1989, sub: Concurrent Engineering—A Total Quality Management Process, WNRC 330–92–0136, USD (A) Chronological Files, 1989, box 3; U.S. Air Force, *Air Force Materiel Command Guide on Integrated Product Development* (n.p., 25 May 1993), pp. 4–10, 95–106; and Defense Science Board *Task Force, Engineering in the Manufacturing Process* (Washington, D.C.: Office of the Under Secretary of Defense for Acquisition, March 1993), ch. 1, pp. 1–13.

[87] Memo, Secretary of Defense Perry for Distribution, 10 May 1995, sub: Use of Integrated Product and Process Development and Integrated Product Teams in DoD Acquisition, Perry Papers, Disk 2, OSD Historical Office. See also OASD (PA), "Department of Defense Announces Bold Reform for Major Systems Oversight and Review, News Release No. 264-95, 16 May 1995. For a description of how IPPD was to be applied to defense acquisition, see *DoD Guide to Integrated Product and Process Development*, version 1.0 (Washington, D.C.: Office of the Under Secretary of Defense for Acquisition and Technology, 5 February 1996).

The various changes to the acquisition organization and process were codified with the release of the 5000-series revision on 15 March 1996.[88] The stark contrast in style and management philosophy between this administration and the previous one was clearly evident in the differences between the 1991 and 1996 versions. The 1991 regulations were contained in three documents (DoD Directive 5000.1, DoD Instruction 5000.2, and DoD Manual 5000.2-M) that totaled almost nine-hundred pages. Although some of the guidelines were discretionary, it was difficult to distinguish them from those that were mandatory. Tailoring the oversight and review process and the documentation was discouraged. The documents appeared to require lockstep movement through the review process. In all, they emphasized discipline.[89]

The two new documents, DoD Directive 5000.1 and DoD Regulation 5000.2-R, had a very different look and feel to them. Together they totaled only one-hundred-forty pages; much of the material from the old documents now appeared in the Defense Acquisition Deskbook. There was one figure, showing the Integrated Test Program Schedule, and no other charts or tables. The documents promoted tailoring the procedures and the documents, with the clear suggestion that the fewer documents, the better. Overall, they emphasized flexibility.[90]

The new documents sought to reflect the themes of the acquisition reform program: teamwork, as opposed to functional stovepiping and adversarial committees; tailoring the process and organization to suit each program's particular circumstances; empowerment of program managers, other acquisition workers, and the industry; cost control; the acquisition of commercial products; and the adoption of best business practices.[91] In terms of specific changes to the process, there occurred some tweaking of the phases and milestones. The basic milestones remained the same (except for Milestone IV—Major Modification Approval, which was deleted).[92]

---

[88] DoD Directive 5000.1, "Defense Acquisition," 15 Mar 1996. See also DoD Regulation 5000.2-R, "Mandatory Procedures for Major Defense Acquisition Programs (MDAPs) and Major Automated Information System (MAIS) Acquisition Programs," 15 Mar 1996.

[89] Charles B. Cochrane, "Defense Acquisition Policy—A More Flexible Management Approach," *Program Manager* (July-August 1996): 16.

[90] Ibid.

[91] Memo, USD (A&T) Kaminski, DOT&E [Director of Operational Test and Evaluation] Philip Coyle, and ASD (C3I) [Assistant Secretary of Defense for Command, Control, Communications, and Intelligence] Emmett Paige Jr. for the Defense Acquisition Community, 15 Mar 1996, sub: Update of the DoD 5000 Documents. Copy in the files of Philip Shiman, OSD Historical Office.

[92] The separate acquisition documents that had previously governed the acquisition of information systems (DoD Directive 8120.1, DoD Instruction 8120.2, and DoD Manual 7920.2-M) were now cancelled, and such systems were subject to the DoD 5000 directives. Milestone IV, Logistics Readiness and Support Review, was deleted in 1991.

Phase I, formerly called Demonstration and Validation, was now Program Definition and Risk Reduction. A new Acquisition Category, ACAT IA, represented major automated information systems (MAIS). Programs requiring milestone review by the MAIS Review Council (MAISRC) were ACAT IAM, and those by the component only were ACAT IAC. The separate acquisition documents that had previously governed the acquisition of information systems (DoD Directive 8120.1, DoD Instruction 8120.2, and DoD Manual 7920.2-M) were now cancelled, and such systems were now subject to the 5000-series directives and instructions.

Results of 1990s Acquisition Reforms[93]

In 2002, the assistant secretary of the Army for acquisition, logistics, and technology sponsored a comprehensive Rand Corporation study of the acquisition reform initiatives adopted by OSD and the military services during the 1990s.

As part of its study, the Arroyo Center of Rand Corporation conducted a thorough review of the latest DoD 5000-series regulations and instructions (i.e., the year 2000 version) to determine which acquisition reform initiatives had been incorporated into the established method of conducting DoD acquisition programs. Rand also interviewed representatives of the Army acquisition headquarters, industry, and the Army program management community (i.e., program managers, program executives, and acquisition functional specialists) to obtain their insights on acquisition reforms. The objective of the study was to understand how well acquisition reform initiatives had been implemented.

In its study, Rand did not attempt to evaluate how acquisition reform initiatives affected acquisition program outcomes (i.e., the cost, schedule, and performance results). Rather, Rand assumed

---

[93] Hanks, et al., *Reexamining Acquisition Reform*, pp. 1–78. The 5000-series documents have been the vehicle for specifying DoD acquisition policy since the early 1970s. (Prior to the 5000 series, DoD relied on the 3200-series documents, which date to the 1960s, to specify R&D and procurement policies and procedures.) The original 5000 series mandated a complicated acquisition process requiring the government to follow specific rules. In 1995, Paul Kaminski, then-Under Secretary of Defense for Acquisition and Technology, issued a memorandum calling for the revision of the series, and a 160-page version was released in 1997 (significantly improving, at least in terms of page count, on the 1991 version, which had 900 pages). The 2001 version of the 5000 series includes DoD Directive 5000.1, "Defense Acquisition System," 4 January 2001, 12 pages; DoD Instruction 5000.2 Change 1, "Operation of the Defense Acquisition System," 4 January 2001, 46 pages; and DoD Regulation 5000.2-R Change 1, "Mandatory Procedures for Major Defense Programs (MDAPs) and Major Automated Information System (MAIS) Acquisition Programs," 10 June 2001, 194 pages. All three of these documents were released in final form in April 2002.

that by studying the acquisition reform initiatives in the 1990s and by enabling acquisition personnel to describe in their own words how their work was affected by the initiatives, they would collect information that would help the Army and the rest of the Defense Department understand what the acquisition reform movement had and had not accomplished in terms of changing the way the acquisition process operated.

The Rand study focused on sixty-three of the 1990s reform initiatives, listed in Appendix D.[94] The list did not include any of the many acquisition reform initiatives aimed solely at improving the quality and training of the defense acquisition workforce.

By the end of the 1990s, it had become clear to the Defense Department and to Rand that additional steps needed to be taken to implement acquisition reform initiatives effectively. First, official DoD acquisition policy had to be rewritten to institutionalize the new approaches, and responsibility had to be fixed somewhere in the system so that a specific and identifiable individual would always be accountable for acting on each initiative and monitoring progress. To accomplish these changes, DoD acquisition reform policymakers arranged for the production of a revised version of DoD's official acquisition policy (the 5000-series directives and instructions). OSD designated acquisition program managers as the parties who would be responsible for the "total life-cycle system management" of all DoD systems, including all new systems still in acquisition, as well as all old (legacy) systems already in the field.

The Rand study found that many of the sixty-three acquisition reform initiatives from the 1990s were not specifically mentioned or described in the June 2003 version of the 5000-series acquisition policy. Representatives of Army headquarters, the Army project management community, and industry were supportive of the goals of acquisition reform and believed that some progress had been made in implementing the reforms. The message that emerged from the Rand interviews, however, was that all three communities believed that much more needed to be done before the acquisition process could be said to be truly reformed.

Under acquisition reform, program managers were being asked to "be more innovative" and "take more risks." But Rand interviews with program management personnel in both the Army and industry clearly reflected a strong view that very little in terms of how resources (funds) were allocated and controlled, either within the Army or in the Defense Department, had changed to encourage program managers to take any more risks than they had before acquisition reform. Army program managers uniformly expressed the view that it made

---

[94] Hanks, et al., *Reexamining Acquisition Reform*, p. 11.

no sense for them to be held "responsible and accountable" for "total life-cycle system management" unless new resourcing methods were put in place that would give them the leverage and management authority to be able to deliver on that responsibility and legitimately be held accountable. The Rand study also indicated that the operational side of the Army resisted making the changes in the military personnel system that would produce a professional acquisition management and program management capability that was comparable to the professional workforce in the Air Force, including the acquisition-related fields of engineering, logistics, auditing, and financial management.

In conducting its study, Rand examined the relevance of each of sixty-three acquisition reform initiatives from the 1990s to the different functional activities that made up or supported the overall acquisition process. The examination began by considering the following twelve acquisition-related career fields:[95]

- Auditing
- Business, Cost Estimating, and Financial Management
- Communications and Computer Systems
- Contracting
- Industrial Property Management
- Logistics
- Manufacturing and Production
- Program Management
- Purchasing and Procurement Assistance
- Quality Assurance
- Systems Planning, Research, Development, and Engineering
- Test and Evaluation

To measure coverage of the sixty-three acquisition reform initiatives from the 1990s, Rand turned to the version of the 5000 series released in 2001. The 2001 version, written by a joint DoD task force working over the 1999–2001 period to prepare a new 5000 series, incorporated and institutionalized what had been accomplished by acquisition reform in the 1990s. The 2001 version thus reflected a consensus among its joint authors about what parts of acquisition reform in the 1990s merited inclusion in the DoD 5000-series acquisition policy documents, as compared to putting them somewhere else, for example, in the Defense Supplement to the Federal Acquisition Regulation.[96]

---

[95] Ibid., pp. 20, 21.
[96] Joseph Ferrara, "DoD's 5000 Documents: Evolution and Change in Defense Acquisition Policy," *Acquisition Review Quarterly*, Fall 1996, available at http:www.dau.mil/pubs/arq/94arq2/ferrar.pdf.

Rand concluded that while the argument for using the DoD 5000-series documents made practical sense (it would be unwieldy to try to capture every detail of all acquisition reform initiatives in these documents), the DoD 5000 series was also the place where program managers were supposed to go for policy guidance on how to perform their jobs and what they could and could not do. Given that program managers had been designated as the responsible parties, that meant they must orchestrate the efforts of the entire acquisition community (requirements determiners, contracting personnel, testers and evaluators, financial managers, and engineers) to make the acquisition process work. Accordingly, Rand took the view that it was not unreasonable to expect the 5000 series to contain, if not detailed guidance on every initiative, at least mention of the initiatives and pointers or references to where guidance could be found.[97]

Rand used electronic (Adobe PDF format) copies of the DoD 5000-series documents and employed keyword searches to find either explicit mention of an initiative or phrases and terms closely enough related to an initiative that one would be justified in saying that the initiative was mentioned. Using the approach described above, Rand found that just under 50 percent of the sixty-three acquisition reform initiatives from the 1990s received mention in the 2001 version of the DoD 5000 series.

Views of Army Headquarters Personnel[98]

For the Army headquarters view, Rand met on three occasions with Kenneth Oscar, the acting assistant secretary of the Army for acquisition, logistics, and technology (ASA [ALT]). Oscar was in that position from January 2001 through March 2002 and was the original sponsor for the acquisition reform study. Rand also met, in separate meetings, with personnel in the ASA (ALT) Directorates for Acquisition Policy and Procurement; Plans, Programs, and Resources; and Integrated Logistics Support. Oscar's views are represented in the paragraphs below.

- Acquisition reform had improved the acquisition process. Acquisition reform made it possible for each acquisition process to work more along the lines that Oscar, as the leader for acquisition in the Army, wanted to see it work. The use of integrated process teams (IPTs) helped mitigate the otherwise natural tendency of functional staff to

---

[97] Rand, *Reexamining Military Acquisition Reform*, pp. 27–28.
[98] Ibid., pp. 35–42.

talk only with their functional counterparts as they communicated up and down the chain of command.
- Many contracts were still being written in ways that produced results opposite to what the government really wanted. To take spare parts contracts as an example, Oscar noted: "If we solicit for 50 spare parts a year for a particular piece of equipment, the only way the contractor can increase his profit is by selling more spare parts. If we instead solicit for the contractor to keep the equipment in spare parts for five years, he can increase his profit by making the parts last longer."
- Much remains to be done with respect to acquisition reform. Acquisition was still "too bureaucratic" and the Army headquarters was still "a problem" in that it is still too slow to approve programs, too quick to change them, and much too quick to take money away and stretch programs out from year to year.
- Although many acquisition reforms were aimed at making life easier for program managers, contracting officers, and others, it did not always work out that way.

Many of the senior personnel in the Rand survey expressed concerns that unless ways were found to preserve and pass on the valuable lessons they had learned, there was a danger that some of what was put in place as acquisition reforms in the 1990s could cause old problems to return, such as waste, fraud, and mismanagement—problems which had motivated much of the reform effort in the 1980s.

VIEWS OF THE ARMY PROGRAM MANAGEMENT COMMUNITY[99]

Rand interviewed a cross-section of both military and civilian personnel working in Army program management. Participants were asked to provide—on a not-for-attribution basis—their views about three issues: what had been good about acquisition reform, what had been bad, and what they would change. Rand conducted one-on-one interviews at two Army locations and conducted a group interview at a third location. Over the course of the interviews, interviewers met and spoke with more than thirty people in the Army program management community and obtained additional written comments from others who were unable to attend the interviews. Interviewees and respondents included one program executive officer, five deputy program executive officers, eight program managers (seven of whom were military),

---
[99] Ibid., pp. 43–60, especially pp. 43–44.

ten deputy program managers (nine of whom were civilians), and roughly a dozen civilian staff members from various Army program management offices.

WHAT HAS BEEN GOOD ABOUT ACQUISITION REFORM?

Several interviewees noted that, in general, the acquisition reform movement had helped "raise consciousness" about the need to "do things differently" in acquisition, thus making some aspects of the job easier than they used to be. Several members of the program management community emphasized the useful role that the Defense Acquisition University (DAU) was playing in "reaching and preaching acquisition reform." However, one person also noted that "most DAU instructors don't have a clue about how PMs actually spend most of their time on each day."[100]

Many of the interviewees cited specific acquisition reform initiatives that they felt had been helpful. The Modified Integrated Program Summary (MIPS) was mentioned as a great help in reducing the number of reports necessary for program management. Best-value contracting was described as a means of making it easier to select a contractor with "the right mix of technical, management, and cost performance." In best-value contracting, contracts were awarded on the basis of best value rather than lowest cost. Thus, all relevant factors—cost, performance, quality, schedule, potential trade-offs—could be taken into account. Elimination of military specifications (milspecs), reduced Contract Data Requirements Lists (CDRLs), electronic processing, and purchase cards were all mentioned as effective means of cutting red tape. Several interviewees expressed approval of Alpha Contracting. One program manager (military) said Alpha Contracting "works to build a team and joint effort." The Single Process Initiative (SPI) was also mentioned as an effective idea for streamlining processes, while Other Transaction Authority (OTA) was cited as being helpful with Future Combat Systems (FCS). Other initiatives described as helpful included Post-Award Debriefing, Parametric Cost Estimating, Multi-Year Contracting, Use of Commercial Warranties, Alternative Dispute Resolution, Revised Cost and Pricing Thresholds, and the use of Cost-Schedule Reporting Standards Tailored to Industry Guidelines.

WHAT HAS BEEN BAD ABOUT ACQUISITION REFORM?[101]

While interviewees described much that they appreciated about the Army's acquisition reform efforts, they were also forthcoming

---

[100] Ibid., p. 45.
[101] Ibid., pp. 47–53.

in depicting many problems that had plagued the acquisition reform (AR) movement.

- Many of the interviewees noted that although innovative AR approaches often generated increased risk, very little had been done to give program managers mechanisms for hedging against that risk. In other words, AR had encouraged program managers to be innovative and take chances, but it had not given them tools—for example, access to additional resources or schedule flexibility or ways to revise technical performance characteristics—that would help them deal with the problems that often arise when those chances are taken.
- Program managers and their staffs lacked the financial flexibility to implement reforms due to constraints on shifting funds from one appropriation category to another.
- Program managers were skeptical about their chances of gaining more control over financial decisions: "Recapitalization—PMs don't control the money. Next year the promise is to send money directly to PMs, but that decision has been delayed a year already, so people are skeptical as to whether it will really happen."
- Many of those interviewed complained that although acquisition reform involved a lot of activity, nothing really new has occurred. The true impact of many of the reforms was questioned. Several of the participants provided frank assessments of the changes—or lack thereof—brought about under AR. A senior deputy program executive officer (PEO) commented that "AR has been good at cranking out policies, but hasn't made anything faster, better, or cheaper, a remark with which many others participating in the group interview concurred."
- One individual submitted a written comment noting, "Acquisition reform will remain suboptimized until they reform the financial, logistics, test, engineering, contracting, and legal communities. These communities can unilaterally kill any AR program, since they have full veto authority in most cases, while not being held accountable for their decisions." A similar view was expressed by a program manager (military) in an interview: "Too many people can say no." The testing community was cited several times for its refusal to change. Among the comments heard: "The testing community is

still in the old ways of doing business. . . . The test community is still living 30 years in the past"
- One deputy PEO (civilian) described a recent experience with a contractor: "The contract wanted to have everything quick, so the contract was vague, and now [we are] spending dearly for that vagueness. The contractor is . . . using the vagueness to do changes—so the vagueness is working to the contractor's benefit, not the government's."
- One deputy PEO (civilian) noted that "Now we have 'CAIV' [Cost as an Independent Variable] and a fixed schedule and are sacrificing performance. We're 'empowering' people but not letting them come back and trade among cost, schedule, and technical performance. Schedule is now king—evolutionary acquisition will sacrifice technical performance and cost."

Summary of Rand Findings[102]

While the people Rand talked to in the Army program management community were supportive of the goals of acquisition reform and acknowledged that some progress had been made, the clear message that emerged from Rand interviews was that many in the Army program management community thought that much more needed to be done before the acquisition process could be characterized as having been truly reformed—or even changed much for the better. Indeed, many of the more senior people expressed concerns that some of the most reasonable-sounding acquisition reforms—the elimination of milspecs, the relaxation of other kinds of data requirements from contractors, the push to outsource as much system support as feasible—all could backfire when DoD found itself having to support the involved systems over the very long life spans that defense systems tended to have once they were operational in the field.

All the program management personnel Rand interviewed pointed out that nothing had changed in the way resources were allocated and controlled, either within the Army or within DoD, in a way that gave them any more reason to adopt reforms than they had in the past. In the same vein, they argued that it made no sense for them to be made "responsible and accountable" for "total life-cycle system management" unless a way was found to give them the commensurate leverage and authority they needed to fulfill that charge.

Rand concluded that whatever happened next, the Army program management community wanted to see other communities

---
[102] Ibid., pp. 58–59.

with whom they worked—including the RD&E, Requirements, Contracting, Testing, Finance, and Logistics communities— brought, through education and training, to the same level of understanding and appreciation of what acquisition reform (and now acquisition excellence) was trying to accomplish in the program management community.

CHAPTER FIVE

CONCLUSIONS

In reflecting on the defense acquisition reform studies of the past five decades, it is clear that the acquisition system has been strongly resistant to change. Major defense programs continue to take ten years or more to deliver less capability than planned, often at two to three times the planned cost.[1] Nearly twenty years ago, in 1992, the U.S. General Accounting Office (GAO) (renamed U.S. Government Accountability Office in July 2004) conducted a comprehensive study of defense acquisition, issuing an insightful report describing why the acquisition reform process had not been more responsive to reform efforts. The report entitled *Weapons Acquisition: A Rare Opportunity for Lasting Change* was based on a review of several hundred weapon system reports conducted during a fifteen-year period and was prepared by a team under project director Paul L. Francis.[2]

In reviewing its own acquisition studies, the GAO offered a valuable and somewhat unusual analysis of a seemingly intractable problem. The report was unique among acquisition reform studies in that it stressed the impact of the acquisition culture as erecting formidable barriers to acquisition reform, thereby enabling persistent problems of cost growth, schedule slippage, and technical performance shortfalls to continue.

The GAO analysis identified counterproductive incentives for government and industry that continue to exist despite the many procedural changes resulting from the acquisition reforms described in the preceding four chapters. It seemed clear to GAO researchers that the Defense Department must remove and replace the counterproductive incentives before improved results could be realistically expected.

The GAO supported the actions taken by the Office of the Secretary of Defense (OSD) to improve acquisition and concluded that the cultural dimension of acquisition problems went beyond

---

[1] U.S. Government Accountability Office (GAO), *Defense Acquisition: Major Weapon Systems Continue to Experience Cost and Schedule Problems under DoD's Revised Policy*, GAO–06–368, April 2006.

[2] GAO Report, *Weapons Acquisition: A Rare Opportunity for Lasting Change*, GAO/NSIAD–93–15, December 1992.

discipline and beyond the control of DoD acting alone, as it involved other participants, such as Congress and the defense industry. The GAO concluded that despite well-meaning attempts to reduce the time and cost of developing and producing weapons systems, "weapons still cost more, take longer to field, and often encounter performance problems." The defense acquisition culture has changed little in almost twenty years since the 1992 report appeared.[3]

In 1992, it was not uncommon for weapon programs to take ten or more years to design, develop, produce, and deploy initial operationally capable units. Reported cost increases of 20 to 40 percent occurred frequently on major weapon programs, with a significant number of programs experiencing larger cost increases.

From the 1950s through the 1980s, the urgency of the military threat and the ability of weapon programs to help participants achieve goals created what the GAO described in 1992 as a culture that preferred continuing an acquisition program irrespective of its problems, to making difficult trade-offs to alleviate cost, affordability, duplication, and risks.

The GAO pointed out that in a collective process that favors compromise, decision makers in the military services preferred to maintain more programs under way at lower funding levels rather than to fund fewer programs. In that culture, program sponsors were motivated to make optimistic (i.e., low-cost) assumptions and to reduce quantities or program scope or prolong schedules to make programs affordable and thereby avoid cancellations.[4]

Most acquisition programs have been initiated to respond to perceived deficiencies in the ability to carry out military missions against a projected threat. Program sponsors in the military services are encouraged to specify demanding performance requirements that further distinguish their weapon as the preferred solution. These demands produce what is known as "goldplating," in which design features are added, even when their cost exceeds their expected value. The GAO found that while it may be easy to criticize the authors of such requirements, it should be kept in mind that "this approach works: it is a successful, if not essential, way to win program support from higher level participants." As a result of their actions, the higher level participants in the services often reinforce the formulation of optimistic schedules and technical performance levels that are exorbitantly expensive, if they are achievable at all. Contractors contribute to the optimism by bidding low in their desire to participate in an acquisition program,

---

[3] Ibid., p. 15
[4] Ibid., pp. 21, 38–39.

CONCLUSIONS

anticipating that government will initiate changes in the contract schedule, funding, or technical performance that will provide opportunities later in the program for the government and contractor to increase the price.

As an acquisition program proceeds through development, it is not surprising for program advocates to forecast program status optimistically. They do so to overcome the challenges a program faces as it experiences schedule, cost, or technical difficulties and encounters criticisms. At the same time, program support grows because the time and money invested in the program build active sponsors for its continuation.[5]

The GAO pointed out that "even when the very underpinnings of a program are badly shaken, strong arguments are made by participants at all levels to continue the program as planned." That tactic is common for programs that have entered the engineering and manufacturing development phase (formerly full-scale development), by which time it is generally conceded that programs are committed to production.

In 2011 as in 1992, it is clear that the incentives inherent in the acquisition culture offer an explanation as to why weapon acquisition problems persist despite numerous attempts at reform. Reforms promoted sound management practices, such as realistic estimating, thorough testing, and accurate reporting. These practices, while recognized as improved acquisition management, had not been widely adopted because they were inconsistent with the very basic and strongly reinforced incentives to continue the development and production of a weapon system. In contrast, practices not normally viewed as good management techniques (concurrency and unrealistically low estimates) could be helpful to continuing acquisition development and production programs because they minimize the risk that programs will be stretched out, reduced, or canceled. There is little doubt that acquisition reforms produce limited, positive effects because they have not changed the basic incentives or pressures that drive the behavior of the participants in the acquisition process.

Despite the more recent acquisition reform initiatives in the late 1980s and 1990s, the same familiar acquisition issues arose: substantial cost growth, schedule slippage, and technical performance shortfalls. Examples included the B–1B and B–2 bombers, V–22 Osprey program, and the belated discovery by DoD of significant cost overruns on the A–12 and F–22 aircraft development programs.

---

[5] Ibid., pp. 21, 35.

As described throughout the past four chapters, procedural and organizational solutions have often been adopted to correct problems without affecting why the problems occurred in the first place. New organizational structures were proposed in attempts to reduce the strong tendency of program managers to report optimistic schedule and cost information to senior defense executives and to Congress. But the recommendations intended to improve the realism of cost estimates had not offset the incentives to submit excessively optimistic cost estimates in the first place. For example, accurate information about the status of the Navy A–12 aircraft development program was withheld by the Navy at the time of the major aircraft review (April 1990) by the secretary of defense.[6]

Acquisition reform proposals calling for prototype competition and the practice of "fly-before-buy" have been resisted, not because they were unsound or because program sponsors had an affinity for increasing technical risks. The resistance to fly-before-buy and testing was a logical reaction to the additional time and up-front cost required and to the reality that testing could jeopardize acquisition programs. This is particularly true of operational testing because it occurs outside the program manager's control, exposes the weapon to harsh operating conditions, and poses the threatening question of whether the weapon can reliably carry out its mission. As such, one of the best ways program sponsors can insulate their program from the perils of the acquisition process is by adopting a strategy of concurrency, rather than fly-before-buy.

Most acquisition reform studies point out that the short tenures of program managers, and particularly the short tenures of high-level DoD acquisition executives, make it difficult for them to change the system of incentives because other participants can wait out the reforms they oppose. Even when acquisition executives take firm stands to restrict specific programs, such as to deny funding, they often do not have the power to make their decisions stick. The Marine Corps' AV–8B Harrier and V–22 Osprey programs are examples. In each case, the secretary of defense excluded the programs from DoD's budget request, believing they were not the most cost-effective solutions to the mission needs. Congress, however, agreed with the Marine Corps' professed need for these new systems and provided funding.

In the 1990s, the GAO reported that to protect programs from criticism, the services were reluctant to provide OSD with current program information, such as updated cost estimates. In

---

[6] Office of General Counsel, Office of the Secretary of the Navy, the Beach Report, 28 November 1990, a study of events leading to the termination of the Navy A–12 aircraft development program.

fact, congressional or OSD demands for more realistic program information can intensify the protectionism of program advocates. For example, in January 1992, a panel of the National Academy of Public Administration reported that congressional demands for DoD to certify cost, performance, and reliability information on the Advanced Medium-Range Air-to-Air Missile, or AMRAAM, program during the 1980s instead yielded more unreliable information.[7]

Since 1959, seventeen defense secretaries have made commitments to bring about effective and efficient management of the defense acquisition process. Indeed, each has taken specific steps to identify problems and to initiate improvements. But each has left office before reform implementation has become institutionalized.

THE DEFENSE MARKETPLACE

The U.S. economic system is built on the concept of free enterprise regulated by competition. The private-sector marketplace is the testing ground for products and methods of production and management. A well-managed, efficient firm will prosper, and a poorly managed one will fail. Lower costs usually mean higher profits. Investors take risks that, if successful, will be rewarded by higher profits. The defense industry does not fit that model.

Many defense acquisition problems are rooted in the mistaken belief that the defense industry and the government-industry relationship in defense acquisition fit naturally into the free-enterprise model. Most Americans believe that the defense industry, as a part of private industry, is equipped to handle any kind of development or production program. They also by and large distrust government "interference" in private enterprise. Government and industry defense managers often go to great lengths to preserve the myth that large defense programs are developed and produced through the free-enterprise system. But major defense acquisition programs rarely offer incentives resembling those of the commercial marketplace. The limited positive effects of efforts to reform defense acquisition fail to address the causes of acquisition problems.

In the defense industry, most of the major producers depend heavily on one customer, the Defense Department, for business. Defense firms hire and maintain throughout their projects large groups of engineers, draftsmen, scientists, technicians, production workers, and managers to retain their capability for defense work and to increase their chances of selection for the next defense contract. Few, if any, commercial projects would enable a firm to

---

[7] National Academy of Public Administration (NAPA). *Beyond Distrust: Building Bridges Between Congress and the Executive* (Washington, D.C.: National Academy of Public Administration, January 1992).

support such a large and varied workforce. On many large defense projects, the federal government also supplies the major part of the working capital and investment. Once a weapon system contract has been signed, a firm risks little likelihood of cancellation for default because the interaction of government and industry managers involved makes it difficult to ascribe separate responsibility. The firms are further protected because contract cancellations would delay and risk program cancellation by Congress.

Relationships Between Government and Industry

The functions of DoD managers of large acquisition programs are not those classically associated with the term *manager*.[8] This is because DoD does not develop or produce its weapon systems in-house; rather, the development and production work is contracted through prime contractors. Hence, the principal functions of the program manager and staff are planning, contracting, monitoring, controlling, and evaluating the schedule, cost, and technical performance of contractors and the government agencies that provide services and support. This range of activities includes design, development, procurement, production, training, testing, and field support. The term *technical performance* is used here in the broadest sense to include not only the engineering aspects of a weapon system but also the contractor's management of resources (costs) and subcontractors.

Managing technical performance, in this sense, poses demanding industrial management challenges. Government managers are required to oversee the performance of several private-sector industries involving many of the largest firms in the country—firms managed by experienced managers, familiar with the defense acquisition process, and with methods of estimating costs, measuring progress, allocating overhead, calculating profits, and measuring return on investment for high-tech programs. Most of the recurring problems of cost growth, schedule delays, and failure to achieve technical performance on large acquisition programs cannot be solved or avoided simply by better engineering, better forms of contracting, multiyear procurement, or more prototypes. Solutions require frequent negotiations between government and industry (monthly, weekly, and sometimes daily) in situations that require government managers to be knowledgeable about their acquisition programs and the industries in which they work, experienced in the acquisition process, and highly skilled in applying the tools of industrial management.

---

[8] Maj. Gen. Howard D. Graves, "The U.S. Army War College: Gearing Up for the 21st Century," *Parameters*, December 1988.

CONCLUSIONS

One of the conclusions from studying the management of defense acquisition is that it requires specific technical knowledge and skills well beyond what many recent government managers, senior military officers, and assistant secretaries have acquired. There has always been an implicit assumption within parts of the Defense Department that natural leaders with little or no advanced training and experience in the management of large industrial programs could function effectively at any management level. This assumption has been a key factor leading to the disappointing results of virtually every acquisition reform program in the past fifty years. If the complex defense acquisition process is to be managed more effectively and efficiently, the Defense Department must develop better trained and more experienced acquisition managers and support staffs to manage the complex, continuing negotiations between one part of government and another and between government and large industrial firms.

The relationship between a government program office and its major contractor is necessarily a close one. Government and industry program managers must work together to solve complex technical problems, and, on finding solutions, initiate contract changes to the work being performed. In this environment, both government and industry must recognize that on most large development and production programs, a contract mechanism, by itself, is an ineffective substitute for rigorous day-to-day evaluations and negotiations between managers in government and industry. A government manager is not simply a partner with private industry but an independent manager charged with supervising the use of public funds.

Defense contractors, though usually motivated by a commitment to a strong defense program as well as economic gain, have three important goals: achieving the technical performance objectives of a program, meeting payrolls, and satisfying stockholders. Therefore, industry managers continually strive to obtain additional contracts that will provide work for their research and development (R&D) and production workforce. Members of Congress, usually beholden to contractors and contractor employees in their districts, often provide increased funding, lest contractors lay off employees.

Meanwhile, Defense Department program managers and contracting officers are nominally responsible for monitoring three areas of contractor activity: achieving technical performance called for in the contract, meeting the schedule requirements, and performing work within the specified budget. If a major defense acquisition program is to run smoothly and efficiently, it should be structured so that contractors have a reasonable opportunity to earn a return on investment comparable to commercial returns, without undermining government program objectives. That is often not the case.

When contractors meet their obligations at reasonable costs, government program managers should be trained and empowered to recognize that performance and to reward contractors with attractive profits and improved opportunities for future defense business. On the other hand, when contractors fail to perform effectively at reasonable costs, government program managers and contracting officers should be sufficiently trained, experienced, and motivated to discover and report inadequate performance to higher echelons of the Defense Department and to take corrective actions. Members of Congress and government officials at all levels from program managers to the secretary of defense must be qualified and motivated to conduct this kind of responsible management. But the current acquisition process is often structured to frustrate that behavior.

Adversarial Relationships. Some government program managers deal with contractors as adversaries, failing to appreciate the need for the informal cooperation so necessary between buyer and seller in managing any large development program—especially a major weapon system under conditions of technical uncertainties and changing requirements. In an adversarial relationship, these managers at times attempt to enforce fixed-price contracts for engineering development work where cost-reimbursement contracts would be far more appropriate. Or they treat cost-reimbursement contracts as if they were fixed-price contracts, trying to enforce rigid task statements when the work inherently requires adaptation.

Partnership Relationships. Other government program managers see themselves as no more than partners with industry. They may even be looking for an employer at the end of their current assignment when they retire from military service at age 45 or 50. And they may be unaware of the mixed motives inherent in the buyer-seller relationship. They share industry's goal of producing a technically excellent product, but they often do not have the required industrial management skills to oversee and control giant contractors performing highly technical work on major acquisition programs. They sometimes are unprepared or lose sight of their role in conducting arm's-length buyer-seller negotiations throughout the life of a program, protecting taxpayer funds on programs where changes occur weekly, sometimes daily. These managers often express the mistaken view that "we know how much the program 'should' cost because that's how much the contractor spent." They seem unaware of how easy it is for contractor costs to increase out of control. Program managers are proud, as they should be, of the technical excellence of their products. But unlike their peers in commercial business, they usually incur no penalty for programs exceeding their original budgets.

The challenge of managing major acquisition programs effectively and efficiently requires government program managers and contracting officers professionally skilled in achieving a critical balance between the adversarial role and the pure partnership role—a balance that produces what is referred to as a *wise buyer*.[9] Achieving that balance requires years of acquisition training and experience; learning to cope with the complexities of the acquisition process; the day-to-day negotiations; and the marketing tactics within government, within industry, and between government and industry. What is needed is not an adversarial relationship characterized by animosity, suspicion, and mistrust, but a business relationship characterized by rigorous analyses, bargaining, and a tenacious regard for the best interests of one's own side.[10] But military and civilian assignment policies often fall short of enabling government program managers and their superiors to acquire these capabilities.

At present, government managers who handle crises effectively are given high performance ratings. Often, however, timely preventive action could have corrected problems before they became crises. Because preventive action requires attention to management detail, inexperienced program managers may be unlikely to appreciate the engineering and development work being performed by contractors. As a result, there is often little motivation to exercise rigorous, systematic control.

The Liaison Manager. Some government and industry acquisition managers and officials describe the job of a government program manager primarily as one of promoting a program, preparing progress reports and briefings, negotiating with officials at the Pentagon and at various military commands, and resolving engineering conflicts between these organizations and contractors. They often act as though the responsibility for cost control belongs solely to the contractor. This is often called the liaison manager view. It is based on the belief that the defense business is part of the free-enterprise system and therefore regulated by competition in the marketplace. Those holding this mistaken view believe that general leadership training and leadership experience added to two or three years of significant acquisition experience are sufficient qualifications to manage a major acquisition program. They mistakenly believe

---

[9] Ltr, General Henry A. Miley, U.S. Army (Ret.), former commander of the U.S. Army Materiel Command, to Jay R. Sculley, Assistant Secretary of the Army, 11 Jul 1984; U.S. Congress, Senate, testimony of General Miley before the Task Force on Selected Defense Procurement Matters of the Committee on Armed Services, *Career Paths and Professional Development for Acquisition Managers in the Department of Defense*, 13 December 1984, pp. 17–22

[10] Richard J. Bednar and John T. Jones Jr., "The Role of the DoD Contracting Officer," Draft Report of the American Bar Association (ABA) Section of Public Contract Law, Ad Hoc Committee, John E. Cavanagh, chairman, 11 January 1987, p. 120.

that knowledge of industry and skills in industrial practices are "nice to have," but not essential, and that relying on functional subordinates and "presiding" over a team of specialists can substitute for personal involvement by the program manager.

The Active Manager. Others describe the program manager's role as one of planning and making key decisions associated with rigorous oversight of, negotiation with, and control of industrial firms performing the development and production work. This is called the active manager view. It is based on the belief that in this environment, the competitive forces of the marketplace do not alone produce the desired cost, schedule, and technical performance, often frustrated by contract changes occurring throughout the life of a program.

Those who hold the liaison manager view often talk about cost control in managing programs but fail to understand that the planning and control of large industrial programs are achieved neither by proclamation nor by good intentions. They occur only as the result of careful analyses and trade-offs associated with their program and with persistent control of engineering changes. The skills needed for these tasks require intensive practical training and acquisition experience in dealing with contractors, users, and other stakeholders, first on smaller acquisition programs, then on larger ones.

In reality, the responsibility for cost control belongs to the government program manager, the contracting officer, and the contractor. Significant cost reductions are often possible, depending on the government manager's knowledge and skills in establishing and implementing challenging productivity and cost incentives, formal and informal, throughout the life of a program.

Not surprisingly, those of the liaison manager view consider the government acquisition job a reasonable alternate assignment, or "shore duty," for combat arms officers until they are next assigned to their primary duties in operational units. Proponents of the active manager view, however, consider the defense acquisition process as too complex, too costly, and too important to national security to be relegated to an alternate assignment.

REEXAMINING THE PROGRAM MANAGER CONCEPT

The program manager concept works well in private industry. Why then does it experience serious problems so often in government? Consider the unique characteristics of industry program managers, who usually report to the company president.

- They have genuine decision-making authority regarding personnel assignments, promotions, technical matters, and budgets.

CONCLUSIONS

- They usually have years of training and experience in the work of their industry (e.g., development and production of missiles, aircraft, tanks, ships, and guidance systems). They understand the goals and constraints of their customers and the ways in which their customers operate.
- They understand the roles performed and the tactics employed within government, within industry, and between government and industry. They are experienced practitioners in dealing with these situations.

Lacking the training, experience, and stature of their private-sector counterparts, DoD program managers often encounter another serious obstacle to performing their jobs. Namely, they are required to respond to (indeed, often placate) many individuals in government capable of influencing their careers: senior officers in the buying commands, the using commands, the service headquarters staff, the service secretariat, OSD, and Congress. Within these groups there are diverse elements: some who support a particular acquisition program, some who oppose it, and some who are undecided. The people representing one or more of these stakeholder groups can change every few months, as assignments change. These groups have voracious appetites for data from DoD program managers: How much will it cost to reduce the aircraft by 200 pounds? What is the consequence of reducing the budget by $100 million? How much can we save by reducing the production rate by 50 percent? What will be the impact of replacing the radar? What caused the program delay? What will it take to regain the lost schedule? How much can we save by competing the next production contract?

It is long past time to reexamine the current method of manning and operating government program management offices. The current job descriptions portray program managers as supermen and superwomen who

- cut through the red tape generated by several hundred "interested" government managers;
- always obtain budget approvals from the service headquarters, OSD, and Congress;
- work as partners with industry in solving technical problems;
- obtain reliable measurement data from which to determine independently the schedule, cost, and technical performance status of a program; and
- provide incentives for industry to perform expeditiously at the lowest reasonable cost.

All this is often expected of relatively inexperienced program managers with modest staffs directing and controlling an acquisition system for complex engineering development programs.

Although there is a pressing need for the Defense Department to perform the active manager role, the current approach to program management is fundamentally flawed. After fifty years, we know that an Army or Air Force colonel or Navy captain (at the rank of O–6) with limited industrial management knowledge and experience is often ill prepared to direct and oversee a first-of-a-kind, multihundred-million-dollar industrial program with hundreds of complex challenges and dilemmas. If DoD is to perform the role of the wise buyer on major acquisition programs, a senior O–6 or a one- or two-star military officer or equivalent government civilian must be highly skilled in the acquisition process and business management, and committed to effective and efficient performance. There is too much at stake for on-the-job training in these positions. Too often, the training and experience have been far too shallow and brief.

On most large engineering development programs, a fixed-price contract jeopardizes the quality of the product and restricts the information available to the Department of Defense. Over the past several decades, the Defense Department has learned repeatedly that fixed-price contracts (including fixed-price incentive contracts) cannot substitute for—indeed they inhibit—the week-to-week evaluations of progress, correlations of cost and progress, and negotiations of the hundreds of changes proposed by both government and contractor personnel.

Differing Perceptions of Defense Acquisition

One impression that stands out from conversations with people involved in defense acquisition is that government and industry managers have very different perceptions of the current condition of the acquisition process. Some describe it as poorly managed and plagued by serious problems; others see it as having few problems. These differing perceptions do not reflect the conventional dichotomies of military versus civilian or government versus industry. Rather, they reflect differing views of the government's role in managing the acquisition process.

Those with the liaison manager view, described earlier, believe government program managers do not need years of training and experience in business management and methods of industrial cost control. If the program manager is limited to promoting the program, preparing progress reports, and performing technical liaison, then experience as a pilot, tank commander, ship captain, or engineer, and possibly ten to fifteen weeks at the Defense Acquisition University may be sufficient. But for those who hold the active manager view, military experience and fifteen weeks of training are far from sufficient for the job.

For decades, many have observed that government program managers and their staffs are intelligent and hardworking. Program managers, along with most other managers in defense acquisition, genuinely want to acquire advanced weapon systems that meet performance standards at reasonable costs. But in practice, too few government managers know much about industry financial incentives or the process of controlling costs, schedules, and technical performance in large industrial firms. As a result, government managers rarely make the difficult decisions required to create and reward lean industrial organizations.

Most of the proposed solutions to defense management problems in the past have been undermined in one of two ways. The first is the lack of continuity. When a Pentagon official introduces specific acquisition reforms, there is often a flurry of activity, and for a year or two progress is made. Then the sponsoring military or civilian official is transferred to another assignment or leaves the government. A new official takes over and shifts the focus to other activities, and the old problems begin to resurface.

The second practice undermining proposed solutions to acquisition problems is the tendency to apply quick-fix solutions to reduce budgets for a particular program. For example, a funding stretch-out, a new contract form, or a new management technique is adopted, in the misguided hope that quick fixes, by themselves, will substitute for better trained, experienced, and more skilled and capable program management personnel.

Many of the so-called centralized or decentralized approaches to improve the acquisition process could succeed if experienced government managers—military and civilian—at each level, from the program office to OSD, understood the intricacies of the acquisition process, were skilled and committed to achieving its objectives, were deeply involved in the process for most of their careers, and received significant rewards for achieving improved performance. As it is, many defense managers often either have limited understanding of the desired improvements or lack the knowledge or skills to implement them. Their attempts to improve the process are often short-lived or ineffective and thus hinder the goals of the improvement program (e.g., imposing expensive reporting requirements on contractors in the hope that vast amounts of detailed data will alone achieve cost control).

Previous acquisition reform efforts described in Chapters Two, Three, and Four all call for more extensive training and experience for program managers. Improvements have been made in recent years, but still more needs to be done as evidenced by the comments made in every acquisition study conducted.

There appears to be no realistic alternative to providing clear and more comprehensive career paths for government acquisition managers from the level of functional managers, program managers, and program executive officers to the senior acquisition positions in the Pentagon. Experience to date indicates that managing taxpayer-funded acquisition programs costing hundreds of millions of dollars is too important and too complex to be conducted by government military and civilian personnel with part-time acquisition careers or acquisition careers so short as to require incumbents to look to their contractors for their next employment or for a referral for the next employment. Acquisition career paths for both military and civilian personnel need to include genuine promotion opportunities at least comparable to those provided in military operational career fields. Short of these steps, the Defense Department can expect yet one or more decades of studies and recommendations for improvements, with little accomplished in the way of lasting change.

It seems only reasonable that the heads of the Army, Navy, and Air Force acquisition organizations should be among the most qualified acquisition managers available, based on years of acquisition training and practical acquisition experience. When selected for these positions, they should have sole responsibility for materiel acquisition and personnel recruitment, selection, and assignments of their acquisition workforce. To separate these responsibilities is to invite the problems of the past four decades.

Although Defense Acquisition University (DAU) courses constitute important steps in training program managers and their staffs, more training time and courses are needed to provide students with extensive practice in analyzing and dealing with real-life examples of the challenges they will encounter on their jobs. Future program managers should be required to complete six months or more of formal advanced training in which they study and learn to deal effectively with hundreds of realistic examples of the challenges and dilemmas both they and contracting officers will encounter on acquisition programs. They should analyze these challenges, discuss the strengths and weaknesses of the options available for dealing with them, and plan the implementation programs for the selected option. Instructors will need to be familiar with industrial management practices, skilled in conducting practical training, comfortable with interactive classroom sessions, and current in practical knowledge of the opportunities and constraints that exist in the field. Instructors do not need to be academics or theorists. The training program should develop the wise buyer skills needed to resolve the complex problems that occur on major engineering development and production programs. The emphasis should be on making analyses and decisions, using simulations of contractor negotiations, exercises, case studies, and other techniques to plan effective implementation programs. DAU courses currently provide a useful start toward accomplishing this goal. An internship in a program management office would ideally precede *and* follow the one-year practical training program, with experienced program managers serving as supervisors.

Military and civil service positions in acquisition usually have few similarities. Too few military program managers remain in their job assignments long enough to develop the required expertise and in-depth knowledge of their programs, while civil servants at times remain for so long in their functional assignments at one location that some resist innovation and change.

Insufficient professional acquisition management training, experience, and incentives can be serious handicaps for civilians in the acquisition workforce. Those who devote their careers to acquisition management and procurement need professional acquisition training. But there should be an effective screening process for selecting candidates for demanding acquisition positions; only those with the requisite talent and motivation should be accepted. In addition, a personnel board, comprising senior military and civilian acquisition officials, should review applicants for all major positions and be authorized and motivated to remove government personnel whose performance is marginal or inadequate. The board should also have the authority to provide significant financial rewards for outstanding performance.

GOVERNMENT AND CONTRACTOR INCENTIVES

If, as has been the case for five decades, the military promotion system will not respond to repeated attempts to provide attractive promotions and career opportunities for acquisition managers to attain flag or civilian equivalent grade, then the Defense Department should provide other incentives, such as additional pay and incentive compensation. If an extra $30,000 or more per year were paid to selected military officers and civilians (at the rank of O–6 and above) and career regulations permitted them to remain in the acquisition field, incentives to retire and join the defense industry would be minimized. The extra cost would be negligible compared to the benefits of retaining experienced acquisition managers.

Such a proposal is not without precedent. Military officers on flight status and submarine duty as well as medical and dental officers and other special-skilled officers currently receive additional pay. Indeed, Sweden's government acquisition agency addresses the problem of attracting and retaining senior people—military and civilian—by a special law that allows an added salary increase for crucial acquisition positions. Thus, a Swedish colonel serving as a program manager can receive a significantly higher salary than other colonels and even the director general of the agency. This incentive provides prestige and draws highly qualified, experienced people to senior acquisition positions.[11]

Were there a more attractive government career in DoD acquisition management, it would then be possible to minimize the conflicts associated with frequent turnover of military personnel and widespread military retirements to industry, while preserving the rights of individuals to careers in acquisition management. The basic goal of any legislative remedy must be achieving and maintaining outstanding competence and integrity to the defense acquisition system.

With respect to contractors, the Defense Department customarily does business with an inverted system of rewards and penalties. As noted earlier, contractors are often rewarded for higher than planned program costs with increased sales, higher contributions to overhead, and higher profits. The system also encourages government and industry managers to place far higher priority on gaining congressional approval to begin new acquisition weapon programs or obtain additional funding for ongoing programs than it does on controlling cost.[12] In a *New York Times* article, Arthur E. Fitzgerald noted that the acquisition cost problems of the 1980s, 1990s, and 2000s are not aberrations; they are the result of many government and industry participants reacting in perfect accord with the distorted rewards and penalties inherent in the acquisition process.[13]

Reluctance to establish more appropriate incentives has been a serious deficiency in most DoD improvement programs during the past five decades.[14] Contractors should be rewarded with higher profits for complying with schedules, satisfying promised technical performance standards, and delivering goods and services at or be-

---

[11] Jacques S. Gansler, "Strengthening Government Acquisition Management Through Selected Use of Experienced Industrial Managers," paper prepared for the Procurement Roundtable, Washington, D.C., 11 June 1987, p. 4.

[12] Charles Mohr, "Critics See Key Flaw in Arms Cost Controls," *New York Times*, 18 May 1985.

[13] Arthur E. Fitzgerald, Deputy for Management Systems, Office of the Assistant Secretary of the Air Force, *New York Times*, 18 May 1985.

[14] *Boston Globe*, 27 July 1986. The Packard Commission reluctance to recommend changed incentives was most clearly seen at a press conference on 2 July 1986, at which David Packard, presenting the final report, said that waste and fraud in defense industries should be rooted out by "self-discipline," not by government regulation.

low contracted cost. Prospects for obtaining future contracts should be closely linked to performance on existing contracts.[15] New contract forms; better planning, control, and reporting systems; and improved cost estimating and change control systems are unlikely to be effective unless government managers are skilled in the implementation and use of these techniques and are rewarded, along with contractors, for effective results.

THE NEED FOR EXTENDED FOLLOW-UP ACTIONS

A persistent problem associated with previous attempts at acquisition reform has been the failure of management to take vigorous action to ensure implementation of the best recommendations. The results of the acquisition reform efforts of the 1970s, 1980s, 1990s, and 2000s have taught us that communicating acquisition reform actions from the Office of the Secretary of Defense down to the services, without significant follow-up by managers throughout the government hierarchy, produces no more than temporary or marginal improvements at best. Much activity is directed toward initiating reform efforts but little toward following through to ensure that lasting change occurs.

Many in government and industry want to improve the acquisition process. But it is unrealistic to expect any lasting improvement if an appropriate system of incentives and disincentives is not established and enforced. Specifically,

- Unless changes are made in the current contractor source selection process, which makes optimistically low-cost estimates a significant advantage in competing for a contract, it is useless to discuss realistic contractor proposals. The source selection process must give far more weight to a contractor's record of realistic cost estimates and past performance.
- Unless changes are made in the current profit system that demands higher costs as a prerequisite for higher profits, it is futile to expect lower costs. Because profits are largely cost based, there is little economic motivation for contractors to reduce direct or indirect costs. The profit system needs a major overhaul to relate a significant portion of profit to contractor investment and performance.[16]

---

[15] Richard A. Stubbing, *The Defense Game* (New York: Harper & Row, 1986), p. 416.
[16] Testimony of Lt. Gen. James Stansberry, United States Air Force (Ret.) (formerly commander, Electronics Systems Division, Air Force Systems Command), before the Senate Subcommittee on Defense Acquisition Policy of the Committee on Armed Services, "Defense Procurement Process," 20 February 1985, p. 20.

- Unless changes are made in the current military personnel system that makes short-term assignments necessary for military officers to acquire the number and variety of assignments required for promotion, any significant reduction in personnel turnover in defense program offices is unlikely.
- Unless changes are made in the current OSD and congressional practice of routinely accepting program stretch-outs as a tactic for funding new programs, it is unrealistic to advocate economical production rates.
- Unless changes are made in the current DoD practice of waiving training requirements and offering only short training courses, which limit coverage to introductory rather than in-depth practical treatment of industrial planning and control, it is unrealistic to expect improved training for acquisition managers.
- Unless changes are made in military careers that currently provide few opportunities beyond age 45 or 50, it is unrealistic to expect military officers not to seek a second career in the defense industry. In addressing this problem, DoD needs to listen to lieutenant colonels and colonels and Navy commanders and captains to learn their views on the advantages and disadvantages of the acquisition career field.
- Without genuine promotion opportunities for individuals who make the difficult decisions associated with successful negotiating and wise buying, it is unrealistic to expect to retain in government service experienced program managers able to do much more than promote their programs, prepare progress reports, and conduct briefings.

After nearly fifty years of initiatives to improve the acquisition process, it is increasingly evident that the schedule, cost, and technical performance problems of defense acquisition programs conducted by thousands of government and industry participants will not be corrected by short-term fixes. The persistence of acquisition problems is not due to lack of understanding of what practices need to be changed. The field of defense acquisition abounds with thoughtful recommendations developed by senior acquisition managers who have studied the acquisition process with care. The underlying stumbling block has been and continues to be one of implementing and institutionalizing the recommendations required to bring about more professional management.

CONCLUSIONS

Future attempts to correct the persistent and costly problems of defense acquisition must include more effective follow-up by senior and mid-level government managers who must understand and agree with the changes that need to be made. Today's practice of reassigning military acquisition managers, at most levels every two or three years on acquisition programs that require ten years or more to complete, is unlikely to produce lasting improvements in managing those programs. The instruments of change must be a strong secretary of defense and senior acquisition executives chosen for industrial experience, with expert knowledge and skills in defense acquisition, who understand why acquisition reform efforts of the past have failed to achieve lasting improvements, and who have strong commitments to achieving efficient as well as effective acquisition program outcomes.

It is clear that military and civilian acquisition managers need more extensive training in the practicalities of acquisition, need tenure longer than two or three years in program manager assignments, and need to be unambiguous in taking steps to improve management of acquisition programs. There is little likelihood that the cost of major acquisition programs will stabilize or decrease unless and until more skilled government acquisition managers, at all levels, have the ability and commitment to accomplish these objectives. Minor adjustments or corrections to the present acquisition process simply will not accomplish this vital job.

High federal deficits at the end of the first decade of the twenty-first century, the continuing need for a strong defense, and a growing awareness to deal more effectively with the high cost of defense acquisition can provide the stimulus to bring about much needed improvements in the control of schedules and costs for defense engineering development and production programs. That view is reinforced by the findings of four insightful studies of defense acquisition, conducted from 2006 to 2009, commissioned by the Office of the Secretary of Defense, the Secretary of the Air Force, the Defense Science Board, and the Government Accountability Office. These studies (in Appendix A) describe the current state of defense acquisition and indicate, once again, the less-than-satisfying results of acquisition reform efforts conducted during the past four decades. The studies suggest that correcting the shortcomings in defense acquisition management deserves urgent and concerted action by the secretary of defense and his key assistants.

APPENDIX A

FOUR ACQUISITION REFORM STUDIES CONDUCTED FROM 2001 TO 2009

From 2001 to 2009, the Office of the Secretary of Defense (OSD), the Army, the Navy, the Air Force, and the U.S. Government Accountability Office (GAO) undertook a number of insightful studies and reports on defense acquisition. Among those were the following four reports whose enduring effects on acquisition performance are still to be determined. A summary of each study is included below in the order in which they were completed.

1. OSD assessment of DoD acquisition management: *Defense Acquisition Performance Assessment*, a report commissioned by Gordon England, Acting Deputy Secretary of Defense, January 2006.
2. *CNA Independent Assessment: Air Force Acquisition*, a report commissioned by the secretary of the Air Force and directed by the assistant secretary of the Air Force for acquisition (ASAF/AQ), February 2009.
3. *Creating a DoD Strategic Acquisition Platform*, a report by the Defense Science Board, an advisory board to the secretary of defense, March 2009.
4. *Defense Acquisitions: Assessments of Selected Weapon Programs*, U.S. Government Accountability Office, GAO–09–0326SP, March 2009.

1. *Defense Acquisition Performance Assessment*[1]
Conducted by the Office of the Secretary of Defense, January 2006

Initiated by Gordon England, Acting Deputy Secretary of Defense, the Defense Acquisition Performance Assessment (DAPA) study was conducted by Defense Department military and civilian personnel, with a report issued in January 2006. In commissioning the report, Secretary England acknowledged that

---

[1] *Defense Acquisition Performance Assessment Report* (Washington, D.C.: January 2006). A Department of Defense study commissioned by the Honorable Gordon England, Acting Deputy Secretary of Defense.

[t]here is a growing and deep concern within the Congress and within the Department of Defense (DoD) Leadership Team about the DoD acquisition processes. Many programs continue to increase in cost and schedule even after multiple studies and recommendations that span the past 15 years. In addition, the DoD Inspector General has recently raised various acquisition management shortcomings.[2]

Among its major findings, the DAPA report found that DoD acquisition processes did not meet the standards set by the Packard Commission and issued by the Department of Defense twenty years earlier. The report acknowledged that in 2006 several "staff oversight organizations, lengthy lines of communication and adversarial relations" resulted in excessive and ineffective exercise of authority without accountability and "inhibit proper execution of our programs. . . . The current decision-making process is flawed."[3]

Explaining this finding, the report concluded that "existing oversight relies upon overlapping layers of reviews and reviewers at the expense of quality and focus." The DAPA report also concluded that "the Department of Defense does not have a single consistent, sufficient set of metrics applicable across programs to manage acquisitions or measure success. Key performance parameters . . . do not correlate with either force or system capability and often are not testable."[4]

The DAPA assessment determined that correcting these vulnerabilities required "implement[ing] the intent of the Packard Commission more fully and regain[ing] stability in the Acquisition System by realigning authority, accountability and responsibility at the appropriate levels."[5] It also determined that increasing the stature and authority of the under secretary of defense for acquisition, technology, and logistics and the service acquisition executives would improve accountability. To successfully accomplish these changes, DAPA acknowledged, would require the personal involvement of the service secretaries, the Army and Air Force chiefs of staff, and the chief of Naval Operations.

In describing other significant shortcomings in the acquisition system, the report stated that the definition of the acquisition workforce did not include requirements and budget personnel, that is, key personnel not covered in the Defense Acquisition Workforce Improvement Act. Requirements personnel were not assigned to

---

[2] Ibid., p. v, introductory letter to the report by Gordon England, and pp. 10, 26, 29.
[3] Ibid., p. 24.
[4] Ibid., p. 25.
[5] Ibid., p. 26.

APPENDIX A

acquisition organizations but to major commands and staff offices. Their mission was to establish and codify acquisition thresholds and objective performance requirements and to sit on requirements generation, control, and approval boards, representing the war-fighting community in acquisition decision-making forums. Budget officers were assigned to the services and OSD to allocate and manage program accounts. "Thus, no single organization is accountable for overall acquisition workforce career development, no consistent training or experience requirements exist for these key skills, and training and certification standards are not enforced."[6]

DAPA concluded that key DoD personnel responsible for requirements, budget, and acquisition did not have sufficient experience, tenure, and training to meet current acquisition challenges. Personnel stability in these key positions was not sufficient to develop or maintain adequate understanding of programs and program issues. The systems engineering capability within the Department of Defense was not sufficient to clearly define the interdependencies of program activities and to manage large-scale integration efforts.

The devaluation of experience and expertise in the acquisition workforce contributed to what the DAPA called a conspiracy of hope, in which the cost, risk, and technical readiness of acquisition programs were understated and could not be conducted within initial estimates. The DAPA report highlighted that "lack of experience and expertise is [particularly] apparent in [the] program management cadre." The declining number of science and engineering graduates willing to enter either industry or government has led to an increase in contractor support in acquisition management, thus resulting in the loss of core competencies among government personnel. The DAPA report recommended "infusing program management expertise into the workforce in the near term by routinely [providing] expert mentoring to Program Managers."[7]

With respect to budgeting, DAPA pointed out that "the variability between annual budget predictions and ultimate budget authority [made] program planning difficult." Congressional inclination to take money from specific program elements for nonprogrammatic reasons as well as the services' propensity to take procurement investment account money to pay military personnel and operations and maintenance bills had combined to create a root cause for program instablility.[8]

---

[6] Ibid., p. 28 (quotation).
[7] Ibid., pp. 29, 31.
[8] Ibid., pp. 29–32, 36.

The DAPA team also cited significant problems with the DoD requirements process. Senior military leadership was not adequately involved in managing the requirements process. "Neither the Joint Capabilities Integration and Development System nor the services requirement development processes were well informed about the maturity of technologies that underlie achievement of the requirement or the resources necessary to realize their developments."[9] This has produced a significant disconnect between "requirements management and development" and the budget and acquisition processes in the acquisition system. Managing the requirements process was identified as the number one area that, if restructured or changed, would have the most positive influence on the overall acquisition system. While 96 percent of the respondents to the DAPA assessment agreed that changes in requirements adversely affected acquisition programs, there was not a common agreement on what drove those changes. Nonetheless, 87 percent of those interviewed believed there was insufficient training for government personnel involved in the requirements process. The lack of input from systems engineering in the requirements development process resulted in inadequate conversion of capability needs into measurable requirements.

The DAPA report contained more than thirty recommendations, including the following:

- Seek legislation establishing the Service Acquisition Executives as Five-Year Fixed Presidential Appointments renewable for a second five-year term. This will add leadership continuity and stability to the Acquisition System.
- Immediately increase the number of federal employees focused on critical skill areas, such as program management, system engineering and contracting. The cost of this increase should be offset by reductions in funding for contractor support.
- Fully implement the intent of the Packard Commission. Create a streamlined acquisition organization with accountability assigned and enforced at each level.
- Adjust program estimates to reflect "high confidence"—defined as a program with an 80 percent chance of completing development at or below estimated cost—when programs are baselined in the Stable Program Funding Account.
- Change [DoD's] preferred acquisition strategy for developmental programs from delivering 100 percent performance to delivering useful military capability within a constrained period of

---

[9] Ibid., p. 36.

APPENDIX A

time, no more than 6 years from Milestone A. This makes time a Key Performance Parameter.
- Direct the Service Acquisition Executives to appoint Program Managers to be held accountable for each baseline from Milestone B through completion of the Beyond Low-Rate Initial Production report.[10]

Although the Defense Department held the DAPA report in high regard, it became clear that significant barriers existed to implementing many of the DAPA recommendations. Three years after the DAPA report was issued, many of the recommendations were not yet implemented.

2. *CNA Independent Assessment: Air Force Acquisition*[11]
Conducted by CNA, February 2009

The CNA report on Air Force acquisition was prepared in 2009 by three former senior DoD officials. The report is based on the analysis and recommendations of a panel consisting of four retired Air Force general officers and three former OSD and Air Force civilian officials.

The CNA report documented significant cost growth on Air Force acquisition programs since the mid-1990s, exceeding the cost growth experienced by Army and Navy acquisition programs during the same period. The authors and their distinguished panel concluded that the apparent failure of the Air Force community to value acquisition as a profession in the Air Force or to enforce accountability or process discipline was a major impediment to achieving significant improvements in Air Force acquisition. They pointed out that it was "imperative that the acquisition profession be seen as a valued component of the Air Force" and that the individuals working in the acquisition function have career opportunities comparable to Air Force operations personnel. Without an effective acquisition function, the ability of the Air Force to provide the capability "demanded by the joint warfighter [was] in jeopardy."[12]

In reviewing the acquisition organizational structure in the Air Force, the CNA team concluded that the SAF/AQ (the Office of the Service Acquisition Executive), the Air Force chief of staff, the commander, Air Force Materiel Command, and the commanders of the

---
[10] Ibid., pp. 9–14.
[11] *CNA Independent Assessment: Air Force Acquisition*, (Alexandria, Va.: CNA, February 2009). This report was commissioned by the secretary of the Air Force on 18 July 2008 and directed by the assistant secretary of the Air Force for acquisition. CNA is a federally funded research and development center.
[12] Ibid., pp. 24–25.

user commands "need to be more actively and personally involved ... in defining requirements and resource priorities."[13]

The CNA team also concluded that the wing/group/squadron structure of the Air Force acquisition workforce was not effective and was a major inhibitor to efficient execution of the acquisition process. Further, the team was frequently told that the command selection process for wing commanders "often [resulted] in wing commanders with limited acquisition experience."[14]

The CNA team unanimously agreed that a return to a matrix structure with acquisition functional home rooms was a necessary ingredient in revitalizing the Air Force acquisition workforce. The team concluded that the current wing structure for the acquisition workforce:

- Inhibits functional management and development of the workforce;
- Inhibits deployment of critical skills and resources across and among wings and centers;
- Adds at least one additional organizational layer; and
- Confuses reporting and rating chains.[15]

The CNA team reported that most of those who discussed requirements with them complained that there were few, if any, constraints on Air Force requirements in terms of numbers, cost, or technological maturity. Acquisition participants in requirements high performance teams (HPTs) tended to feel either ignored or intimidated. They said acquisition members "are frequently chosen based on the fact that they are simply available and often were replaced at the next meeting." With respect to the weapon system requirements process, the CNA team concluded that the process was seriously flawed.

- There [are] excessive numbers of KPPs [Key Performance Parameters].
- Evaluability and testability is often neglected.
- Technical feasibility is often overestimated.
- Performance trades are often not emphasized in requirements generation.
- There are disconnects between requirements, acquisition, and resource communities and processes

---

[13] Ibid., pp. 5–6.
[14] Ibid., p. 6.
[15] Ibid., p. 7.

APPENDIX A

- There is inadequate stratification of requirements to enable and institutionalize the concept of block acquisition.[16]

The CNA team was surprised to discover that the program control function in Air Force program management offices had been reduced to little more than a "budget shop." The consensus opinion of the team was, "How can anyone run a program without the program control function?" When combined with the consequent move to place earned value functional personnel into financial job series, "it was no surprise that the earned value function had virtually disappeared from the Air Force."[17] The team recommended that the program control function be restored or revitalized, or both, within program offices.

3. *Creating a DoD Strategic Acquisition Platform*[18]
Conducted by the Defense Science Board, an advisory board to the secretary of defense, April 2009

The Defense Science Board (DSB) report was published in April 2009 to inform the new administration that "fixing the acquisition process is a critical national security issue—requiring the attention of the Secretary of Defense. The incoming leadership must address this concern among its top priorities as the nation's military prowess depends on it."[19]

The DSB report pointed out that typical major defense system acquisitions still require ten to fifteen years to develop, though new product development in the commercial sector of similarly complex systems took one-third to one-half that time. The DSB explained that

> [t]hese development times are far outpaced by the rapid advances in technology, which means that subsystems technology can be one or two generations old by the time a system is provided to warfighters in the field—unless upgrades are incorporated before the system is fielded. Furthermore, DoD acquisition programs often have large cost overruns, long schedule delays, and unsatisfactory product quality and performance.[20]

---

[16] Ibid., p. 9.
[17] Ibid., p. 11.
[18] Defense Science Board (DSB), *Creating a DoD Strategic Acquisition Platform* (Washington, D.C.: March 2009). The DSB is a federal advisory committee established to provide independent advice to the secretary of defense. Ronald Kerber was the chair of the ten-person committee that conducted the study and prepared the report.
[19] Ibid., introduction.
[20] Ibid., p. 1.

In exploring the causes of these problems, the DSB team asked why previous acquisition reform efforts had failed so often. Team members determined that it was, in part, because they did not address the root causes of the problems and focused instead on reengineering the mechanics of the acquisition decision process. "Many problems appeared to be caused by the use of immature technology, [changing] requirements, or funding instability. Such problems, however, were really only symptoms of the lack of experienced judgment on the part of [DoD] personnel who structured acquisition programs in a way that would almost certainly lead to failure."[21]

The DSB report also observed that perhaps the most important reason previous acquisition reform efforts had failed was that the problems had been left to the under secretary of defense for acquisition, technology, and logistics. Effective acquisition is a challenge that exceeds the authority of the under secretary.

> Fixing defense acquisition is a challenge that can only be successfully addressed by the Secretary of Defense and it should be among his top priorities. The Secretary not only had to lead the charge within DOD to fix the acquisition process, but also to inform Congress of departmental actions and enlist its support for his agenda, lest Congress act independently in a way that undermined his efforts.[22]

Consequently, proven, relevant experience was needed in the Office of the Secretary of Defense, the military departments, and defense agencies. The DSB pointed out that many people were inexperienced in acquisition, from the leadership to program managers. Very few had a personal track record of repeated successes at acquisition. Trial-and-error and on-the-job training could be expensive.[23]

In supporting this observation, the DSB cited a key point from the 1986 Packard Commission on the need for acquisition leadership to have "a solid industrial background." Yet the commission's intent was often ignored. The rules had been stretched so that acquisition executives in OSD and the services were appointed with little or no proven, relevant, or successful business experience. "Without relevant experience to guide decision-making, those leaders often rely on the bureaucracy to make decisions for them."[24]

The DSB expressed the view that today's acquisition leaders required a combination of business, technical, and human resource management capabilities and skills. Without these skills they might lead in some other field but would fail in managing the acquisition of major de-

---

[21] Ibid., p. 4.
[22] Ibid., p. 5.
[23] Ibid., p. 13.
[24] Ibid., pp. 13–14.

fense engineering development and production programs. Along with experienced leaders and program managers, acquisition functional specialists, military and civilian, needed upgrading as well.

The DSB report stated that the first step was to select program managers of major systems programs who had demonstrated successful performance in managing acquisition programs of increasing complexity. Program success was more likely, even when delayed, if the right leadership could be put in place from the start so that the program began with goals and objectives that could be realized.

> The Secretary of Defense should issue guidance that top [senior] acquisition appointments be filled with individuals who have proven, successful, and relevant [acquisition] experience.
>
> The Under Secretary of Defense for Acquisition, Technology, and Logistics, should require that program executive officers and program managers have demonstrated successful performance in managing programs of increasing complexity before appointments are made [in which they are responsible for the conduct of] major systems programs.[25]

Experienced leadership needed the support of a well-trained and experienced workforce. But the acquisition workforce in general—both civilian and military—lacked the experience needed.

The DSB also reported that the personal interests of many individuals involved in the acquisition process did not always align with the interests of the nation—their incentives could be counterproductive. "It is in the self interest of too many people not to fix the acquisition system: they are financially rewarded and their career is sustained by keeping things as they are."[26] Those responsible for technical performance usually had no organizational responsibility for meeting cost and schedule requirements. Yet their input could have a significant impact on program decisions and, in turn, program schedule and cost.

4. *Defense Acquisitions: Assessments of Selected Weapon Programs*[27]
Conducted by the U.S. Government Accountability Office, March 2009

This report for Congress contained the GAO's seventh annual assessment of selected Department of Defense weapon programs.

---
[25] Ibid., pp. 14–15.
[26] Ibid., p. 15.
[27] U.S. Government Accountability Office (GAO) Report, *Defense Acquisitions: Assessments of Selected Weapon Programs*, GAO-09-326SP (Washington, D.C.: March 2009). The GAO's seventh annual assessment of selected weapon programs provides a snapshot of how well the Department of Defense plans and executes its major weapon acquisition programs—an area that has been on GAO's high-risk list since its inception in 1990.

The report examined how well DoD planned and executed the development and production of its weapon acquisition programs. While the overall performance of weapon system programs "was still poor," the GAO reported that there had been some modest improvements in DoD's acquisition outcomes. The report included an analysis of the overall performance of DoD's portfolio of ninety-six major defense acquisition programs.[28] Total cost growth for the 2008 portfolio of ninety-six major defense acquisition programs had decreased marginally compared to the 2007 portfolio, and programs started in recent years were based on more knowledge about technology and design at key points in the acquisition process.

The GAO pointed out that since 2003, DoD's portfolio of major defense acquisition programs had grown from seventy-seven to ninety-six programs; its investment in those programs had grown from $1.2 trillion to $1.6 trillion (fiscal year 2009 dollars). The five-year cumulative cost growth for these programs compared to original estimates was $296 billion in fiscal 2009 dollars—and the problems were pervasive. For these programs, research and development costs were 42 percent higher than originally estimated, and the average delay in delivering initial capabilities had increased to twenty-two months.[29]

The report also pointed out that for forty-seven programs the GAO assessed in-depth, the amount of knowledge that programs attained by key decision points had increased in recent years. However, most programs still proceeded with far less technology, design, and manufacturing knowledge than best practices suggested and faced a higher risk of cost increases and schedule delays. Programs that exhibited early system engineering, stable requirements, and disciplined software management had smaller cost increases and shorter schedule delays on average. Workforce challenges could also impair program execution. Most of the programs the GAO assessed were unable to fill all authorized program office positions, resulting in increased workloads, a reliance on support contractors, and fewer personnel available to conduct oversight.

The under secretary of defense commented on the 17 March 2009 GAO report in a letter to the acting comptroller general. The letter explained how current Defense Department practices were not the only cause of cost increases on acquisition programs, citing lengthy older programs, budget pressures, and the actions of Congress. The under secretary's letter ended with the following paragraph:

---

[28] Ibid., p. 7.
[29] Ibid., p. 13.

APPENDIX A

We must continue to improve the acquisition process to more effectively and efficiently deliver products to our customers, and we need to continue to develop better metrics. The Department looks forward to working with the GAO in both important endeavors.[30]

---

[30] Ltr, John J. Young Jr., Undersecretary of Defense, to Gene L. Dodaro, Acting Comptroller General, 17 Mar 2009, app. II to GAO Report, *Defense Acquisitions: Assessment of Selected Weapon Programs*, GAO–09–326SP, p. 171.

Appendix B

CHANGES TO THE ACQUISITION PROCESS
DOD DIRECTIVE 5000.1, 1971 TO 2008

Deputy Secretary of Defense David Packard signed the first DoD Directive 5000.1 in 1971. This eight-page document created the Defense Systems Acquisition Review Council (DSARC) and required three major decision points (milestones) with one supporting document. Over the next thirty-seven years, this DoD 5000 process was revised fourteen times, reflecting frequent changes in personnel in the Office of the Secretary of Defense (OSD).

During the past four decades, the 5000-series documents have been issued and reissued as a directive; two directives; a directive and an instruction; a directive and a regulation; a directive and instructions and a manual; and a directive, an instruction, and a regulation. The 5000-series documents had a combined page count of as few as eight (1971) to as many as eight hundred and forty (1991). In 2008, DoD Directive 5000.01 (formerly 5000.1) and DoD Instruction 5000.02 (formerly 5000.2) totaled ninety pages.

Phases of the acquisition process have ranged from three (1971 to 1977), to four (1977 to 1991 and 1996 to 2000), to five (2003 to 2008).

The phases of the acquisition process include:

- Conceptual Effort
- Full-Scale Development
- Production/Deployment

The milestones include:

- Program Initiation
- Full-Scale Development Decision
- Production Go-Ahead Decision

Milestones that indicate the beginning of a major acquisition program have been identified as follows: secretary of defense approval of the MENS (Mission Element Need Statement) (1977 to 1980) and the POM (Program Objective Memorandum) (1982 to 1985), as well as secretary of defense or under secretary of defense approval at Milestone 0 (1985 to 1991), Milestone I (1991 to 2000), and Milestone B (2000 to 2008).

The number of milestones and other decision points requiring an OSD-level review has ranged from three (1971 to 1975), to as few as two (1982 to 1985), and as many as seven (2008).

The Secretary of Defense was the Milestone Decision Authority (MDA) for MDAPs (Major Defense Acquisition Programs) from 1971 to 1991. (In 2009, the MDA was the under secretary for acquisition, technology, and logistics.)

The first DoD-level requirements document, entitled the Mission Element Need Statement (MENS), appeared in 1977. The second, entitled the Operational Requirements Document (ORD), appeared in 1991. The format and content of both documents were directed by OSD until authority was transferred to the Joint Staff in 1996.

The major events in the acquisition reform process from 1971 through 2008 are as follows:

1971

- The Defense Systems Acquisition Review Council (DSARC) is created.
- SECDEF (Secretary of Defense) decisions are documented in an approved Decision Coordinating Paper (DCP).
- Major programs are defined as $50 million for RDT&E (research, development, test, and evaluation) or $200 million for procurement.

1975

- Milestones are defined as:
  - "Program Initiation"
  - "Full-Scale Development Decision"
  - "Production Go-Ahead Decision"
- Major programs are redefined as $75 million for RDT&E or $300 million for procurement (in FY 1972 dollars).
- Milestones are unchanged or redefined as follows:
  - Milestone one remains unchanged: "Program Initiation."
  - Milestone two is redefined from "Full-Scale Development Decision" to "Full-Scale Engineering Development Decision."
  - Milestone three is redefined from "Production Go-Ahead" to "Production and Deployment Decision."
- The acquisition phases are redefined:
  - From "Conceptual Effort" to "Validation Phase."
  - From "Full-Scale Development" to "Full-Scale Engineering Development."
  - "Production/Deployment" phase remains the same.

1977

- The names of the acquisition phases are changed and numbered as follows:
  - Phase 0 is redefined as "Exploration of Alternative System Concepts."
  - Phase I is redefined as "Demonstration and Validation."
  - Phase II is redefined as "Full-Scale Engineering Development."
  - Phase III is redefined as "Production and Deployment."
- Milestones are redefined and numbered as follows:
  - Milestone 0 becomes "Mission Element Need Statement" (MENS), Program Initiation approved by the secretary of defense.
  - Milestone I becomes "Approval to Enter Demonstration and Validation."
  - Milestone II becomes "Approval to Enter Full-Scale Engineering Development."
  - Milestone III becomes "Approval to Enter Production and Deployment."
- MENS appears as the first DoD-level requirements document.

1980

- Major programs are now defined as $100 million for RDT&E or $500 million for procurement (FY 1980 dollars).
- Phases:
  - Phase 0 is changed from "Exploration of Alternative System Concepts" to "Concept Exploration."
  - Phase II is changed from "Full-Scale Engineering Development" to "Full-Scale Development."
  - Phase III remains the same, "Production and Deployment."
- Milestones:
  - Milestones 0, I, II, and III remain unchanged.
  - SECDEF Decision Memorandum (SDDM) is implemented to document milestone decisions.

1982

- Major programs are now defined as $200 million RDT&E or $1 billion procurement (FY 1980 dollars).
- Milestones:
  - Milestone 0 is changed from "Million Element Need Statement" to "Approval of JMSNS (Joint Materiel System Need Statement) in PPBS, Program Initiation." The designation "Milestone 0" is discontinued. (PPBS = Planning, Programming, and Budgeting System)
  - Milestone I is changed from "Enter Demonstration and Validation" to "Concept Selection."
  - Milestone II is changed from "Approval to Enter Full-Scale Development" to "Program Go-Ahead."
  - Milestone III is changed from "Enter Production and Deployment" to "Production Decision" (Delegated to Components).

- Programs may proceed to FSD (Full-Scale Development) with delayed MS II (Milestone II). Contracts must be written so program can be terminated at least cost to the government.

1985

- Milestone 0 returns and is named "Approval of JMSNS in PPBS, Program Initiation."
- Production Decision (may be delegated to Components).

1987

- Phases:
  - Phase 0 is changed from "Concept Exploration" to "Concept Exploration/Definition."
  - Phase I is changed from "Demonstration and Validation" to "Concept Demonstration/Validation."
  - Phase II is changed from "Full-Scale Engineering Development" to "Full-Scale Development and LRIP (Low-Rate Initial Production)."
  - Phase III is changed to "Production, Fielding/Deployment, Operational Support."
- Milestones:
  - Milestone 0 remains the same: "Approval of JMSNS in PPBS, Program Initiation."
  - Milestone I is changed from "Concept Selection" to "Approval to Enter Concept Demonstration/Validation."
  - Milestone II is changed from "Program Go-Ahead" to "Approval to Enter Full-Scale Development and LRIP."
  - Milestone III is changed from "Production Decision" (Delegated to Components) to "Approval for Full-Rate Production and Deployment."
  - Milestone IV is introduced as "Logistics Readiness and Support Review."
- Competitive Prototyping Strategy is required by law and by DoD Instruction 5000.2.
- Joint Requirements Management Board (JRMB) is renamed JROC (Joint Requirements Oversight Council).
- Defense Systems Acquisition Review Council (DSARC) is renamed JRMB.
- JRMB is renamed Defense Acquisition Board (DAB).

1991

- Major programs are now defined as $300 million for RDT&E or $1.8 billion for procurement (FY 1980 dollars).
- Milestones:
  - Milestone 0 is redefined as "Approval to Conduct Concept Studies."
  - Milestone I is redefined as "Concept Demonstration Approval."
  - Milestone II is redefined as "Development Approval."

APPENDIX B

- Milestone II redefined as "Production Approval."
- Milestone IV is redefined as "Major Modification Approval."
- Phases:
  - A new phase, "Determination of Mission Need," is inserted before Milestone 0.
  - Phase I is redefined as "Demonstration and Validation."
  - Phase II is redefined as "Engineering and Manufacturing Development."
  - Phase III is redefined as "Production and Deployment."
  - A new Phase IV is introduced as "Operations and Support."
- Acquisition Decision Memorandum (ADM), signed by the USD (A), replaces SDDM (SECDEF Decision Memorandum).
- The provision for a delayed Milestone II is eliminated.
- The acquisition category (ACAT) structure is created.
- The JROC-approved MENS replaces the secretary of defense–approved JMSNS at Milestone 0.
- Operational Requirements Document (ORD) appears in DoD Instruction 5000.2 and is required at Milestone II and Milestone III.

1996

- Phases:
  - Phase 0 is redefined as "Concept Exploration."
  - Phase I is redefined as "Program Definition and Risk Reduction."
  - Phase II is redefined as "Engineering and Manufacturing Development."
  - Phase III is redefined as "Production, Fielding/Deployment, and Operational Support."
  - A new phase appears following Phase III: "Demilitarization and Disposal."
- Milestones:
  - Milestone I is redefined as "Approval to Begin a New Acquisition Program."
  - Milestone II is redefined as "Approval to Enter Engineering and Manufacturing Development."
  - Milestone II is redefined as "Production or Fielding/Deployment Approval."
- Program Initiation is moved to Milestone I.
- Automated Information System (AIS) acquisition programs are folded into the DoD 5000 process.
- Competitive Prototyping requirement is eliminated.

2000

- Major programs are redefined as $365 million for RDT&E or $219 billion for procurement (FY 2000 dollars).
- Milestone identifications are changed from numbers to letters "A," "B," and "C."

- Phases:
  - Phase A becomes "Concept and Technology Development (Decision Review)."
  - Phase B becomes "System Development and Demonstration (Interim Progress Review)."
  - Phase C becomes "Production and Deployment (FRP Decision Review)."
  - A phase following Phase C appears and is named "Operations and Support."
- Milestones:
  - Milestone A is defined as "Approval to Enter Concept and Technology Development."
  - Milestone B is defined as "Approval to Enter Systems Development and Demonstration."
  - Milestone C is defined as "Approval to Enter LRIP/Production and Deployment."
- Program Initiation occurs at Milestone B.
- Commitment to Production occurs at Milestone C (LRIP).
- Evolutionary Acquisition (EA) becomes the preferred approach to major systems acquisition.

2002

- "Technology Opportunities and User Needs" is changed to "User Needs and Technology Opportunities."
- "Critical Design Review" is added to Phase B.
- Deputy Secretary of Defense cancels all three DoD 5000 documents.
- Interim Guidance documents are issued: "Defense Acquisition" for basic policy and "Operation of the Defense Acquisition System" for implementation procedures.
- DoD 5000.2-R becomes the "Interim Defense Acquisition Guidebook."

2003

- Phases:
  - A phase preceding Milestone A becomes "Concept Refinement (Concept Decision)."
  - Phase A becomes "Technology Development."
  - Phase B becomes "System Development and Demonstration (Design Readiness Review)."
- Milestones:
  - A new milestone is created at the beginning of the Concept Refinement Phase. The milestone is named "Approval to Enter Concept Refinement."
  - Milestone A is redefined as "Approval to Enter Technology Development."

- The Defense Acquisition Guidebook (DAG) is made available online.
- "Joint Capabilities Integration and Development System" (JCIDS) is created. MNS (Mission Need Statement) and ORD (Operational Requirements Document) are replaced.
- "Initial Capabilities Document" is required at Milestone B; the "Capability Production Document" is required at Milestone C.

2008

- Definition of major acquisition programs remains the same: $365 million for RDT&E or $2.19 billion for procurement (FY 2000 dollars).
- "User Needs and Technology Opportunities" becomes "User Needs and Technology Opportunities and Resources."
- Phases:
  - The phase preceding Milestone A is redefined to "Materiel Solution Analysis (Materiel Development Decision)."
  - Phase B is redefined as "Engineering and Manufacturing Development" with two submilestones: "Post-PDR A" and "Post-CDR A."
- Milestones:
  - The milestone at the beginning of the Materiel Solution Analysis Phase is redefined as "Approval to Enter Acquisition Process."
  - Milestone B is redefined as "Approval to Enter Engineering and Manufacturing Development."
- The Materiel Development Decision precedes entry into any phase of the acquisition process.
- Competitive Prototyping returns and is required during the Technology Development Phase.
- A Preliminary Design Review (PDR) after Milestone B requires a Post-PDR. The assessment is made by the Milestone Decision Authority.

APPENDIX C

CARLUCCI THIRTY-TWO ACQUISITION REFORM INITIATIVES, 1983

1. Reaffirm Acquisition Management Principles
2. Increase Use of Preplanned Product Improvement
3. Implement Multiyear Procurement
4. Increase Program Stability
5. Encourage Capital Investment to Enhance Productivity
6. Budget to Most Likely Costs
7. Use Economical Production Rates
8. Assure Appropriate Contract Type
9. Improve System Support and Readiness
10. Reduce Administrative Costs and Time
11. Budget for Technological Risk
12. Provide Front-End Funding for Test Hardware
13. Reduce Governmental Legislation Related to Acquisition
14. Reduce Number of DOD Directives
15. Enhance Funding Flexibility
16. Provide Contractor Incentives to Improve Reliability and Support
17. Decrease DSARC Briefing and Data Requirements
18. Budget for Inflation
19. Forecast Business Base Conditions
20. Improve Source Selection Process
21. Develop and Use Standard Operation and Support Systems
22. Provide More Appropriate Design-to-Cost Goals
23. Implement Acquisition Process Decisions
24. Reduce DSARC Milestones
25. Submit MENS with Service POM
26. Revise DSARC Membership
27. Retain USDRE as Defense Acquisition Executive
28. Raise Dollar Thresholds for DSARC Review
29. Integrate DSARC and PPBS Process
30. Increase PM Visibility of Support Resources
31. Improve Reliability and Support
32. Increase Competition

APPENDIX D

RAND CORPORATION STUDY OF SIXTY-THREE ACQUISITION REFORM INITIATIVES, 2002

(in Chronological Order)

Date Issued	Acquisition Reform Initiatives
March 1966	Competitive Sourcing
1989	DoD Purchase Card
September 1991	Performance-Based Service Acquisition
1993	Prime Vendor Delivery
January 1993	Improved Pre-Solicitation Phase Communication
1994	Advanced Concept Technology Demonstration
1994	Electronic Data Interchange
February 1994	Elimination of Mil Specs and Mil Standards
February 1994	Elimination of Non-Value-Added Receiving/In-Process/Final Inspection and Testing
February 1994	Elimination of Non-Value-Added Reporting Requirements/CDRLs
February 1994	Integrated Product and Process Development
February 1994	Program Stability
February 1994	Multi-Year Contracting
February 1994	Rights in Technical Data and Computer Software
March 1994	Contractor-Maintained Design Configuration
June 1994	Single Process Initiative
October 1994	Risk-Based Approach to DCAA Oversight
November 1994	Concurrent Developmental/Operational Testing
November 1994	Open Systems Approach

Date Issued	Acquisition Reform Initiatives
November 1994	Rapid Prototyping for Software Development
January 1995	Streamlined Defense Industrial Security Program Requirements
February 1995	Commercial Engineering Drawing Practices
February 1995	Streamlined ECP Review/Approval
March 1995	RFP Streamlining
March 1995	Streamlined Documentation/Resolution of Nonconforming Material Issues
March 1995	Streamlined Government Property Management Requirements
April 1995	Elimination of Redundant Oversight (PMO/Services/DCMC)
April 1995	Past Performance Data
June 1995	Commercial Sourcing: FAR Part 12 Procurements
June 1995	Reduction/Elimination of Contractor Purchasing System Reviews
June 1995	Survivability/Lethality Below End-Item Level
July 1995	Streamlined Contract Close-Out Process
August 1995	Parametric Cost Estimating
September 1995	Better Post-Award Debriefing
September 1995	Commercial Warranties and Other Product Liability Issues
September 1995	Performance-Based Progress Payments
September 1995	Reduced Number of TINA Sweeps
October 1995	Commercial Data and Other Exemptions for Cost or Pricing Data
October 1995	Cost Accounting Standards Exemptions
October 1995	Joint Government/Industry IPTs
October 1995	Reduction of Multiple Software Capability Evaluations
October 1995	Revised Thresholds for Certified Cost and Pricing

APPENDIX D

Date Issued	Acquisition Reform Initiatives
December 1995	CAIV (Cost as an Independent Variable)
March 1996	Best-Value Contracting: Consideration of Cost/Performance Tradeoffs
March 1996	Simulation-Based Acquisition
May 1996	Direct Submission of Cost Vouchers to DFAS (or other disbursing office)
June 1996	Alternative Dispute Resolution
June 1996	Tailored Negotiation of Forward Pricing Rates
June 1996	Evolutionary Acquisition
October 1996	Commercial Quality Standards (e.g., ISO 9000)
October 1996	Elimination of Non-Value-Added Packaging Requirements
December 1996	Other Transaction Authority
1997	Modernization Through Spares
March 1997	Cost-Schedule Reporting Standards Tailored to Industry Guidelines
October 1997	Alpha Contracting
1998	Logistics Transformation
1998	Contractor Total System Performance Responsibility
April 1998	Reduction in Total Ownership Cost
June 1998	Enterprise Software Initiative
1999	Oral Presentations
November 1999	Virtual Prime Vendor
November 2000	Price-Based Acquisition
May 2001	Contractor Cost Sharing

Abbreviations and Acronyms

ACAT	Acquisition category
ACO	Administrative contracting officer
AFLC	Air Force Logistics Command
AFSC	Air Force Systems Command
AIP	Acquisition Improvement Program
AIS	Automated information system
AMRAAM	Advanced Medium-Range Air-to-Air Missile
AoA	Analysis of Alternatives
AR	Acquisition reform
ARPA	Advanced Research Projects Agency
ASA (ALT)	Assistant secretary of the Army for acquisition, logistics, and technology
ASA (RD&A)	Assistant secretary of the Army for research, development, and acquisition
ASAF (A&L)	Assistant secretary of the Air Force for acquisition and logistics
ASD (A&L)	Assistant secretary of defense for acquisition and logistics
ASD (D&S)	Assistant secretary of defense for development and support
ASD (ES)	Assistant secretary of defense for economic security
ASD (I&L)	Assistant secretary of defense for installations and logistics
ASD (MI&L)	Assistant secretary of defense for manpower, installations, and logistics
ASPR	Armed Services Procurement Regulation
B&P	Bid and proposal
BENS	Business Executives for National Security
C/SCSC	Cost and Schedule Control System Criteria
C3	Command, Control, and Communications
C3I	Command, Control, Communications, and Intelligence
CAE	Component acquisition executive
CAIG	Cost Analysis Improvement Group
CAIV	Cost as an Independent Variable
CDD	Capability Development Document
CDRL	Contract Data Requirements List

CIA	Central Intelligence Agency
CINC	Commander in chief
CITE	Contractor independent technical effort
CJCS	Chairman of the Joint Chiefs of Staff
CRS	Congressional Research Service
CSDR	Cost and Software Data Reporting
CTE	Critical technology element
DAB	Defense Acquisition Board
DAE	Defense acquisition executive
DAHP	Defense Acquisition History Project
DARCOM	Department of the Army Readiness Command
DARPA	Defense Advanced Research Projects Agency
DAU	Defense Acquisition University
DCAA	Defense Contract Audit Agency
DCAPE	Director, Cost Assessment and Program Evaluation
DCAS	Defense Contract Administration Service
DCMA	Defense Contract Management Agency
DCMC	Defense Contract Management Command
DCP	Development Concept Paper
DCS (RD&A)	Deputy chief of staff for research, development, and acquisition
DDR&E	Director of defense research and engineering
DFARS	Defense Federal Acquisition Regulation Supplement
DoD	Department of Defense
DOT&E	Director of operational test and evaluation
DRB	Defense Resources Board
DSARC	Defense Systems Acquisition Review Council
DSB	Defense Science Board
DSMC	Defense Systems Management College
DT&E	Development testing and evaluation
DUSD (AR)	Deputy under secretary of defense for acquisition reform
EMD	Engineering and Manufacturing Development
EVMS	Earned Value Management System
FACNET	Federal Acquisition Network
FAIA	Federal Acquisition Improvement Act
FAR	Federal Acquisition Regulation
FARA	Federal Acquisition Reform Act
FASA	Federal Acquisition Streamlining Act

ABBREVIATIONS AND ACRONYMS

FCRC	Federal contract research center
FCS	Future Combat Systems
FFRDC	Federally funded research and development center
FY	Fiscal year
GAO	Government Accountability Office, formerly General Accounting Office
GDP	Gross domestic product
GNP	Gross national product
GPRA	Government Performance and Results Act
GSA	General Services Administration
HASC	House Armed Services Committee
HP	Hewlett-Packard Company
HumRRO	Human Resources Research Organization
IAC	Industry Advisory Council
ICBM	Intercontinental ballistic missile
IDA	Institute for Defense Analyses
IPD	Integrated product development
IPPD	Integrated product and process development
IPT	Integrated product team
IR&D	Independent research and development
ITMRA	Information Technology Management Reform Act
IWSM	Integrated Weapon System Management
JCIDS	Joint Capabilities Integration and Development System
JCS	Joint Chiefs of Staff
JDAM	Joint Direct Attack Munition
JPATS	Joint Primary Aircraft Training System
JRMB	Joint Requirements Management Board
JROC	Joint Requirements Oversight Council
LRIP	Low-Rate Initial Production
MAIS	Major Automated Information System
MAISRC	MAIS Review Council
MDA	Milestone Decision Authority
MDAP	Major Defense Acquisition Program
MIPS	Modified Integrated Program Summary
NASA	National Aeronautics and Space Administration
NATO	North Atlantic Treaty Organization

NAVMAT	Navy Material Command
NPOESS	National Polar-Orbiting Operational Environmental Satellite System
NSDD	National Security Decision Directive
OASD (PA)	Office of the Assistant Secretary of Defense for Public Affairs
ODUSD (AR)	Office of the Deputy Under Secretary of Defense for Acquisition Reform
OIPT	Overarching Integrated Product Team
OJCS	Office of the Joint Chief of Staff
OMB	Office of Management and Budget
OSD	Office of the Secretary of Defense
OTA	Other Transaction Authority
OUSD (A&T)	Office of the Under Secretary of Defense for Acquisition and Technology
OUSD (A)	Office of the Under Secretary of Defense for Acquisition
P3I	Preplanned product improvement
PAT	Process action team
PDR	Preliminary design review
PDUSD (A&T)	Principal deputy under secretary of defense for acquisition and technology
PEO	Program executive officer
PERT	Program Evaluation and Review Technique
PM	Program manager
PPBES	Planning, Programming, Budgeting, and Execution System
PPBS	Planning, Programming, and Budgeting System
R&D	Research and development
RDT&E	Research, development, test, and evaluation
RFP	Request for proposal
RG	Record Group
SAE	Service acquisition executive
SALT	Strategic Arms Limitation Treaty
SAMSO	Space and Missile Systems Organization
SLBM	Submarine-launched ballistic missile
SPI	Single Process Initiative
SSA	Source selection authority
SSAC	Source Selection Advisory Council
SSEB	Source Selection Evaluation Board

ABBREVIATIONS AND ACRONYMS

TDS	Technology Development Strategy
TPM	Technical Performance Measurement
TPP	Total Package Procurement
TQM	Total Quality Management
USAF	United States Air Force
USD (A&T)	Under secretary of defense for acquisition and technology
USD (A)	Under secretary of defense for acquisition
USD (AT&L)	Under secretary of defense for acquisition, technology, and logistics
USD (R&E)	Under secretary of defense for research and engineering
WBS	Work breakdown structure
WIPT	Working integrated product team
WNRC	Washington National Records Center
ZBB	Zero-based budgeting

Selected Bibliography

Government Publications, Correspondence, and Congressional Hearings and Testimony

Assistant Secretary of Defense (Comptroller). Memo for Assistant Secretary of Defense for Installation and Logistics (ASD [I&L]), 19 May 1969. Major Weapon System Acquisition. Comptroller Subject Decimal File, 1969 (75–0089), Box 54, 400.13 (May 1969), Record Group (RG) 330, Washington National Records Center (WNRC), Suitland, Maryland.

Assistant Secretary of Defense (I&L). Memo for Melvin Laird and David Packard, 9 October 1969. Industry Advisory Council, 10–11 October 1969. Comptroller Subject Decimal File, 1969 (75–0089), Box 43, 334 Industry Advisory Council (July 1969), RG 330, WNRC.

Augustine, Norman. U.S. Senate testimony of president of Martin Marietta and former under secretary of the Army, hearing before the Committee on Governmental Affairs, *Acquisition Process in the Department of Defense*, 21–27 October and 5 November 1981.

Carlucci, Frank C. Memo for Distribution List, 13 February 1981. WNRC, Series 330–83–0102, Box 26/48, Folder: "100.5 (January-April 1981)."

———. Letter to D. A. Stockman, 22 April 1981, WNRC, Series 330–83–0102, Box 26/48, Folder: "100.5 (January-April 1981)."

Claytor, W. Graham Jr. Memo for Undersecretaries and Assistant Secretaries of Defense, 4 December 1980, Office of the Secretary of Defense Historical Office, Box 561, Folder: "OSD/DoD 1980-81, Transition to Reagan Era."

CNA Independent Assessment: Air Force Acquisition. Commissioned by the Secretary of the Air Force and directed by the Assistant Secretary of the Air Force for Acquisition, February 2009.

Conahan, Frank C., Assistant Comptroller General (National Security and International Affairs Division, Government Accounting Office). Statement before the Congressional Military Reform Caucus, "Defense Management: Streamlining the Acquisition Process," 2 August 1989.

Congressional Research Service. Report RL34026. "Defense Acquisition: Overview, Issues, and Options for Congress." Washington, D.C.: Congressional Research Service, 20 June 2007.

Defense Acquisition: Major U.S. Commission Reports (1949–1988), vol. 1. Prepared for the Defense Policy Panel and Acquisition Policy Panel of the Committee on Armed Services, House of Representatives, 100th Cong., 2d sess., November 1988.

"Defense Acquisition Improvement Program (Weinberger/Carlucci Initiatives): Army Implementation Activities." In *Acquisition Improvement Program: General Army Implementation*. Fort Belvoir, Va.: Defense Systems Management College, March 1982.

Defense Acquisition Performance Assessment Report. Washington, D.C.: Office of the Secretary of Defense, January 2006.

"Defense Resources Board Meeting, 2 February 1981, Talking Points—Carlucci," (undated). Office of the Secretary of Defense Historical Office, Box: "Defense Resources Board, May-August 1981, Puritano-Bureau Files," Folder: "Defense Resources Board, 6 May 1981."

Defense Science Board. Report of the Acquisition Cycle Task Force, 1977 Summer Study, 15 March 1978.

Defense Systems Management College. "Acquisition Strategy Guide." Fort Belvoir, Va.: Defense Systems Management College, July 1984.

Department of Defense Appropriations for 1973. Hearings before a Subcommittee of the Committee on Appropriations, 92d Cong., 2d sess., 22 February 1972.

Department of Defense Directive 5000.1, "The Defense Acquisition System." Office of the Secretary of Defense, 4 January 2001.

Department of Defense Directive 5000.1, "Acquisition of Major Defense Systems." Office of the Secretary of Defense, 13 July 1971.

Department of Defense Directive 7045.14, "The Planning, Programming, and Budgeting System," 22 May 1984.

Department of Defense Instruction 7045.7, "Implementation of the Planning, Programming, and Budgeting System," 23 May 1984.

Department of Defense Instruction 5000.2 Change 1, "Operation of the Defense Acquisition System," 4 January 2001.

Department of Defense Manual 4245.7-M. *Transition from Development to Production*, Assistant Secretary of Defense (A&L), September 1985.

Department of Defense Regulation 5000.2-R Change 1, "Mandatory Procedures for Major Defense Programs (MDAPS) and Major Automated Information System (MAIS) Acquisition Programs," 10 June 2001.

Deputy Secretary of Defense. Statement to the Press, 9 June 1970. Appendix to "Policy Changes in Weapon System Procurement," House Committee on Government Operations, 91st Cong., 2d sess., 22 September 1970.

Federal Acquisition Regulation (FAR) System, July 2009, and U.S. Department of Defense, Defense Federal Acquisition Regulation

Supplement (DFARS). Washington, D.C.: U.S. Government Printing Office, 21 July 2009.
Federal Acquisition Streamlining Act of 1993, S. 1587. Joint Hearings U.S. Senate, Committee on Governmental Affairs and Committee on Armed Services, 103d Cong., 2d sess., S. Hearing 103–849. Washington, D.C.: U.S. Government Printing Office, 1994.
Foster, John S. Memo for David Packard, 7 July 1969. Management of Weapons Systems Acquisition. Comptroller Subject Decimal File, 1969 (75–0089), Box 54, 400.13 (June 1969), RG 330, WNRC.
———. Memo for Listed Recipients, 29 July 1970. Application of New Policy Guidance to Major Weapon Systems. Appendix to "Policy Changes in Weapon System Procurement," House Committee on Government Operations, 91st Cong., 2d sess., 22 September 1970.
———. Memo for Packard, 18 July 1969. Report by Panel A of the Industry Advisory Council. Comptroller Subject Decimal File, 1969 (75–0089), Box 54, 400.13 (July 1969), RG 330, WNRC.
Goldwater, Senator Barry. Letter to Melvin Laird, 21 August 1969. Comptroller Subject Decimal File (75–0089), Box 57, 452 (June–August 1969), RG 330, WNRC.
Laird, Melvin R., Secretary of Defense. Memo for Listed Parties, 24 January 1969. Matters Involving the Hewlett-Packard Company. Comptroller Subject Decimal File, 1969 (75–0089), Box 11, 020 OSD, 69, RG 330, WNRC.
———. Outline of Remarks to Blue Ribbon Defense Panel, 24 July 1969. Comptroller Subject Decimal File, 1969 (75–0089), Box 10, Blue Ribbon Defense Panel, RG 330, WNRC.
———. Letter to Senator John C. Stennis, 18 March 1971, with attachment, DoD Steps Taken to Improve the Acquisition of Major Weapon Systems. Comptroller Subject Decimal File, 1971 (76–0197), 400.13 (February 1971), RG 330, WNRC.
Laird, Packard, and Darden. Hearings before the Senate Armed Services Committee. 91st Cong., 1st sess., 14 January 1969.
Lowenthal, Mark M. "Defense Department Reorganization: The Fitzhugh Report, 1969–1970." Congressional Research Service, CRS–76–153F, 19 August 1976.
Lynn, Laurence E., Professor of Public Policy, Harvard University. Hearings before the U.S. Senate Committee on Governmental Affairs, 21–27 October and 5 November 1981.
Moore, John Norton, and Robert F. Turner. *The Legal Structure of Defense Organization: Memorandum Prepared for the President's Blue Ribbon Commission on Defense Management*. Washington, D.C.: U.S. Government Printing Office, 15 January 1986.

News Release. "Assistant Secretary of Defense (Acquisition and Logistics) Named." Office of the Secretary of Defense Historical Office, 5 July 1985.

News Release. "Secretary of Defense Weinberger Announces Management Streamlining," Office of the Secretary of Defense Historical Office, 29 January 1985.

Nunn, Senator Sam. Remarks, *Congressional Record*, 93d Cong., 2d sess., S. 7575–7577, 1974.

Office of the Assistant Secretary of Defense (Comptroller). *National Defense Budget, Financial Summary Tables*, 2008 and 2009.

Office of the Assistant Secretary of Defense for Economic Security. *Implementation Plan for the Process Action Team Report on Specifications and Standards*. Washington, D.C., 23 June 1994.

Office of the General Counsel, Office of the Secretary of the Navy. The Beach Report. Washington, D.C., 28 November 1990.

Office of Management and Budget. Executive Office of the President. *Management of the United States Government, Fiscal Year 2007*. Washington, D.C.: U.S. Government Printing Office, 2008.

———. *Special Analyses of the Budget of the U.S. Government, Fiscal Year 1972 and Fiscal Year 2007*. Washington, D.C.: U.S. Government Printing Office, 1972 and 2008.

Office of the Secretary of Defense. Memo for Industry Advisory Council and Defense Participants, 4 November 1969. Summary Minutes of the 10–11 October 1969 Meeting, Table B, Chart 1, VIII G, Installations and Logistics (1969–2000), Industry, 1969–1971, Box 1022, Office of the Secretary of Defense Historical Office Subject Files.

Packard, David, Deputy Secretary of Defense. Address to the Armed Forces Management Association, Los Angeles, Calif., 22 August 1970. Appendix to "Policy Changes in Weapon System Procurement," House Committee on Government Operations, 91st Cong., 2d sess., 22 September 1970.

———. Memo for Listed Parties, 14 May 1970. Reports to the Secretary of Defense by the Military Departments and Defense Agencies on Approved Major Weapon Systems during Development. Appendix to "Policy Changes in Weapon System Procurement," House Committee on Government Operations, 91st Cong., 2d sess., 22 September 1970.

———. Memo for Listed Parties, 28 May 1971. DoD Directive on the Acquisition of Major Defense Systems. Comptroller Subject Decimal File, 1971 (76–0197), 400.13 (April-May 1971), RG 330, WNRC.

———. Memo for Listed Parties, 23 September 1971. Defense Systems Acquisition Policy. Comptroller Subject Decimal File,

1971 (76–0197), 400.13 (August-September 1971), Box 47, RG 330, WNRC.
———. Memo for Listed Parties, 3 November 1970. Blue Ribbon Decision Memorandum No. 1, IV B. Blue Ribbon Defense Panel, 1969–1970 (1), Box 549, Office of the Secretary of Defense Historical Office Subject Files.
———. Memo for Listed Parties, 28 May 1970. Policy Guidance on Major Weapon System Acquisition. IV B, OSD/DOD Organization, 1969–1972, Box 558 (1970–1971), Office of the Secretary of Defense Historical Office Subject Files.
———. Memo for Service Secretaries, ASD Comptroller, ASD I&L, DDRE, and ASD Systems Analysis. Establishment of a Defense System Acquisition Review Council, 30 May 1969, with attachment, Charter, Defense System Acquisition Review Council, VIIIA, Box 992: Management, 1969–1970, Office of the Secretary of Defense Historical Office Subject Files.
———. Memo for Service Secretaries, 31 July 1969. Improvement in Weapon System Acquisition. Comptroller Subject Decimal File 1969 (75–0089), 400.13 (July 1969), RG 330, WNRC.
———. Memo for Service Secretaries, 15 December 1969. Responsibilities in the Process of Acquiring Major Weapon Systems. Appendix to "Policy Changes in Weapon System Procurement," House Committee on Government Operations, 91st Cong., 2d sess., 22 September 1970.
———. Message to all DoD Personnel, 14 February 1969, IV B, Box 558: OSD/DOD Organization, 1969–1972, Office of the Secretary of Defense Historical Office Subject Files.
———. Press Conference on *A Quest for Excellence*. President's Blue Ribbon Commission on Defense Management. Washington, D.C.: U.S. Government Printing Office, 2 July 1986.
Perry, William J., Secretary of Defense. Memo for Distribution, 15 March 1994. Vertical File: "Defense Acquisition—Reform." Defense Systems Management College, Acker Library, Fort Belvoir, Va.
———. "Acquisition Reform: A Mandate for Change," 9 February 1994. Vertical File: "Defense Acquisition—Reform." Defense Systems Management College, Acker Library, Fort Belvoir, Va.
Pope, Joseph Kevin. "Measuring the Effect of the Defense Acquisition Workforce Improvement Act." Master's thesis: Naval Postgraduate School, June 1997.
President's Blue Ribbon Commission on Defense Management. *An Interim Report to the President*. Washington, D.C.: U.S. Government Printing Office, 28 February 1986.
———. *A Quest for Excellence: Final Report to the President*. Washington, D.C.: U.S. Government Printing Office, June 1986.

―――. *A Formula for Action*. Washington, D.C.: U.S. Government Printing Office, April 1986.

―――. *National Security Planning and Budgeting*. Washington, D.C.: U.S. Government Printing Office, June 1986.

―――. *Conduct and Accountability*. Washington, D.C.: U.S. Government Printing Office, June 1986.

President's Private Sector Survey on Cost Control: A Report to the President. Washington, D.C.: U.S. Government Printing Office, 1983.

Pryor, Senator David. Statement of 8 June 1994. *Congressional Record*, 103d Cong., 2d sess., S. 6587.

Report by Panel A of the Industry Advisory Council on the Major Systems Acquisition Process, 14 June 1969. Comptroller Subject Decimal File, 1969 (75–0089), Box 54, 400.13 (July 1969), RG 330, WNRC.

Report of the Commission on Government Procurement, vols. 1 and 2. Washington, D.C.: U.S. Government Printing Office, 31 December 1972.

Report to the President and the Secretary of Defense on the Department of Defense, Blue Ribbon Defense Panel. Washington, D.C.: U.S. Government Printing Office, 1 July 1970.

Resor, Stanley R. Memo for David Packard. Improvement in Weapon System Acquisition, 2 October 1969, attached to Memo, Packard for Resor, 10 October 1969. Comptroller Subject Decimal File (75–0089), Box 54, 400.13 (October 1969), RG 330, WNRC.

Richardson, Elliott L., Secretary of Defense. Testimony before the Committee on Armed Forces, FY 1974 Defense Budget and FY 1974–1978 Program, 10 April 1973.

Rivers, Congressman L. Mendel. Letter to David Packard 7 May 1969, Deputy Secretary Subject File, 1969 (74–132), Box 2, RG 330, WNRC.

Roth, Senator William V. Jr. Statement before the Senate, 26 October 1993, *Congressional Record*, 103d Cong., 1st sess., S. 14376 and S. 1598, *The Department of Defense Acquisition Management Reform Act of 1993*.

Seamans, Robert C. Jr. Memo for David Packard, 5 December 1969, with attached letter, Gen. J. C. Meyer to Seamans, Improvement in Weapon Systems Acquisition (20 October 1969). Comptroller Subject Decimal File 1969 (75–0089), 400.13 (September 1969), RG 330, WNRC.

Secretary of Defense. Statement to Industry Advisory Council, 13 July 1970. Summary Minutes of the Industry Advisory Council Meeting on 12 and 13 June 1970. VIII G, Installations and Logistics (1969–2000), Industry, 1969–1971, Box 1022, Office of the Secretary of Defense Historical Office Subject Files.

Senate Committee on Armed Services, Staff Report. "Defense Organization: The Need for Change," 16 October 1985.
Shillito, Barry. Memo for John Foster, 22 July 1969. Comptroller Subject Decimal File 1969 (75–0089), 400.13 (July 1969), RG 330, WNRC.
Stubbing, Richard, U.S. Bureau of the Budget. Hearing before the U.S. Congress Joint Economic Committee on Defense Procurement. Washington, D.C., 10 March 1969.
U.S. Army Materiel Command Annual Historical Review, Fiscal Year 1987. Fort Belvoir, Va.: Headquarters, U.S. Army Materiel Command Historical Office, August 1989.
U.S. Congress. House. Committee on Armed Services. *Military Posture*, part 1. 91st Cong., 1st sess., 1970.
———. Committee on Armed Services. *Acquisition Reform: Fact or Fiction.* HASC No. 103–26. 103d Cong., 1st sess., 1994.
———. Committee on Government Operations. 91st Cong., 2d sess. "Policy Changes in Weapon System Procurement," 22 September 1970.
———. Committee on Government Reform and Oversight. *Oversight of Implementation of Federal Acquisition Streamlining Act of 1994.* 104th Cong., 1st sess., 1995.
U.S. Congress. Senate. Committee on Armed Services. "Military Procurement for Fiscal Year 1971." 91st Cong., 2d sess., 10 March 1970.
———. Committee on Governmental Affairs. *Government Performance and Results Act of 1993*, Senate Report 103–58. 103d Cong., 1st sess., 16 June 1993.
———. Committee on Governmental Affairs and Committee on Armed Services. S. 1587, *Federal Acquisition Streamlining Act of 1993.* Joint Hearings, 103d Cong., 2d sess., S. Hearing 103–849, 1994.
U.S. Government Accountability Office. *Legislative Recommendations of the Commission on Government Procurement: 5 Years Later.* PSAD–78–100. Washington, D.C.: U.S. Government Printing Office, 31 July 1978.
———. *Impediments to Reducing the Costs of Weapon Systems.* PSAD–80–6. Washington, D.C.: U.S. Government Printing Office, 8 November 1979.
———. *Can the United States Major Weapon Systems Acquisition Process Keep Pace with the Conventional Arms Threat Posed by the USSR?* GAO/PSAD/GP. Washington, D.C.: U.S. Government Printing Office, 27 May 1980.
———. *Technical Risk Assessment.* GAO/EMD–86–5. Washington, D.C.: U.S. Government Printing Office, 3 April 1986.
———. *DoD Acquisition: Strengthening Capabilities of Key Personnel in Systems Acquisition.* GAO/NSIAD–86–45. Washington, D.C.: U.S. Government Printing Office, May 1986.

---. *DoD's Defense Acquisition Improvement Program: A Status Report*. GAO/NSIAD-86-148. Washington, D.C.: U.S. Government Printing Office, July 1986.

---. *Status of the Defense Acquisition Improvement Program's 33 Initiatives*. GAO/NSIAD-86-178BR. Washington, D.C.: Government Printing Office, September 1986.

---. *Reorganization of the Military Departments' Acquisition Management Structures*. GAO/T-NSIAD-88-28. Statement of William W. Thurman, Deputy Director for Planning and Reporting (National Security and International Affairs Division, General Accounting Office), before the U.S. House of Representatives, Subcommittee on Investigations, Committee on Armed Services. Washington, D.C.: U.S. Government Printing Office, 20 April 1988.

---. *Major Acquisitions: Summary of Recurring Problems and Systematic Issues: 1960–1987*. GAO/NSIAD-88-135BR. Washington, D.C.: Government Printing Office, September 1988.

---. *Status of Recommendations. Blue Ribbon Commission on Defense Management*. NSIAD-89-19FS. Washington, D.C.: U.S. Government Printing Office, November 1988.

---. *Weapons Acquisition: A Rare Opportunity for Lasting Change*. GAO/NSIAD-93-15. Washington, D.C.: U.S. Government Printing Office, December 1992.

---. *Acquisition Reform: DoD Begins Program to Reform Specifications and Standards*. GAO-NSIAD-95-14. Washington, D.C.: U.S. Government Printing Office, October 1994.

---. *Defense Acquisition: Continue to Experience Cost and Schedule Problems under DoD's Revised Policy*. GAO-06-368. Washington, D.C.: U.S. Government Printing Office, April 2006.

---. *Defense Acquisitions: Assessments of Selected Weapon Programs*. GAO-09-326SP. Washington, D.C.: U.S. Government Printing Office, 30 March 2009.

Warner, John W. Memo for David Packard, 20 October 1969. Improvement in Weapon System Acquisition. Comptroller Subject Decimal File 1969 (75–0089), 400.13 (October 1969), RG 330, WNRC.

Weinberger, Caspar, Secretary of Defense. Testimony before the U.S. Senate Armed Services Committee on the FY 1983 Budget, FY 1984 Authorization Request, and FY 1983–1987 Defense Programs. Office of the Secretary of Defense Historical Office, 2 February 1982.

Books, Articles, and Monographs

Acker, David D. *A History of the Defense Systems Management College*. Washington, D.C.: U.S. Government Printing Office, 1986.

SELECTED BIBLIOGRAPHY

———. "The Maturing of the DoD Acquisition Process," *Defense Systems Management Review* (Summer 1980).
Acker, David D., and G. R. McAleer Jr. "The Acquisition Process: New Opportunities for Innovative Management." *Concepts* 5 (Summer 1982).
———. "Defense Systems Acquisition Review Process: A History and Evaluation." *Program Manager* 13 (January-February 1984).
———. "Issues and Actions Affecting the Systems Acquisition Process (July 1983–July 1984)." *Program Manager* 13 (September-October 1984).
———. *Acquiring Defense Systems: A Quest for the Best.* Fort Belvoir, Va.: Defense Systems Management College Press, July 1993.
Adams, Gordon, Paul Murphy, and William Grey Rosenau. *Controlling Weapons Costs: Can the Pentagon Reforms Work?* New York: Council on Economic Priorities, 1983.
Alpern, D. M., and J. J. Lindsay. "Fighting to Win the War." *Newsweek* 98 (14 September 1981): 27.
Art, Robert J. "Bureaucratic Politics and American Foreign Policy: A Critique." *Policy Sciences*, December 1973.
———. "Congress and the Defense Budget: Enhancing Policy Oversight." *Political Science Quarterly* 100 (Summer 1985): 227–48.
Atkinson, Rick, and Fred Hiatt. "Military in a Fix." *Washington Post*, 18 August 1985.
Beck, Charles L. Jr., Nina Lyn Brokaw, and Brian A. Kelmar. *A Model for Leading Change: Making Acquisition Reform Work.* Report of the Defense Systems Management College Military Research Fellows, 1996–1997. Fort Belvoir, Va.: Defense Systems Management College Press, December 1997.
Bedard, P. "Pentagon Acquisition Czar." *Defense Week* 7 (4 February 1985).
Black, Brig. Gen. Richard A. "Colleen Preston on Acquisition Reform." *Program Manager*, Defense Systems Management College (Special Issue: January-February 1997): 22–31.
Brabson, Col. G. Dana, USAF. "Department of Defense Acquisition Improvement Program." *Concepts: The Journal of Defense Systems Acquisition Management* 4 (Autumn 1981).
Brown, W. D. "Program Instability: Fighting Goliath." *Program Manager* (November-December 1983).
Caldwell, John S. Jr. "Reengineering the Oversight and Review Process for Systems Acquisition." *Program Manager* (May-June 1995): 3–5.
Carter, Ashton B., and William J. Perry. *Preventive Defense: A New Security Strategy for America.* Washington, D.C.: Brookings Institution Press, 1999.

Center for Strategic and International Studies, Working Group on Military Specifications and Standards. *Road Map for Milspec Reform.* Washington, D.C.: Center for Strategic and International Studies, 1993.

Cochrane, Charles B. "Defense Acquisition Policy—A More Flexible Management Approach." *Program Manager* (July-August 1996): 16.

Crock, S. "Military Reform: Congress May Steal Reagan's Thunder." *Business Week* (14 October 1985): 53.

Day, Kathleen. "Streamlining Procurement Begins Phase 2." *Washington Post* (9 February 1996): 19.

Drewes, Robert W. "SPI, Progress Made and Lessons Learned." *Program Manager* (Special Issue, January-February 1997): 37.

Eisenstadt, S. "Wade to Close Curtain on Career in Pentagon." *Defense News* (22 September 1986): 1.

———. "Officials Do the Procurement Post Shuffle." *Defense News* (13 October 1986): 1.

Enthoven, Alain C., and K. Wayne Smith. *How Much Is Enough: Shaping the Defense Program, 1961–1969.* New York: Harper & Row, 1971.

Ferrara, Joseph. "DoD's 5000 Documents: Evolution and Change in Defense Acquisition Policy." *Acquisition Review Quarterly* (Fall 1996, available at http:www.dau.mil/pubs/arq/94arq2/ferrar.pdf).

Foelber, Robert. "Cutting the High Cost of Weapons." *Backgrounder No. 72.* Washington, D.C.: Heritage Foundation, 16 March 1982.

Ford, Gerald R. *A Time to Heal: The Autobiography of Gerald R. Ford.* New York: Harper & Row, 1979.

Fox, J. Ronald. *Arming America: How the U.S. Buys Weapons.* Boston: Division of Research, Graduate School of Business Administration, Harvard University, 1974.

———. *Managing Business-Government Relations.* Homewood, Ill.: Richard D. Irwin, Inc., 1982.

———. *The Defense Management Challenge: Weapons Acquisition.* Boston: Harvard Business School Press, 1988.

Fox, J. Ronald, Edward Hirsch, and George Krikorian. *Critical Issues in the Defense Acquisition Culture.* Fort Belvoir, Va.: Defense Systems Management College, 1994.

Fox, J. Ronald, and Donn B. Miller. *Challenges in Managing Large Projects.* Fort Belvoir, Va.: Defense Acquisition University Press, 2006.

Galbraith, John Kenneth. "The Big Defense Firms Are Really Public Firms and Should be Nationalized." *New York Times Magazine* (16 November 1969).

Gansler, Jacques S. *The Defense Industry.* Cambridge, Mass.: MIT Press, 1980.

———. "Program Instability: Causes, Costs, and Cures." Paper prepared for the Defense Acquisition Study, Center for Strategic and International Studies, Georgetown University, Washington, D.C., 1 March 1986.

———. *Affording Defense.* Cambridge, Mass.: MIT Press, 1989.

"Godwin Proposes to Abolish Hicks' Job in New 'USDA' Reorganization." *Inside the Pentagon* (26 September 1986).

"GPRA Spurs Efforts to Measure Results." *Acquisition Reform Today* 2, no. 4 (July/August 1997).

Griffiths, D. "An Unlikely Alliance Takes on the Pentagon." *Business Week* (5 August 1985): 54–55.

Hanks, Christopher H., et al. *Reexamining Military Acquisition Reform: Are We There Yet?* Santa Monica, Calif.: Rand Arroyo Center, 7 December 2005.

Hart, G. "What's Wrong with the Military?" *New York Times Magazine*, 14 (February 1982): 16–19.

———. "The Need for Military Reform." *Air University Review* 36 (September-October 1985): 41–46.

Hitch, Charles J. "Evolution of the Department of Defense." In *American Defense Policy*, 3d ed., eds. Richard Head and Eavin J. Rokke. Baltimore: Johns Hopkins University Press, 1973.

Holt, D. D. "Cap Weinberger's Pentagon Revolution." *Fortune* (18 May 1981): 79–82.

Kelman, Steven. *Implementing Federal Procurement Reform.* Cambridge, Mass.: Ash Institute for Democratic Governance and Innovation, John F. Kennedy School of Government, Harvard University, Spring 1998.

———. *Unleashing Change: A Study of Organizational Renewal in Government.* Washington, D.C.: Brookings Institution Press, 2005.

Kitfield, J. "Sizing Up Godwin." *Military Logistics Forum* 3 (March 1987).

Komons, Nick A. *Science and the Air Force: A History of the Air Force Office of Scientific Research.* Arlington, Va.: Historical Division, Office of Information, Office of Aerospace Research, 1966.

Kovacic, William E. "Blue Ribbon Defense Commissions: The Acquisition of Major Weapon Systems." In *Arms, Politics, and the Economy: Historical and Contemporary Perspectives*, ed. Robert Higgs. New York: Holmes and Meier, 1990.

Lassman, Thomas C. *Sources of Weapons Systems Innovation in the Department of Defense: The Role of In-House Research and Development, 1945–2000.* Washington, D.C.: U.S. Army Center of Military History, 2008.

Logistics Management Institute. *The DoD-Contractor Relationship—Preliminary Review*. Task 69–21. McLean, Va.: Logistics Management Institute, March 1970.

Lynn, Laurence E. Jr., and Richard I. Smith. "Can the Defense Secretary Make a Difference." *International Security* 7 (Summer 1982): 45–69.

Malone, Michael S. *Bill & Dave: How Hewlett and Packard Built the World's Greatest Company*. New York: Portfolio, 2007.

Mann, P. "Congress Continues Drive for Procurement Reform." *Aviation Week and Space Technology* 125 (3 November 1986): 36–37.

Marsh, A. K. "Military Reform Caucus Seeks Targets." *Aviation Week and Space Technology* 116 (29 March 1982): 55–56.

McNaugher, Thomas L. *New Weapons, Old Politics: America's Military Procurement Muddle*. Washington, D.C.: Brookings Institution, 1989.

Mohr, Charles. "Critics See Key Flaw in Arms Cost Controls." *New York Times*, 18 May 1985.

Packard, David. *The HP Way: How Bill Hewlett and I Built Our Company*, eds. David Kirby and Karen Lewis. New York: HarperBusiness, 1995.

"Paul Kaminski on Acquisition Reform." *Program Manager* (Special Issue, January-February 1997): 2–12.

Peck, Merton J., and Frederic. M. Scherer. *The Weapons Acquisition Process: An Economic Analysis*. Boston: Division of Research, Harvard Business School, 1962.

"Pentagon: Waste Probers Faulted." *Boston Globe* (27 July 1986): 73–74.

Pinker, Aron, Charles G. Smith, and Jack Booher. "Selecting Effective Acquisition Process Metrics. *Acquisition Review Quarterly* 4 (Spring 1997): 189–208.

Proxmire, Senator William. *Report from Wasteland*. New York: Praeger Publishers, 1970.

Puritano, Vincent. "Getting Ourselves Together on Systems Acquisition." *Defense '81* (October 1981).

———. "Streamlining PPBS." *Defense '81* (August 1981).

Rasor, Dina, ed. *More Bucks, Less Bang: How the Pentagon Buys Ineffective Weapons*. Washington, D.C.: Fund for a Constitutional Government, 1983.

Reagan, Ronald. *An American Life*. New York: Simon and Schuster, 1990.

Ricks, Thomas E. "Pentagon, in Streamlining Effort, Plans to Revamp Its Purchasing Procedures." *Wall Street Journal* (30 June 1994).

"Running the Pentagon—Aspin Style." *Navy News & Undersea Technology* (27 September 1993).

Sapolsky, Harvey M. *Science and the Navy: The History of the Office of Naval Research.* Princeton: Princeton University Press, 1990.

Scherer, Frederic M. *The Weapons Acquisition Process: Economic Incentives.* Boston: Division of Research, Harvard Business School, 1964.

Schultze, Charles L. "Economic Effects of the Defense Budget." *Brookings Bulletin* (Fall 1981).

Schutt, H. J., and David D. Acker. "Program Stability: An Essential Element in Improved Acquisition." *Concepts: The Journal of Defense Systems Acquisition Management* 5 (Summer 1982): 148, 150.

"SECDEF Weinberger's Planning, Programming, and Budgeting System Brings Practical Management to the Defense Program." *Program Manager* 10 (May-June 1981).

Smith, Giles K., and E. T. Friedmann. *An Analysis of Weapon System Acquisition Intervals, Past and Present.* Report R–2605–DR&E. Santa Monica, Calif.: Rand Corporation, 1980.

Smith, R. J., and M. Moore. "Pentagon Purchasing Chief to Quit." *Washington Post* (14 September 1987): 1.

Stubbing, Richard A. *The Defense Game.* New York: Harper & Row, 1986.

Sullivan, Leonard. "Characterizing the Acquisition Process." Paper prepared for the Defense Acquisition Study, Center for Strategic and International Studies, Georgetown University, Washington, D.C., January 1986.

"Taft Tightens His Grip." *Defense Week* 9 (December 1985): 15.

Towell, P. "Pentagon Gets a New Procurement 'Czar.' " *Congressional Quarterly* (25 October 1986).

Trask, Roger R., and Goldberg, Alfred. *The Department of Defense: Organization and Leaders, 1947–1997.* Washington, D.C.: Office of the Secretary of Defense Historical Office, 2000.

Tsipis, Kosta, and Penny Janeway, eds. *Review of U.S. Military Research and Development.* Washington, D.C.: Pergamon-Brassey's, 1984.

Weisskopf, M. "Defense 'Procurement Czar' Named." *Washington Post* (6 July 1985): 7.

———. "Pentagon's New Troubleshooter." *Washington Post* (16 July 1985): 13.

"Who's in Charge?" *Washington Post* (4 April 1986): 17.

"Why the 'Carlucci Initiatives' Aren't Working." *Government Executive* (August 1982): 30.

Yoder, John C., and Jan Horbaly. "Department of Defense Procurement Alternatives." Paper prepared for the Defense Acquisition Study, Center for Strategic and International Studies, Georgetown University, Washington, D.C., 17 March 1986.

INTERVIEWS

Defense Acquisition History Project (DAHP) Interviews
- Foster, John S., 19 February 2003.
- Laird, Melvin R., 18 November 2004.
- Schlesinger, James R., 7 February 1991.
- Shillito, Barry, 6, 8 June 2005.

Office of the Secretary of Defense (OSD) Historical Office Interviews
- Laird, Melvin R., 2 September 1986.
- Packard, David, 9 and 28 November 1987.
- Rumsfeld, Donald H. (Alfred Goldberg and Roger R. Trask, interviewers), 12 July and 2 August 1994.
- Schlesinger, James R. (Alfred Goldberg and Maurice Matloff, interviewers), 12 July 1990.

UNPUBLISHED MANUSCRIPTS

Moody, Walton S., and David G. Allen. "Department of Defense Acquisition History, Volume III: 1969–1980."

Lassman, Thomas C., and Andrew J. Butrica. "Department of Defense Acquisition History, Volume IV: 1981–1990."

Shiman, Philip L. "Department of Defense Acquisition History, Volume V: 1991–2000."

INDEX

A–12 aircraft, 191
Abrams M–1 battle tank, 101, 114
ACATs (acquisition categories), 17–18, 134, 180
Acker, David D., 9
Acquisition. *See entries at* Defense acquisition.
Acquisition categories (ACATs), 17–18, 134, 180
Acquisition Improvement Program (AIP, or Carlucci initiatives)
   background to, 106–08
   development of, 108–14
   DSARC reform, 108, 111–14, 118
   implementation and execution of, 114–20
   Packard Commission and, 130, 133
   purpose of, 99–100
   resistance of military services to, 109, 114–17, 122
Acquisition Reform Benchmarking Initiative, 162
Acquisition Reform Day and Week, 164–65
Acquisition Reform Now bulletins, 164
Acquisition Review Quarterly, founding of, 164
Active manager view, 198, 199, 200–201
Adams, Gordon, 119
Advanced Medium-Range Air-to-Air Missile (AMRAAM), 114, 193
Advanced Research Projects Agency (ARPA), 73
Adversarial relationships
   between OSD and military services, 102, 118, 133
   between program managers and contractors, 195–96
Aerospace Corporation, 88, 92
AFLC (Air Force Logistics Command), 107
AFSC (Air Force Systems Command), 107
AIP. *See* Acquisition Improvement Program.

Air Force
   budget authority, share of, 3
   FCRCs, 88
   IPD (Integrated Product Development) in, 178
   Packard reforms, resistance to, 55–56
   program managers in, 33, 77–78
   reorganization of internal acquisition functions by, 137
   See also Military services.
Air Force Logistics Command (AFLC), 107
Air Force Systems Command (AFSC), 107
Aldridge, Edward "Pete," 143–44, 146
Alpha Contracting, 185
Alternative Dispute Resolution, 185
AMRAAM (Advanced Medium-Range Air-to-Air Missile), 114, 193
Analysis of Alternatives (AoA), 25, 28
Annual or single-year appropriations, 19
AoA (Analysis of Alternatives), 25, 28
Appropriations process, 19–20
Armed Services Procurement Act, 84
Armed Services Procurement Regulation (ASPR), 14, 90–91
Army
   budget authority, share of, 3
   DARCOM (formerly Army Materiel Command), 107, 137
   FCRCs, 88–89
   Packard reforms, resistance to, 55
   program managers in, 33, 78, 184–85
   reforms of 1990–2000, Rand study of, 183–88
   reorganization of internal acquisition functions by, 136–37
   See also Military services.
ARPA (Advanced Research Projects Agency), 73
Art, Robert J., 13
ASD (A&L) (assistant secretary of defense for acquisition and logistics), 121–24, 134

ASD (D&S) (assistant secretary of defense for development and support), 123

ASD (MI&L) (assistant secretary of defense for manpower, installations, and logistics), 122, 132

Aspin, Leslie "Les," 125, 142, 151, 153, 154, 158

ASPR (Armed Services Procurement Regulation), 14, 90–91

Assistant secretary of defense for acquisition and logistics (ASD [A&L]), 121–24, 134

Assistant secretary of defense for development and support (ASD [D&S]), 123

Assistant secretary of defense for manpower, installations, and logistics (ASD [MI&L]), 122, 132

Atomic Energy Commission, 80, 83

AV–8B Harrier, 192

B–1 bomber, 101, 105n17
B–1B bomber, 191
B–2 bomber, 191
B–52 bomber, 101
B&P (bid and proposal) work, 89–91
Bechtel Group, 139–40
Benson, Robert, 40
Bid and proposal (B&P) work, 89–91
"Big A" acquisition, 5
Block change agreements, 173–74
Blue Ribbon Commission on Defense (1985–1989). *See* Packard Commission.
Blue Ribbon Defense Panel (Fitzhugh Commission, 1969–1970), 41, 45–47, 57, 62–69, 71–73, 77, 82, 83
Blueprint for Change (1994), 171–72
Boeing Company, 124
Brookings Institution, 141
Brown, Harold, 52, 95, 99, 140n99
Budget Act of 1974, 93–94
Budget authority, 1, 3
Budget fluctuations, program instability due to, 98–99, 102, 109, 115–16
Business environment of defense acquisition, 12–13, 32–33, 98, 193–94

Buy American Act, 87

C–5A cargo transport, 37, 45, 55, 57
CAIG (Cost Analysis Improvement Group), 78
CAIV (Cost as an Independent Variable), 187
Career paths and training for program managers, 33, 39–40, 54–55, 66, 131, 194–204
Carlucci, Frank C., 99, 102–06, 115–17, 120, 146–47
Carlucci initiatives. *See* Acquisition Improvement Program.
Carter, Jimmy, and administration, 95, 96, 97, 101, 102
CDRLs (Contract Data Requirements Lists), 185
Center for Naval Analyses, 88, 188
Centralization/decentralization approaches
  OSD, centralization of decision-making authority under, 36, 38–39, 98, 104
  Packard on, 39–40, 47, 68, 72, 74, 95
  political system in United States, decentralized nature of, 98–99, 150
  program manager understanding of, 201
  under Weinberger, 99–100, 104, 106, 113
Charles, Robert, Jr., 40
Chiles, Lawton M., 83, 87, 91
Chrysler Corporation, 114
CINC (commander in chief) participation in PPBS reform, 105n17
Circular A–76, OMB, 85, 94–95
Circular A–109, OMB, 95, 107
CITE (contractor independent technical effort), 89–91
Clark, John Russell, 83, 91
Claytor, W. Graham, 102
Clean Air Act, 87
Clements, William P., Jr., 80–81, 93
Clinger-Cohen Act, 170
Clinton, William J. "Bill," and administration, 151, 163. *See also* Defense acquisition reform, 1990 to 2000.

INDEX

Cohen, William, 167, 168, 170
Cold War, 98, 101
Commander in chief (CINC)
   participation in PPBS reform, 105n17
Commercial operation versus defense acquisition, 12–13, 32–33, 98, 193–94
Commission on Procurement. *See* Congressional Commission on Government Procurement.
Communications program to engage workforce, 163–65
Competition in Contracting Act (1983), 154–55, 169
Conahan, Frank C., 145–46
Concurrent engineering, 178
Configuration management, 14, 38
Congress
   AIP and, 109
   authorization and appropriation by, 16–17
   changes in program funding and, 17, 20, 31
   on cost estimates, 6
   increased defense spending in 1980s and, 100, 118
   legislative reforms
      of 1960s and 1970s, 93–95
      of 1980s, 128–29, 132, 133, 141
      1990 to 2000, 165–70
   Packard reform proposals promoted to, 69–73
   as participant in defense acquisition process, 14–15, 16–17, 100, 109n24
   production rate constraints, 32
   USD (A), establishment of, 132, 133, 141–42
Congressional Budget Office, 15, 94
Congressional Commission on Government Procurement (McGuire-Holifield Commission), 41, 82–95
   legislative reform following, 93–95
   Office of Federal Procurement Policy and, 84–88
   organization of, 82–84
   report, presentation and implementation of, 92–93
   on research and development procurement, 88–91
   on systems acquisition reform, 91–93
Congressional Research Service, 15
Continuity, problem of lack of, 201, 206–07
Contract Data Requirements Lists (CDRLs), 185
Contracting
   Blue Ribbon Panel report (1969–1970) on, 65
   Congressional Commission on, 86–87
   cost efficiency incentives for contractors, 11, 31–32, 204–06
   development and production overlap, 27
   DoD Directive 5000.1 on, 75
   economics of defense acquisition and, 12–13, 32–33, 98, 193–94
   historical background (before 1960), 7–9
   Logistics Management Institute report on, 41–42
   McNamara reforms, 36–37
   multiyear appropriations and, 19
   Packard on, 79
   profits of contractor, basis for, 31–32
   proposals to reduce oversight of, 176, 177
   relationships between government and contractors, 193–98
   role in defense acquisition, 1
   selection of contractor, 29–30
   social objectives and, 32
   stages in acquisition process, involvement in, 21, 27
   timely payment of contractors, 86, 93–94
   for weapon systems, 11
Contractor Funds Status Reporting, 37
Contractor independent technical effort (CITE), 89–91
Conyers, John, Jr., 165
Cost Analysis Improvement Group (CAIG), 78
Cost and Schedule Control System Criteria (C/SCSC), 37
Cost and Software Data Reporting (CSDR) Plan(s), 26

Cost as an Independent Variable (CAIV), 187
Cost efficiency
  incentives for contractors, 11, 31–32, 204–06
  as major problem, 6, 192
  multiyear appropriations and, 19
  nature of relationship between government and contractors affecting, 193–98
  scheduling and, 29, 35
  systemic issues affecting, 30–31
  timing and length of acquisition process affecting, 29
  uniform cost accounting standards, Congressional Commission on, 86
Cost estimates
  Blue Ribbon Panel (1969–1970) on, 67
  inadequate methodology for, 6, 35
  parametric cost estimating, 36
  reforms of 1960s–1970s and, 40
  tendency of programs to exceed, 30–31
Cost Information Reports, 37
Cost-plus-fixed-fee contracts, 9, 36
Cost-reimbursement contracts, 9, 60, 89, 90–91, 196
Costello, Robert, 143, 146–47, 178
Critical technology elements (CTEs), 25
C/SCSC (Cost and Schedule Control System Criteria), 37
CSDR (Cost and Software Data Reporting) Plan(s), 26
CTEs (critical technology elements), 25
Currie, Malcolm R., 81

DAB (Defense Acquisition Board), 134–35, 175–77
DAE (defense acquisition executive), 17, 107, 112, 121, 124, 130
DARCOM (Department of the Army Readiness Command, formerly Army Materiel Command), 107, 137
DARPA (Defense Advanced Research Projects Agency), 131
DAU (Defense Acquisition University), 6, 55, 156, 185, 202
Davis-Bacon Act, 168–69
DCAPE (director, cost assessment and program evaluation), 23
DCAS (Defense Contract Administration Service), 37, 86–87, 94–95
DCMC (Defense Contract Management Command), 176, 177
DCP. *See* Development Concept Paper.
DDR&E. *See* Director of defense research and engineering.
De Poix, V. Adm. Vincent, 70–71, 74
Deadeye program, 143, 144
Decentralization. *See* Centralization/decentralization approaches.
Defense acquisition, 1–33, 189–207
  ACATs (acquisition categories), 17–18
  budgeting authorities and defense establishment, 1–4
  changes in funding, schedules, and technical performance requirements, 15–16, 31
  congressional authorization and appropriation, 19–20
  as consensus-building exercise, 16
  continuing problems associated with, 189–92
  continuing study of problems associated with, 188
  continuity problems in, 201, 206–07
  contracting. *See* Contracting.
  cost efficiency in. *See* Cost efficiency.
  differing perceptions of current state of, 200
  economics of, 12–13, 32–33, 98, 193–94
  federal deficit and, 207
  historical background (before 1960), 7–11
  implementation and follow-up of reform recommendations, 205–07
  incentives inherent in, 11, 32–33, 191, 203–05
  media and public scrutiny of, 100, 120–21, 125–28
  participants in process, 14–17
  production, limited rates of, 32–33
  program management. *See* Program management offices and program managers.

INDEX

quick fixes to reduce budgets, problem of, 201
regulations and directives applicable to. *See* Regulations and directives.
stages in acquisition process, 20–27, 95
timing and length of acquisition process, 27, 29, 192
transition between stages, 28–29
weapon systems. *See* Weapon systems.
Defense Acquisition Board (DAB), 134–35, 175–77
Defense Acquisition Deskbook, 164, 179
Defense acquisition executive (DAE), 17, 107, 112, 121, 124, 130
Defense Acquisition Improvement Act of 1986, 135
Defense Acquisition Pilot Programs, 158–60
Defense Acquisition Policy Subcommittee, 127
Defense Acquisition Process ("little a" acquisition), 5
Defense acquisition reform, 1960s and 1970s, 35–96
    Blue Ribbon Defense Panel (Fitzhugh Commission), 41, 45–47, 57, 62–69, 71–73, 77, 82, 83
    centralization of decision-making authority under OSD, 36, 38–39
    Congressional Commission on. *See* Congressional Commission on Government Procurement.
    Defense Resource Board study, 96
    DoD Directive 5000.1, 74–78
    DSARC, creation of, 47–49
    IAC, 50–53
    under Laird, 40–48, 63, 68, 71–74, 78–80
    legislative reforms, 93–95
    McNamara innovations, 35–40, 45, 48
    Office of Federal Procurement Policy, 84–88, 93–95
    OMB Circular A—109, 95
    Packard and. *See* Packard, David.
    post-Laird/Packard changes of appointees, 79–82
    PPBS, 36, 38, 96
Defense acquisition reform, 1980s, 97–150
    Blue Ribbon Commission on Defense (1985–1989). *See* Packard Commission.
    Carlucci initiatives. *See* Acquisition Improvement Program.
    expansion of military services and defense spending, 97, 100–01
    fraud, waste, and mismanagement charges, 120–21, 125–27
    legacy of, 146–50
    OSD leadership reorganization, 120–25
    PPBS, 101–06
    program instability due to budget fluctuations, 98–99, 102, 109, 115–16
    Reagan's mandate for change and, 97–100
    USD (A). *See* Under secretary of defense for acquisition.
    Weinberger and. *See* Weinberger, Caspar W.
Defense acquisition reform, 1990 to 2000, 151–88
    acquisitions process, changing, 175–80
    advantages and disadvantages, 185–87
    broad-based nature of, 166, 170
    communications program to engage workforce, 163–65
    Defense Acquisition Pilot Programs, 158–60
    legislative reform, 165–70
    metrics development, 160–63
    milspec reform, 171–75
    organization of reform process, 154–58
    Perry and. *See* Perry, William J.
    Rand study of, 180–88
    white paper "The Mandate for Change" (1994), 153–54, 170
Defense Acquisition University (DAU), 6, 55, 156, 185, 202
Defense Acquisition Workforce Improvement Act, 155
Defense Advanced Research Projects Agency (DARPA), 131

Defense Authorization Act of 1986, 131
Defense budget, 1–4
Defense Contract Administration Service (DCAS), 37, 86–87, 95
Defense Contract Audit Agency (DCAA), 37, 82, 86, 94
Defense Contract Management Agency, 1
Defense Contract Management Command (DCMC), 176, 177
Defense Department. *See* Department of Defense.
Defense Enterprise Programs, 158–59
Defense Federal Acquisition Regulation Supplement (DFARS), 13–14, 159
Defense Logistics Agency, 122
Defense Procurement Act of 1984, 155
Defense Procurement Improvement Acts of 1985 and 1986, 155
Defense Resources Board, 96, 105, 116, 133
Defense Science Board (DSB), 163, 178, 188
Defense Standards Improvement Council, 162
Defense Supply Agency, 37, 87
Defense Systems Acquisition Review Council (DSARC)
  in 1960s and 1970s, 56, 61, 70, 71–72
  AIP reform of, 108, 111–14, 118
  creation of, 47–49, 108, 134
  DoD Directive 5000.1, 74, 75, 76
  JRMB modeled on, 1342
  membership, 108n22
Defense Weapons Systems Management Center (later Defense Systems Management School/ College), 52, 54–55, 156
Definition of the Requirement, 20–22
DeLauer, Richard D., 112, 114, 122–24
Department of Defense (DoD), 1–3
  Blue Ribbon Panel report (1969–1970) proposing reorganization of, 63–64, 68, 72–73
  on cost estimates, 6
  historical background (before 1960), 9–11
  as participant in defense acquisition process, 15

profits of contractor, basis for, 31–32
Reagan, expansion under, 97–98
Department of Defense Reorganization Act of 1958, 35
Department of Justice, 15
Department of the Army Readiness Command (DARCOM, formerly Army Materiel Command), 107, 137
Deputy under secretary for acquisition reform, 154–58
Deutch, John M., 152, 155
Development Concept Paper (DCP)
  Laird-Packard reforms and, 49, 56, 66, 71–73, 75, 76
  McNamara reforms and, 37
Development testing and evaluation (DT&E), 89–90
DFARS (Defense Federal Acquisition Regulation Supplement), 13–14, 159
Dickinson, William, 142
Director, cost assessment and program evaluation (DCAPE), 23
Director of defense research and engineering (DDR&E)
  in 1960s and 1970s, 44, 52, 53, 56–57, 61, 64, 73, 75, 90
  re-creation of, 140
  USD (R&E), upgraded to, 107, 140n99
Director of operational test and evaluation, 26, 169
DoD. *See* Department of Defense.
DoD Directive 5000.01, 22
DoD Directive 5000.1, 14, 74–78, 107, 179
DoD Directive 5134.1, 135–36
DoD Directive 8120.1, 180
DoD Instruction 5000.01, 17
DoD Instruction 5000.2, 14, 17, 107, 179
DoD Instruction 8120.2, 180
DoD Manual 5000.2-M, 179
DoD Manual 7920.2-M, 180
DoD Regulation 5000.2-R, 175, 179
Douglas Aircraft Corporation, 88
DSARC. *See* Defense Systems Acquisition Review Council.

INDEX

DSB (Defense Science Board), 163, 178, 188
DT&E (development testing and evaluation), 89–90
Earned Value Management System (EVMS), 37
Economics of defense acquisition, 12–13, 32–33, 98, 193–94
Engineering and Manufacturing Development (EMD), 22, 24, 26
Enthoven, Alain C., 44–45
EVMS (Earned Value Management System), 37
Evolutionary acquisition, 23, 28n57, 111

F-14A Tomcat fighter aircraft, 37
F-15 aircraft, 7, 56
F-15E tactical fighter, 105n17
F-22 aircraft, 7, 191
F-52G strategic bomber, 105n17
F-111 fighter-bomber, 37, 55
FACNET (Federal Acquisition Network), 168
FAIA (Federal Acquisition Improvement Act), 165–66
FAR (Federal Acquisition Regulation), 13–14, 159
FAR supplements, component-unique, 13
FARA (Federal Acquisition Reform Act), 170
FASA (Federal Acquisition Streamlining Act), 160, 166–70
"Faster, better, cheaper," 154
FCRCs (federal contract research centers), 88–89
FCS (Future Combat Systems), 185
Federal Acquisition Improvement Act (FAIA), 165–66
Federal Acquisition Network (FACNET), 168
Federal Acquisition Reform Act (FARA), 170
Federal Acquisition Regulation (FAR), 13–14, 159
Federal Acquisition Streamlining Act (FASA), 160, 166–70
Federal contract research centers (FCRCs), 88–89

Federal Property and Administrative Services Act, 84–85
Federally funded research and development centers (FFRDCs), 88–89
Fitzgerald, Arthur E., 204
Fitzhugh Commission (Blue Ribbon Defense Panel, 1969–1970), 41, 45–47, 57, 62–69, 71–73, 77, 82, 83
Fitzhugh, Gilbert W., 46, 47, 63, 67, 73
Fixed-price contracts, 36, 37, 38, 75, 89, 90, 110, 119, 196, 200
Fly-before-buy, 78, 131, 135, 191
Ford, Gerald P., and administration, 81–82, 96
Forrestal, James V., 10
Foster, John S., 44, 50, 52–54, 62, 64, 81
Francis, Paul L., 189
Fubini, Eugene G., 52
Future Combat Systems (FCS), 185

Galbraith, John Kenneth, 85
GDP (gross domestic product), 1, 2
General Dynamics Corporation, 114, 120
General Services Board of Contract Appeals, 170
Germany, defense acquisition in, 12
GDP (gross domestic product), 1, 2,
GNP (gross national product), U.S. defense share of, 12
Godwin, Richard P., 139–44, 146, 148
Goldwater, Barry M., 45, 125, 139–40
Goldwater-Nichols Department of Defense Reorganization Act (1986), 132, 135–37, 146, 169
Gore, Al, 167
Government Accountability Office (GAO, formerly General Accounting Office)
  on AIP, 117–20
  on cost estimates, 6, 31, 40
  as participant in defense acquisition process, 15
  profits of contractor, basis for, 31
  on proposal to consolidated DCAS and DCAA, 87
  on USD (A), 145–46
  on weapon systems, 6, 188, 189–90

Government regulations. *See* Regulations and directives.
Governmental Affairs Committee, 168
Grace Commission (Private Sector Survey on Cost Control, 1982), 126
Gramm, William Philip "Phil," 139
Grassley, Charles E., 125, 147, 167–68
Gross domestic product (GDP), 1, 2
Gross national product (GNP), U.S. defense share of, 12
Gurney, Edward J., 83

Harry Diamond Laboratory, 88
Hart, Gary, 126, 145
Harvard University study of defense acquisition (1962), 30, 35
HASC (House Armed Services Committee), 125, 151–55, 166
Hewlett-Packard (HP), 43–44, 47, 78, 138, 149
Hicks, Donald, 124–25, 139–40, 141, 144
Holifield, Chet E., 83, 87, 91
Horton, Frank, 83, 91
House. *See* Congress.
House Armed Services Committee (HASC), 125, 151–55, 166
HP (Hewlett-Packard), 43–44, 47, 78, 138, 149
Hughes Aircraft, 114
Human Resources Research Organization (HumRRO), 88

ICBMs (intercontinental ballistic missiles), 10, 14, 98, 101, 105n17
IDA (Institute for Defense Analyses), 88, 178
Impediments to Reducing the Costs of Weapon Systems (GAO, 1979), 31
Incentives
 acquisition culture, problems inherent in, 11, 31–32, 189, 191, 204–05
 for contractors, 11, 31–32, 204–06
 for program managers, 203–04
Independent research and development (IR&D), 89–91, 95
Information Technology Management Reform Act (ITMRA), 170
Initial Capabilities Document, 23

Institute for Defense Analyses (IDA), 88, 178
Integrated Priority Lists (IPLs), 105n17
Integrated product and process development (IPPD), 160, 177–78
Integrated product teams (IPTs), 176–77
Integrated Weapon System Management (IWSM), 178
Intercontinental ballistic missiles (ICBMs), 10, 14, 98, 101, 105n17
Iowa-class battleships, 101
IPLs (Integrated Priority Lists), 105n17
IPPD (integrated product and process development), 160, 177–78
IPTs (integrated product teams), 176–77
IR&D (independent research and development), 89–91, 95
ITMRA (Information Technology Management Reform Act), 170
IWSM (Integrated Weapon System Management), 178

Jackson, Henry M., 83
Japan, defense acquisition in, 12
JCIDS (Joint Capabilities Integration and Development System), 5, 28
JDAM (Joint Direct Attack Munition), 160
Johns Hopkins University Applied Physics Laboratory, 88
Johnson, Lyndon B., and administration, 36
Joint Capabilities Integration and Development System (JCIDS), 5, 28
Joint Chiefs of Staff
 in 1960s and 1970s, 45, 46, 62, 63n70
 in 1980s, 102–06, 129, 132–35
Joint Direct Attack Munition (JDAM), 160
Joint Primary Aircraft Training System (JPATS), 160
Joint Requirements Management Board (JRMB), 134, 135
Joint Requirements Oversight Council (JROC), 23, 134

INDEX

JPATS (Joint Primary Aircraft Training System), 160
JRMB (Joint Requirements Management Board), 134, 135
JROC (Joint Requirements Oversight Council), 23, 134
Justice Department, 15

Kaminski, Paul, 163, 164–65, 174–75, 176–77, 178, 180n93
Kelman, Steven, 169
Kennedy, John F., and administration, 36
Kissinger, Henry A., 81
Kleindienst, Richard G., 80
Korb, Lawrence J., 115, 122
Korean War, 10
Kunzig, Robert L., 83

Laird, Melvin, 40–48, 63, 68, 71–74, 78–80
Lawrence Berkeley National Laboratory, 124
Lehman, John F., 101, 141, 143–44, 146
Length and timing of acquisition process, 27, 29, 192
Liaison manager view, 197–98, 200
Lincoln Laboratory, 88
"Little a" acquisition (Defense Acquisition Process), 5
Lockheed, 37, 57
Logistics Management Institute, 31, 41–42, 88
Low-Rate Initial Production (LRIP) quantity, 26–27
LTV Aerospace Corporation, 83, 91

M–1 battle tank, 101, 114
MAIS Review Council (MAISRC), 180
Major Automated Information Systems (MAISs), 17, 27, 180
Major Defense Acquisition Programs (MDAPs), 17, 22
Major weapon systems. *See* Weapon systems.
Management by objectives, 47, 48, 61, 74
Management of programs. *See* Program management offices and program managers.

"The Mandate for Change" (Perry, 1994), 153–54, 170
Marine Corps AV–8B Harrier and V–22 Osprey programs, funding for, 192. *See also* Military services.
Marsh, John, 144
Materiel Development Decision, 22, 23
Materiel Solution Analysis, 22, 23, 24, 28
Maverick missile, 115
McClary, Terence E., 81
McCurdy, Dave, 120
McGuire-Holifield Commission. *See* Congressional Commission on Government Procurement.
McGuire, Perkins, 83
McLucas, John L., 81
McNamara, Robert S., 5, 35–40, 45, 58, 100, 104
McNaugher, Thomas L., 141
MDA (Milestone Decision Authority), 18, 22, 23, 25, 26
MDAPs (Major Defense Acquisition Programs), 17, 22
Media scrutiny of defense acquisition process, 100, 120–21, 125–28
Mendolia, Arthur L., 81
Metrics development, 160–63
Milestone Decision Authority (MDA), 18, 22, 23, 25, 26
Military Reform Caucus, 126–27, 145–46, 148
Military Retirement Reform Act of 1986, 132, 135
Military services
  AIP, resistance to, 109, 114–17, 122
  competition between, 98
  directives supplementing government regulations, 14
  government regulations applicable to acquisition by, 13
  historical background (before 1960) to acquisition programs in, 10–11
  organization of reform process under Clinton, 158
  OSD, adversarial relationship with, 102, 118, 133
  Packard Commission's proposal to reform command structure for acquisitions purposes, 133–34

Military services—*Continued*
　Packard reforms, resistance to, 53–57
　as participants in defense acquisition process, 14–15
　production rate constraints, 32
　Reagan, expansion under, 97, 100–101
　reorganization of internal acquisition functions by, 136–37
　USD (A), resistance to, 132–33, 139, 141–46, 148
　See also Air Force; Army; Marine Corps; Navy.
Military specifications and standards (milspecs), 170–74, 185
Minuteman missile system, 101
Modified Integrated Program Summary (MIPS), 185
Mondale, Walter, 120
Moot, Robert C., 44, 48
Multiyear appropriations and contracting, 19, 99, 108, 110
MX (Peacekeeper) ICBM, 105n17

National Defense Authorization Act for Fiscal Year 1987, 135
National Performance Review, 166
National Polar-Orbiting Operational Environmental Satellite System (NPOESS), 120
National policies, use of procurement to implement, 87
National Security Decision Directive (NSDD) 219, 134–35, 138
NATO (North Atlantic Treaty Organization), 32, 81
Naval Weapons Center, 88
NAVMAT (Navy Material Command), 108
Navy
　A-12 development program information, withholding of, 192
　budget authority, share of, 3
　DSARC review process and, 114
　expansion program for submarine and surface fleets, 101, 143
　FCRCs, 88
　Packard reforms, resistance to, 55
　program managers in, 33, 78
　reorganization of internal acquisition functions by, 136–37
Navy Material Command (NAVMAT), 108
Nixon, Richard M., and administration, 41, 42, 46, 79–81, 82, 83, 93, 96. *See also* Defense acquisition reform, 1960s and 1970s.
No-year appropriations, 19
Non-defense versus defense outlays, 3, 4
North Atlantic Treaty Organization (NATO), 32, 81
Northrop Corporation, 124
NPOESS (National Polar-Orbiting Operational Environmental Satellite System), 120
NSDD (National Security Decision Directive) 219, 134–35, 138
Nuclear weapons, 42, 83, 98, 100, 101, 120
Nunn-McCurdy Amendment to Defense Authorization Act of 1982, 119–20
Nunn, Sam, 119, 125, 142, 169

Office of Federal Procurement Policy, 87, 93–95
Office of Management and Budget (OMB)
　Circular A–76, 85, 94–95
　Circular A–109, 95, 107
　on cost estimates, 6
　Defense Acquisition Pilot Programs submitted to, 158
　as participant in defense acquisition process, 14, 15
　production rate constraints, 33
Office of Systems Analysis, 36, 44
Office of Technology Assessment, 15
Office of the Secretary of Defense (OSD)
　AIP and, 110, 117–18, 120
　centralization of decision-making authority under, 36, 38–39, 98, 104
　directives supplementing government regulations, 14
　DoD Reorganization Act of 1958 expanding role of, 35
　military services, adversarial relationship with, 102, 118, 133

INDEX

265

as participant in defense acquisition process, 14
production rate constraints, 32
responsibility for defense acquisition, development of, 10
Test and Evaluation Oversight List, 26
Weinberger reorganization of executive leadership, 120
Office of the Service Secretary, 14
OMB. *See* Office of Management and Budget.
Open systems approach, 174–75
Open Systems Joint Task Force, 174
Operational test and evaluation (OT&E), 28
Operations and Support, 22, 24, 27
Oscar, Kenneth, 183–84
OSD. *See* Office of the Secretary of Defense.
Other Transaction Authority (OTA), 185

P3I (preplanned product improvement), 111
Packard Commission (Blue Ribbon Commission on Defense, 1985–1989), 125–32
    Defense Enterprise Programs, 158–59
    fraud, waste, and mismanagement charges, in response to, 120, 125–26
    legacy of, 148, 149
    legislation implementing, 134–35
    Perry on, 151–52
    on USD (A), 124, 127, 129, 131–32, 142
Packard, David
    on Blue Ribbon Commission on Defense (1985–1989), 120, 138–39
    on centralization versus decentralization of acquisitions process, 39–40, 47, 68, 72, 74, 95
    Congressional Commission report and, 87, 90, 92
    as deputy secretary of defense appointment as, 43–45
        Blue Ribbon Panel report (1969–1970) and, 57, 63, 64, 67–69

        broad policy memorandum of 1970, 57–62, 75–76
        Congress, promotion of proposed changes to, 69–73
        departure from DoD, 78–79
        DoD Directive 5000.1 and, 74–78
        DSARC, creation of, 47–49, 108, 134
        IAC and, 50–53
        internal push by, 45
        services resistance to reforms of, 53–57
        systems acquisition process under, 54, 58
    HP (Hewlett-Packard) and, 43–44, 47, 78, 138, 149
    legacy of, 148–49
    Perry and, 152
"Panel A," IAC, 50–52
Parametric cost estimating, 36
Participatory management, concept of, 101, 103
Partnership relationships between program managers and contractors, 196–97
PATs (process action teams), 157–58, 162, 171–72, 175–78
PDR (preliminary design review), 22
Peacekeeper (MX) ICBM, 105n17
Peck, Merton J., 35
PEOs (program executive officers), 129, 130, 137, 186–87
Perry, William J.
    acquisitions process, changing, 175, 178
    Clinton acquisition reforms, as driving force of, 151–53
    Defense Acquisition Pilot Programs and, 159, 160
    metrics development and, 162
    on milspec reform, 171–74
    white paper "The Mandate for Change" (1994), 153–54, 170
PERT (Program Evaluation and Review Technique), 37
Planning, Programming, Budgeting, and Execution System (PPBES, formerly PPBS), 5
    in 1960s and 1970s, 36, 38, 96
    in 1980s, 101–06

PPBES/PPBS. *See* Planning, Programming, Budgeting, and Execution System.
Prediction and performance, gap between, 11
Preliminary design review (PDR), 22
Preplanned product improvement (P3I), 111
Preston, Colleen A., 153–56, 158–65, 167, 171
Private Sector Survey on Cost Control (Grace Commission, 1982), 126
Process action teams (PATs), 157–58, 162, 171–72, 175–78
Production and Deployment, 22, 24, 26–27
Production, limited rates of, 32–33
Program Evaluation and Review Technique (PERT), 37
Program executive officers (PEOs), 129, 130, 137, 186–87
Program instability due to budget fluctuations, 98–99, 102, 109, 115–16
Program management offices and program managers, 10–11
  Blue Ribbon Panel (1969–1970) on, 66–67
  DoD Directive 5000.1 and, 74, 77–78
  fundamental flaws in current approach, 198–200
  incentives for program managers, 203–04
  limitations of, 33
  McNamara reforms, 37, 39–40
  Packard Commission on, 131
  Packard-Laird reforms, 49, 50–53, 54–55, 59, 70
  as participants in defense acquisition process, 14
  Rand study of views on reform efforts, 180–82, 184–87
  relationships between government and contractors, 194–98
  short tenure of program managers, 192, 202–03
  stages of acquisition process, involvement in, 22, 26, 27
  training and career paths for program managers, 33, 39–40, 54–55, 66, 131, 194–204
Project on Military Procurement, 127
Proxmire, William, 45, 80–81
Public scrutiny of defense acquisition process, 100, 120–21, 125–28
Purchasing power, concept of, 12
Puritano, Vincent, 102, 103, 108, 110–13, 115, 120

Qualified government personnel
  Harvard Study on lack of, 35
  program managers, training limitations of, 33
  training and career paths for program managers, 33, 39–40, 54–55, 66, 131, 194–204
Quayle, James Danforth "Dan," 127, 139–40

Rand Corporation, 9, 36, 80, 88, 170, 180–88
Rasor, Dina, 127
RDT&E (research, development, test, and evaluation), 5, 17–19, 107, 113
Reagan, Ronald W., and administration, 96–101, 120, 124, 125, 126, 127, 134–35, 138–39, 146–48. *See also* Defense acquisition reform, 1980s.
Reform activities. *See entries at* Defense acquisition reform.
Regulations and directives, 13–14
  Congressional Commission on Government Procurement report on, 82–85
  Defense Acquisition Pilot Programs required to follow, 159
  Defense Enterprise Programs required to follow, 158
  review of 5000-series regulations and instructions (2002), 180–83
  revisions of 5000-series regulations and instructions, 175–76, 178–79, 180n93, 181
  See also specific DoD Directives and Instructions.
Requests for proposals (RFPs), 21, 29

INDEX

Research and development procurement, Congressional Commission on, 88–91
Research, development, test, and evaluation (RDT&E), 5, 17–19, 107, 113
Resor, Stanley R., 55
RFPs (requests for proposals), 21, 29
Richardson, Elliot L., 79–80, 81
Rickover, Admiral Hyman G., 59
Rivers, L. Mendel, 44–45
Roth, William V., Jr., 167–68
Rumsfeld, Donald R., 81, 82
Rush, Kenneth, 79–80

SAE (service acquisition executive), 29, 129
SALT (Strategic Arms Limitation Treaty), 81
Sampson, Arthur F., 83, 91
SAMSO (Space and Missile Systems Organization), 88
Sanders, Frank P., 83, 91
Scheduling
    delays and slippage, problem of, 29, 35, 188, 189, 191
    length and timing of acquisition process, 27, 29, 192
    McNamara reforms addressing, 37
Scherer, Frederic M., 35
Schlesinger, James R., 80–81
Schriever, Brig. Gen. Bernard A., 10
Schultze, Charles L., 12
Seamans, Robert C., Jr., 81
Second World War, 8, 14, 98
Selin, Ivan, 45
Senate. *See* Congress.
Senate Armed Services Committee, 57, 101, 116, 127, 140, 169
Service acquisition executive (SAE), 29, 129
Shillito, Barry, 44, 48, 52–53, 63
Shultz, George P., 59, 139
Simpson, Alan, 121
Single Process Initiative (SPI), 173–74, 185
Single-year or annual appropriations, 19
SLBM (submarine-launched ballistic missile), 101

Small businesses, interests of, 86, 87, 94, 167
Small ICBM, 15
Social objectives and contracting, 32
Source Selection Advisory Council (SSAC), 29
Source selection authority (SSA), 29–30
Source Selection Evaluation Board (SSEB), 29–30
Soviet Union, 42, 82, 101
Space and Missile Systems Organization (SAMSO), 88
SPI (Single Process Initiative), 173–74, 185
SSA (source selection authority), 29–30
SSAC (Source Selection Advisory Council), 29
SSEB (Source Selection Evaluation Board), 29–30
Staats, Elmer B., 83, 87, 91
Stennis, John C., 71, 72
Stockman, David A., 103n12
Strategic Arms Limitation Treaty (SALT), 81
Submarine-launched ballistic missile (SLBM), 101
Sullivan, Leonard, 81
Systems acquisition. *See entries at* Defense acquisition.

Taft, William H., IV, 121, 123–25, 143–44
Taxation to cover defense acquisition, 12–13
TDS (Technology Development Strategy), 25, 28
Technical leveling, 30
Technical performance issues, 40, 190, 194
Technical Performance Measurement (TPM), 37
Technology Development, 22, 24, 25–26
Technology Development Strategy (TDS), 25, 28
Texas Instruments, 120–21, 173
Threat analysis, 21
Thurman, William W., 136, 137, 144–45
Tiger Team on Metrics, 162
Timing and length of acquisition process, 27, 29, 192

Tomahawk missiles, 114
Total obligational authority, 1
Total Package Procurement (TPP), 37–38, 41
Total Quality Management (TQM), 154, 178
TPM (Technical Performance Measurement), 37
TPP (Total Package Procurement), 37–38, 41
TQM (Total Quality Management), 154, 178
Training and career paths for program managers, 33, 39–40, 54–55, 66, 131, 194–204
Trimble, Robert, 114
Tucker, Gardiner, 45, 81

Under secretary of defense for acquisition (USD [A]), 132–42
  ASD (A&L), downgrading of, 124–25
  business model proposed for, 138–39
  constraints on, 147
  establishment of, 132–36
  Godwin's tenure as, 139–44, 146, 148
  military services' resistance to, 132–33, 139, 141–46, 148
  Packard Commission on, 124, 127, 129, 131–32, 142
Under secretary of defense for acquisition technology and logistics (USD [AT&L]), 17, 130, 134
Under secretary of defense for research and engineering (USD [R&E]), 107, 122, 123, 124, 132, 139, 140
U.S. Department of Defense. See Department of Defense.
U.S. Department of Justice, 15
U.S. military services. See Military services, and also Air Force, Army, Marine Corps, and Navy.
USD (A). See Under secretary of defense for acquisition.
USD (AT&L) (under secretary of defense for acquisition technology and logistics), 17, 130, 134
USD (R&E) (under secretary of defense for research and engineering), 107, 122, 123, 124, 132, 139, 140

V–22 Osprey, 191, 192
Vietnam War, 42–43, 79

Wade, James P., Jr., 123–25, 140, 141
Walsh-Healey Act, 168
Warner, John W., 55, 142
Watergate, 80
Weapon systems, 5–7
  contracting process, 11
  cost estimates for, 6
  defined, 5–6
  GAO assessment of selected programs, 6, 188, 189–90
  nuclear weapons, 42, 83, 98, 100, 101, 120
Weapons acquisition. See entries at Defense acquisition.
The Weapons Acquisition Process: An Economic Analysis (Peck and Scherer, 1962), 35
The Weapons Acquisition Process: Economic Incentives (Scherer, 1964), 35
Webb, James E., 83, 87, 91
Weinberger, Caspar W.
  AIP under, 99–100, 110, 112, 115
  centralization/decentralization patterns under, 99–100
  fraud, waste, and mismanagement charges, 120, 125–26
  legacy of, 147–48
  on military expansion and increase in defense spending, 101
  OSD leadership, reorganization of, 120–25, 132
  Packard Commission recommendations, initial opposition to, 132
  PPBS reform and, 104
  USD (A) and, 139, 141–42, 144, 146
Wilson, Pete, 139–40
WIPTs (working IPTs), 176
Witt, Hugh E., 94
Woolsey, R. James, 142
Working IPTs (WIPTs), 176
World War II, 8, 14, 98

Zero-based budgeting (ZBB), 101, 103

www.ingramcontent.com/pod-product-compliance
Lightning Source LLC
Chambersburg PA
CBHW050212240426
43671CB00013B/2301